. . . AND JUNE WHITFIELD

...AND JUNE WHITFIELD

Merry Christmas Mary

June Whitfield

BANTAM PRESS

LONDON · NEW YORK · TORONTO · SYDNEY · AUCKLAND

TRANSWORLD PUBLISHERS
61–63 Uxbridge Road, London W5 5SA
a division of The Random House Group Ltd.

RANDOM HOUSE AUSTRALIA (PTY) LTD
20 Alfred Street, Milsons Point, Sydney
New South Wales 2061, Australia

RANDOM HOUSE NEW ZEALAND
18 Poland Road, Glenfield, Auckland 10, New Zealand

RANDOM HOUSE SOUTH AFRICA (PTY) LTD
Endulini, 5a Jubilee Road, Parktown 2193, South Africa

Published 2000 by Bantam Press
a division of Transworld Publishers

A catalogue record for this book is available from the British Library
ISBN 0593 045823

Typeset in 11/14¼ pt Ehrhardt by Falcon Oast Graphic Art

Printed in Great Britain
by Mackays of Chatham PLC, Chatham, Kent

1 3 5 7 9 10 8 6 4 2

For my mum and dad

. . . AND JUNE WHITFIELD

CONTENTS

Unless otherwise stated photographs are from the author's collection

Preface

HAVING REACHED THE AGE WHEN I DON'T BEND MY KNEES TOO far without making sure there's something or someone to hang on to when I get up, and having been invited by Bantam Press to write my autobiography, this seems to be the right moment.

I thought it might not prove too difficult a task as I have kept diaries since 1942, but when I referred to them I discovered they weren't exactly bristling with information and observation; entries like, 'Rehearsal 10 a.m.' offered no hint of what the show was, where or with whom. Was it theatre, radio, television or film? CV cross-referencing then began and gave me some idea of the order of things. There were other entries like, 'Had drinks after show with J and M,' 'Drinks p.m. Sheila and George.' They were obviously bosom buddies at the time, but who were they? I seem to have spent an inexcusable amount of time in the 1940s having 'drinks with . . .' and, as I recall, it wasn't too easy to get hold of the stuff in those days. I also made some mysterious shorthand notes which I can no longer interpret, and I'm certainly not letting anyone do so for me, though I suspect they probably translate as 'More drinks with . . .' or 'Loved him, hated her,' but unless I take a Pitman's refresher course we'll never know.

So I'm setting off down memory lane with scrapbooks and photo albums with help and guidance from my editor, Sally Gaminara. Thanks also to Tim and Suzy who have helped considerably with the memory-jogging, and to Bantam Press for publishing me, to my agents April and Lesley, and to everyone who has kindly helped me research and relive my theatrical life.

Roy Hudd has affectionately christened me 'The Comics' Tart', and it's certainly true that I have been of service to many of them. I have been a 'with' or an 'and' to Arthur Askey, Benny Hill, Frankie Howerd, Dick Emery, Tony Hancock, Jimmy Edwards, Dick Bentley, Stanley Baxter, Bob Monkhouse, Leslie Crowther, Ronnie Barker, Terry Scott and Julian Clary, to name a few.

Playing second fiddle has kept me going into the third millennium, and I have thoroughly enjoyed my lengthy career, but since this is an autobiography, I shall, just for once, give myself top billing. My story begins long before I was a 'with' or an 'and', or even the butt of the odd joke, way back in the 1920s.

I am now in my seventy-fifth year. A kind friend said recently, 'That's just middle-aged.' Yes, but who ever heard of a 150-year-old woman? So I'd better get on with it.

Chapter One

THE DANCING YEARS

THE VOICE OF FRANK CRUMIT ON A CRACKLY OLD 78 COMING through my bedroom wall is one of my earliest memories. The source was Uncle Billy's gramophone. He and my Auntie Bea had a sitting room next to my bedroom, and they were just two of a large collection of my mother's relatives with whom I shared my child-hood home. In the room on the other side were my mother's parents, who came to join us after Grandad's business failed, bringing with them Auntie Bea, who was Granny's sister. The cast list also included my mum and dad, my brother John, a cook and a housemaid. In retrospect, I find it amazing that we didn't all come to blows, but at the time I didn't give it much thought. My father was a saint to have housed all the extras, but he adored my mum and would have done anything for her.

Actually, it worked out rather well as Granny took over the running of the house, leaving Mum free to enjoy her amateur dramatics, which were a major part of her life. Gran was a rather formidable lady who stood no nonsense from anyone, particularly the staff, who seemed to change with alarming regularity.

My life began in neither the squalor nor the genteel poverty that are sometimes thought to be requisites for a theatrical career, but in comfortable circumstances. I was born in St Wreatham – or Streatham as it was known then, in the days before Balham and Clapham were christened 'Baahm' and 'Claahm' by the yuppie invasion. My earliest years were spent at Mount Ephraim Lane, and when I was about two we moved to a larger house, 'Calderwood', at number 5 Palace Road, and that was where I first heard Frank Crumit singing 'The Prune Song'. Later on, it was 'Nessun dorma' that came drifting through my bedroom wall, as Uncle Billy had broad musical tastes, and the lyric tenor voice of Jussi Bjoerling ensured that none of us got a wink of *dorma* until he'd finished.

Calderwood was a solid, eight-bedroomed Victorian residence in a leafy avenue, protected from the rest of the world by a gate across the end of the road, which was raised and lowered by a uniformed attendant. It's a block of flats now and at one point it was a Church of England home for unmarried mothers so, like the rest of us, it has had to adapt to changing times. The house had a huge drawing room – used by my parents for amateur-dramatics rehearsals and parties – which was linked to the dining room by a conservatory at the rear. There was also a morning room, a cellar – more about that later – and the property even aspired to the grandeur of a billiards room, where Grandad taught me to play snooker. In our garden was a tennis court where my parents used to give occasional weekend tennis parties, as was the fashion then, and until I was old enough to play, I was allowed, if I was good, to hand round lemonade and buns to the players.

Many children are afraid of certain rooms or parts of their houses, and there was one area of Calderwood that gave me the creeps. It was an open lobby in the hallway with dark panelling, which housed a WC at the end. Since the lobby entrance was at the foot of the stairs, it was impossible to avoid, and I had to go past it at least twice a day. Every time I did so, especially at night, I was convinced that something would jump out at me from the shadows. I'd make a run for it going up, and would jump the last two steps on the way down, landing safely on the far side of the opening – a sort of junior long jump.

My favourite room was the drawing room – my mum's exotic creation. It contained Chinese lacquered furniture and grass-green, ruched satin curtains, complementing the black wallpaper which was decorated with cerise-and-turquoise peacocks, edged in gold. The overall impression was of a Chinese emporium – a very fashionable theme for the 1930s. It was highly theatrical and a perfect setting for the rehearsals that took place when my mother was directing plays.

Before I was old enough to take part in the rehearsal evenings at home, I'd sometimes have a friend to stay, and when we were supposed to be in bed we'd have our ears glued to the drawing-room door to hear what was going on, always ready to dash upstairs if we thought someone was about to come out. We also pilfered the sand-wiches prepared for the actors during their break, peeking over the banisters at them at half-time. We thought the rehearsals were great fun, and I couldn't wait to join in.

The Whitfields were a Yorkshire family originally. My paternal grandfather, whom I never knew, was the founder of Dictograph Internal Telephones. My dad started as a junior installer and ended up as managing director and vice-chairman. He came south and was based at Thornton Heath. Mum lived in Streatham, and it was in this south London suburb that John Whitfield, known as Jack, met and fell in love with Bertha Flett. She hated the name Bertha, maybe because, during the First World War, there was a gun called Big Bertha, and 'big' she certainly wasn't. Dad, for reasons best known to himself, called her Puff, Gran called her Puffie, John called her Mother, she called me Muffet and I called her Mum or Muff – a name which, in the Thirties, had not yet acquired the connotation it has today. To her friends, she remained Bertha until one of her am-dram group suggested she should use her middle name, Georgina, and in due course she became known as Georgie.

Mother/Muff/Puff/Bertha/Georgie had a brief career as a draughtswoman at the Admiralty, but her real ambition was to become a professional actress. Her father wouldn't hear of it, being convinced that all members of that profession were rogues and vagabonds. According to Muff, far worse things happened at the Admiralty than in any theatre – 'You would see two pairs of feet under a locked cloakroom door and that sort of thing,' she'd say, mysteriously. I still have the official Admiralty certificate, signed by the Director of Ship Repairs, commending her work, but there's no doubt that, instead of the certificate, she would have much preferred to have her name on a playbill outside a West End theatre.

It must have been very frustrating for her; she had the looks and figure of a Gaiety Girl – the glamorous, up-market chorus girls of the day – many of whom became good actresses, were well-respected and some even married into the aristocracy. It was certainly a way in to the theatre, and Muff would have qualified. I could imagine her surrounded by stage-door Johnnies, sipping champagne from her slipper. Although I was destined to enjoy the career she never had, my slippers have remained disappointingly dry!

Sadly, I didn't inherit Muff's good looks or her ability to turn high-street fashion into haute couture. If I wanted to look expensive I had to pay the full price. As a child I was constantly being told, 'You're a real Whitfield; you look just like your father,' which didn't exactly boost my confidence. I loved him very much, but would rather have looked like my pretty mum. Dad had a kind face and a great sense of humour – I didn't mind inheriting that bit – but he looked more like Alfred Hitchcock than Cary Grant. I grew up knowing I was no glamour girl and, to me, that meant I couldn't possibly be leading-lady material, as I thought they all had to be as attractive as my mother. This could explain why, during my early career, I was seldom without a wig or glasses to cover my lack of confidence. Looking back at early photographs, I now realize there wasn't much wrong with my appearance, but as a child I thought everyone was better looking than me.

My parents married on 1 June 1921, and a year later to the day their baby was born. Mum decided to christen her first-born accordingly – only the baby was my brother John! He enjoyed his parents' undivided attention until I appeared, three and a half years later, in November – bad timing as Muff was set on the name June. She was never very good at remembering dates or times; I once asked her what time I was born and she said, 'I don't know, dear. It was probably in the early hours, most things happened then.'

Whenever it was, Muff decided to stick with the name June, and the only time I ever regret her choice is when I walk onto the set of a chat show and have to smile through gritted teeth while they play 'June is Busting Out All Over'. Alice was nearly my middle name, after Gran, but my ever practical Auntie Bea spotted that my initials would have been J.A.W. – highly appropriate, some might say – so J.A.W. was dropped – sorry! – and for no reason at all, Rosemary was chosen instead.

Gran not only took command of the housekeeping, she also held sway in the kitchen and would often move in to prepare food herself – a possible reason for the brisk turnover of cooks. She did produce some mouth-watering dishes in those pre-cholesterol-conscious days. One taste firmly lodged in my memory is her Queen of Puddings made according to a Mrs Beeton recipe – the Delia of her day. The ingredients were a healthy combination of eggs, cream, sponge cake, suet, sugar and strawberry jam – yummy! There were also pots of Ambrosia Jam – I never knew how to make it, but peaches were involved and it really was the food of the Gods. The jars were scraped clean and demand always exceeded supply.

Grandad's contribution to the household was less clear. I had no idea what his job was, just something to do with exports. He had travelled a lot when he was younger and Muff had a collection of dolls he'd brought her from various countries he'd visited. He was a handsome man, and a bit of a lad, I think. His objection on moral grounds to Muff's theatrical aspirations could well have been based on his own experience of actresses in foreign lands!

I have only the fondest memories of him in his later years. He was a most patient babysitter and answered endless calls for 'a glass of water' or some other excuse when I was supposed to be asleep. There was a connecting door between my room and his and Gran's, which was left ajar when he was on duty. I used to hear strange hissing noises coming from his direction, and when curiosity finally got the better of me one night, I crept out of bed and, missing the creaky floorboard, took a quick look into his room. He was reading his newspaper, smoking his pipe and occasionally spitting, with amazing accuracy, into the gas fire, hence the hissing noise. I went back to bed impressed by his skill, thinking it a rather good game. The next day, when the room was unoccupied, I stole in and had a go myself, but disappointingly there was no satisfactory hissing noise as the fire was not alight. Before I could explore further, I heard my grandparents coming upstairs and nipped back into my room through the communicating door, hoping I'd left no evidence behind. Shortly afterwards, the door was locked from their side. I didn't try it again.

My small bedroom was situated between their larger one and Uncle Billy and Auntie Bea's sitting room. Uncle Billy was a very distinguished-looking man, tall, powerfully built with a shock of white hair. He was a ship's doctor and to me seemed very old, but he was probably only about forty-five. He had met Auntie Bea when she was a nursing sister in the First World War, during which she was decorated for her bravery at Salonika. Whenever she was expecting Uncle Billy home on leave she would fly into a panic, spending hours dusting, polishing and making sure everything was spick and span. I remember the effort she put into ironing his handkerchiefs, changing over the flat irons heating on the stove, and making sure each corner of his hanky was perfect. I heard her say more than once, 'When a doctor visits his patient and takes out his handkerchief, it makes the correct impression if it's pristine.' As he was in the Merchant Navy, I didn't quite see the significance and I couldn't help wondering if he did, either. I was very fond of Auntie Bea. She taught me to play Bezique, and we enjoyed many card games when Uncle was on the high seas. She was always humming little non-tunes to herself as she went about her business. That habit went down in my book of characteristics and has been used by me in a role or two since.

She was often visited by a friend who had also been a nurse in the war. I loved Miss Kenny's quiet Irish accent and, in the privacy of my room, I would imitate her whispering, slightly sibilant tones, imagining her saying to a patient as she was about to administer a painful injection, 'Now just relax, this won't hurt at all.' To this day, if a nurse is required in a *News Huddlines* sketch, I always remember Miss Kenny and automatically slip into whispering Irish.

*

As a child, I didn't spend a lot of time with my brother John; he was, after all, three and a half years older than me and he had his own gang of friends who had no time for 'rotten girls'. He had a shed at the back of the house which he proclaimed his domain with a large notice pinned to the door saying: 'Private. Keep Out'. I think he and his wretched gang used to dissect frogs in there and goodness knows what else, but it was certainly forbidden territory for little sisters. I was intrigued by my big brother and was thrilled when, one day, after a lot of pleading, I was allowed into his bedroom to see his pet mice, which were running around the room. I couldn't believe it when I accidentally knelt on one. I was mortified and John ended up consoling me in my misery, even though I had murdered one of his pets. He was a typical older brother, chasing me up and down the stairs, half strangling me on occasion and throwing cushions at me if I interrupted his homework. We are now the best of friends but, when asked if he is my brother, John replies, 'No. She is my sister.' I know my place!

Dad's brother, Uncle Ron, was the musical member of the family. He lived with Auntie Mary and my cousins, Richard and Verena, in Huddersfield – Dad's home town – and he was in charge of Whitfield's in Ramsden Street, which sold musical instruments and sheet music. I always looked forward to his visits as we would have great musical evenings.

Uncle Ron played the piano and sang old favourites like 'Jonah and the Whale' and songs from the shows, and we all joined in. There exists an old, flickering film of me dancing at an impromptu family concert, taken by Uncle Ron at Christmas 1929.

Monologues were Dad's party piece, and he delivered them brilliantly. One, called 'The Optimist', was about a factory worker who received compensation for the loss of a finger, then, realizing he was on to a good thing, he proceeded to dispense with various other parts of his body and lived off the proceeds. It was a macabre little tale, but its black comedy always raised a laugh. Dad also gave us his 'Church Notices' such as, 'We are indebted to the late Mrs Entwistle for the endowment of a second font at the rear of the church. Henceforth babies will be baptized at both ends.' His pièce de résistance was about a titled lady who wished to rent lodgings in a remote village in Germany. She wrote to the local schoolmaster, asking for suitable accommodation with a WC attached. He knew no English and consulted the pastor, who was unfamiliar with the abbreviation, but decided the lady must be seeking the nearest Wesleyan Chapel. He replied to her letter as follows: 'Dear Ladyship, the WC is situated seven miles from your habitat in the midst of a pine forest and is open on Tuesdays and Thursdays . . .' The letter continued in that vein. I read it out when I appeared on *Countdown* and the reaction was splendid. The monologue must have been around for at least sixty years, so the moral is, always hang on to good material, you never know when it might come in handy.

It was Muff rather than Dad who had a real passion for performing. It began when she was at school and continued for the rest of her life. She appeared in, or produced, hundreds of amateur shows and was a great success as an amateur actress. A reviewer once wrote of a play she was in, 'The highest honours go to Bertha Whitfield as the middle-aged woman whose generosity in giving hospitality to an apparent down-and-out leads to her being dominated by him and eventually becoming neurotic.' Strong stuff indeed. Muff adored and was proud of her family, but she lived for her amateur dramatics. If a part she had set her heart on went to a rival, gloom and doom set in for at least twenty-four hours. It's perhaps just as well she wasn't a professional actress as she would have found the rejection hard to take, and it happens quite often in this business. Maybe her intense and somewhat theatrical reactions had the effect of encouraging me to remain calm in awkward situations. Or it could have been the influence of my father; he was a good actor, always relaxed onstage and, although he enjoyed performing, he certainly didn't view it as his whole life. In fact, he was just as happy backstage sorting out the sound and lighting and ensuring that everything ran smoothly. Calm, cool and collected, Dad complemented Mum's tendency to over-dramatize, always managing to make her see the funny side of situations. She in turn supported him, attending his business dinners and functions, which she also thoroughly enjoyed. There was often a little game played before many of these occasions, when Muff decided she needed a new dress.

'What? Another one?' Dad would say. 'Surely not. What's happened to the last one? I'm not made of money, you know.'

But after a couple of days of wheedling, Muff would always get her way, arriving home with carrier bags after a shopping spree. Exhausted after these verbal battles, she'd say to me, 'I hate having to ask your dad for money every time I need something special. You must try to make sure you can rely on your own resources so you don't have to go through all that when you get married.'

In pursuit of the career denied her, Muff steered me towards dancing classes and, at the ripe old age of three and a half, I was enrolled at The Robinson School of Dancing, Elocution, Pianoforte and Singing, an excellent school where I was to spend much of my time over the next ten years. It was housed in a two-storey building behind the Howie sisters' coffee shop, off Streatham High Road. The mothers would deliver us to our classes and then, while we disappeared into the basement studio to practise our echappés and arabesques, they repaired to the café to chat and speculate on their daughters' prospects of becoming the next Pavlova or Jessie Matthews. I'm afraid I can't say I hated it, or that I used to come home crying or was forced to attend by a pushy mother who was determined I live out her dream. I loved every minute of it, and in due course took my ballet and tap exams. Muff encouraged me, but I never felt forced into it and couldn't wait for the next lesson.

'June will end up on the stage,' various mums would remark, and I gradually came to believe them. That was what I would do. I certainly didn't want to do anything else, like nursing, teaching or being a vet. So that was it, I *would* end up on the stage.

Miss Nancy Robinson, who ran the school with the help of her sister, was a strict but excellent teacher. 'Point those toes, bend those knees, watch your arms, stretch.' I can hear her now. Muff leaped to my defence on one occasion, saying, 'What June needs is a little encouragement, not criticism.' She was so right. Good old Mum!

Miss Nancy's bloomers always caused a giggle; she wore a blue or green tunic with matching knickers held at the knee with elastic. Sometimes her elderly mother, Mrs Robinson, would attend the classes, her arrival heralded by the unmistakable aroma of Yardley's 4711 scent. We were all on our best behaviour as we thought she had great influence over who did what in the annual dancing display at the Brixton Empress. Mrs Robinson was a regal figure, enveloped in blue silk with no visible beginning or end, and all the pupils were in awe of her.

Looking at the programme of one of the Brixton Empress shows, I see that when I was five or six I appeared as an elfin pedlar and, rather bewilderingly, as clockwork mice. My best friend then, and to this day, is Margaret Faithful, known as Mog. She was listed as a princess, with Felicity Bell-Bonnett, who became an actress, as her prince. As the years went by, I was promoted to the more sophisticated roles of a rabbit or pirate, and eventually to monologues. I can dimly remember delivering a charlady routine with the obligatory piece of fur round my neck. The Empress is now a bingo hall; I wonder if the players know what they missed.

Granny was a brilliant needlewoman and the dancing displays put a heavy demand on her sewing skills. Over the years she must have made nearly a hundred costumes for me; in addition to the ones already mentioned, there were sailors, fairies, tutus, a Spanish lady, a Red Indian, and many others for ensembles and solo costumes. I stood on a chair for what seemed like hours while she patiently tried to interpret the paper patterns provided by the Robinson School. Her efforts were heroic, but I hated the endless fittings and couldn't wait for them to finish. I didn't appreciate her kindness and expertise and can still hear her saying, 'Keep still, dear!'

I had a bit of an argument with her one day. I'd entered an elocution competition and Gran had made me a beautiful white dress for the occasion, but on the day the weather was bitterly cold and she insisted that I wore thick black stockings – an affront to my eleven-year-old dress sense. I was furious, embarrassed and moody all day, and was only consoled by the fact that my stockings didn't prevent me from winning a medal. What a brat!

Neither Muff nor I inherited Gran's skills, though Muff was a dab hand at making dolls' clothes, and I can sew on a button and even turn up a hem in an emergency.

There was a certain rivalry among the mothers at the annual Brixton displays. Muff and I always arrived at the theatre early to claim an advantageous position in the wings, close to the stage so that I could make the numerous costume changes in the shortest time. We would lay the costumes out on a large wicker basket, known as a skip, or hang them on the nearest hook. When I came offstage after a number, Muff was always ready with the next costume. One time, when I had about thirty seconds to shed the Rabbit and wriggle into the Spanish Lady, a hook broke on the skirt and, in her haste to secure my skirt with a safety pin, Mum stuck it through my skin. After a yelp, I was on, petticoats twirling and castanets a-clatter. Mum was mortified, but these things happen only too easily in the scramble of a quick change. I still have a numb patch on one side and wouldn't feel a thing if a pin stuck into me now – which it probably does from time to time as I endeavour to accommodate my expanding waistline.

My very first appearance in a play was at the age of five and a half. I had been 'borrowed' by Audrey Reeves, an am-dram friend of Muff's, to take part in *Hidden Power* by Charles Russ. The part was 'A Boy', and I was required to cry silently and stand still while doing so – or else!

Somehow I managed to find a window in my schedule to go to school, first to kindergarten in Wavertree Road, where the delightful Miss Collins was in charge, then across the road to the big school. I can remember very little about Streatham Hill High School, maybe because my main interest at the time was at Miss Robinson's and I was quite often excused for dancing competitions or similar displays. My strongest subjects were spelling and reading aloud, and I had quite a good French accent, sadly not backed up by the grammar or vocabulary. The performing subjects were my favourites but sustained mental application to facts and figures was somehow beyond me. I showed a brief flicker of interest in geography, and even geometry, but that fizzled out after my first brush with Pythagoras.

Our maths teacher was Miss Hartnell. She was very tall, with a loping walk, and wore woolly stockings in summer and winter. She favoured pleated skirts and brown home-knit jumpers on which she allowed herself the indulgence of a brooch. Her hair was cropped and held back with a large slide. If you remember Joyce Grenfell as Miss Gossage, you've got the picture. I was always imitating her rather stentorian voice.

'Is that June Whitfield again?' she roared out one day to our giggling group at the back of the classroom.

'Yes, Miss Hartnell,' I replied in the same tone.

'Was that supposed to be an impression of me?'

In a voice now small and quavering, I said, 'Yes, Miss Hartnell.'

After a moment she half grinned and said, 'Well, it was very good.'

She must have realized that I had a more promising future in mimicry than maths.

I continued to make progress beyond the school gates, and as well as advancing from animal to human characterizations at the Robinson School, I began taking the short tram ride along Streatham High Road for my first acting and elocution lessons with the renowned teacher and eminent local personage Miss E. C. Massey.

Miss Massey was a large, woollen three-piece lady with a hint of a moustache, who lived and taught in a big house on Streatham Common, which she shared with her slight, birdlike companion Melrose – not Miss Melrose or Miss Hunter, just Melrose; they signed their Christmas cards 'Miss E. C. Massey and Melrose'. Miss Massey was a highly respected drama teacher with an awe-inspiring knowledge of Shakespeare, and it was said that the young Edith Evans was numbered among her former pupils. She also produced large-scale community plays for which dainty Melrose did the choreography.

I was very nervous when I mounted the stairs to the first-floor drawing room on my first visit, but I was soon made to feel welcome and offered tea and biscuits, which Melrose was dispatched to conjure up. For an hour a week over the next few years I was coached by Miss Massey in voice production and verse speaking. In this pleasant room overlooking the common, with its heavy velvet curtains, lived-in armchairs and sofas, and the traditional aspidistra, Miss Massey strove to eliminate my south London vowels and encouraged me, as she did her other private pupils, to enter competitions and participate in local amateur dramatics.

I was a few weeks short of my tenth birthday when Miss Massey cast me as Puck in a Shakespeare evening she was producing at Toynbee Hall. The production photo shows me sitting proudly in the midst of the fairies, some rather noticeably of a certain age – not that there's anything wrong with that, I hasten to add. Were it not generally understood that fairies are ageless, all of us elderly panto fairies would have been done out of a job.

One of Miss Massey's greatest triumphs was the 1936 Pageant Play of Streatham, a historical documentary which recreated such momentous events as the coming of the monks to Tooting Bec and Dr Johnson's visits to Streatham Place. It was presented for only two nights at Streatham Hall and involved over a hundred locals, who were recruited to play assorted villagers, monks and fairies to swell the choir. I was cast as 'A Sweyne', an important role since the sweynes were among the first to get wind that the monks were heading for Tooting.

The pageant was rehearsed for weeks, the schedule being arranged to accommodate everybody's availability, which, as anyone who has been involved in amateur dramatics will know, can be a nightmare. Miss Massey managed it partly by brilliant organization and partly by being extremely fierce and frightening the life out of the less-enthusiastic members of the company. She spared no-one; she would even chastise poor little Melrose in public if she thought the dancing wasn't up to scratch.

Streatham Hall was packed to capacity with relatives who had declined to be on stage. The two performances were a great success and yet another triumph for Miss Massey and Melrose. My sweyne was instructed to stand awe-struck while the monks processed onto the crowded stage to the sonorous accompaniment of a Benedictus.

In another scene, Dad appeared as David Garrick and Muff featured in the grand finale as the châtelaine of Thrale Hall, a favourite haunt of Dr Johnson's. Brother John was even roped in to play the Marquis of Tavistock, much to his disgust until, having reluctantly attended the first rehearsal, he discovered that the Marchioness of Tavistock was going to be played by the extremely glamorous Hyacinth Hazell, another of Miss Massey's finds. John suddenly developed a consuming passion for the cultural heritage of Streatham. Hy Hazell made her name in musicals like *Expresso Bongo* and *Lock Up Your Daughters*, and as a superb principal boy in pantomime. She and John had a few teenage dates and he was able to cut quite a dash escorting his elegant co-star.

Miss Massey and Melrose gave me a small part in their next hundred-strong epic, an adaptation of *A Christmas Carol*, then, in November 1937, Miss Massey cast me as Moth in a production of *Love's Labours Lost* at the old St George's Hall in Carlisle Street. My photo appeared in the *Star* newspaper underneath the headline: SEE A LITTLE GENIUS. The review in the 'Star Man's Diary', which was a bit strong perhaps, but very satisfying for a twelve-year-old, said:

> June Whitfield . . . is a normal, eager, suburban child who lives in Streatham, yet she is astonishing in every way; confident of her words, performance and articulation. Her zest for the play, her slight figure in green hose, a silvery doublet, a silver cap with a green feather left a child, but her acting placed her above all but two of the performers.

It is to the eternal credit of the cast that they didn't throttle me with my green hose.

My parents were already established members of the Comedy Club, an amateur society founded in 1882 and still going strong. Mum and Dad were associated with the club for many years, and I am now their president. I watched most of their performances at the Cripplegate Theatre in the City, which was later demolished to make room for the Broadgate development. My début with the club came in 1939 in *The Housemaster*, a play by Ian Hay which is set in a boys' school. The title role was played by my dad, and I was his schoolgirl daughter who had the dreadful habit of keeping forbidden chocolate inside her knicker elastic. She offered some to one of the boys, who took it and said, 'You haven't got a cold piece, I suppose?' My brother John actually made a brief appearance in that play, too, but on discovering that I was the only girl in the cast, he became increasingly disenchanted, and at the end of the play's short run, he took the decision to retire from the stage altogether and turned his attention to golf.

At this time I couldn't say that I had a burning ambition or a yearning to make it, or any of the other cravings that are the stuff of show-business mythology. I certainly loved what I did, and I just assumed that I would end up on the stage. This was a goal towards which my mother and father encouraged me, although Dad always doubted the wisdom of depending on the theatre for a living. Some years later, when I proudly showed him a new contract, he said, 'Very nice, but you're keeping up your shorthand and typing, aren't you?'

My social life had to be squeezed in between school, dancing and lessons with Miss Massey, and what little free time I had was spent at the cinema or the ice rink. My girlfriends and I often gathered at the rink on a Saturday morning in the hope that we might see the three Jacobs brothers, John, David and Dudley, who were all excellent skaters.

Having slithered our way onto the centre of the ice, there we would stand, occasionally setting off on a wobbly figure of eight, watching for David or his brothers, hoping they might spot us while we were still upright. David was very kind to our gaggle of giggling girls, dancing with us in turn and waltzing us round so easily that we felt like ballerinas on ice rather than the hesitant stumblers we were. Even when I persuaded Dad that I needed my own white boots to fall over in, instead of the hired, ill-fitting black ones, I knew I was never going to be Sonja Henie. Dudley Jacobs, however, was good enough to turn professional, while John became a distinguished television and film producer. David made a name for himself by acting and presenting shows like *Juke Box Jury* which was a great hit. He has also chaired numerous radio programmes, been a DJ, and still presents radio programmes. We have remained friends, and when we meet, we thank our lucky stars that we are still around and working.

One of my favourite teenage activities was going to the local pictures with my Gran. We had three cinemas within striking distance; the Astoria, the Gaumont, both of which were frequent haunts, and the Golden Domes, but we only went there once as it was rather dilapidated and known affectionately as 'the flea pit'. The Astoria was our first choice because they served fish and chips in the restaurant, which made any visit quite an outing. It was at the Astoria that I fell madly in love for the first time. He was tall, dark and handsome, and totally unaware of my existence. His name was Glenn Ford, and since he was an American movie star who wasn't very likely to come to Streatham in person, I persuaded Gran to take me to lots of his films. Later on, I transferred my affections to Spencer Tracy. I loved seeing him and Katharine Hepburn working together and delivering those spellbinding, quick-fire exchanges in *Woman of the Year* and *Pat and Mike* – wonderful, witty films. I used to enjoy imitating Katharine Hepburn while envying her long neck. But my idol, in common with most of the girls in my class, was Judy Garland. I wanted to play all her parts, and watching her made me work harder at my dancing and singing. Eve Arden was an actress who intrigued me. I loved her deadpan delivery and snappy one-liners – when *Ab Fab* came along I had the chance to deliver a few myself. Thanks, Jennifer. A cinema visit in those days was a real treat. We not only had the feature but also British Movietone News, a 'B' picture and a travelogue, all perfectly audible, without the ear-splitting sound forced on us in cinemas today. Are those decibels really necessary? The travelogues took us to exotic foreign lands, rather like the holiday programmes on television now. However, we weren't offered instructions on how to get there or given the price as very few families ventured further than Cornwall or Skegness.

Our family holidays were spent at Felpham near Bognor Regis in Sussex, and my first recollection is of the old thatched cottage we rented. It belonged, and was next to, the Summerley Barn Café, where they sold the most delicious blackcurrant ice-cream cornets, made from their own blackcurrants grown in the garden. After a few summers, Dad bought a house in Felpham and the school holidays were spent there. It was a few minutes' cycle ride from the beach, but there was a snag: the beach was entirely made up of pebbles, until the tide was way out and stony sand appeared. Muff, Dad, John, Granny and usually a few friends would trundle down to the shore for a swim and a picnic, the grown-ups in bathrobes and the smalls in swimsuits and more often than not a cardigan. It was generally blowing a gale and freezing, and on the odd occasion when the sun shone, I was hauled under cover to avoid getting sunburned. I clearly remember crawling unwillingly on all fours over the pebbles to the freezing sea, circumnavigating the terrifying seaweed that seemed to gather exactly where I intended to put a toe in the water, the scream of delight as I finally went under and then the endless, painful clamber up the pebbles to the haven of an enormous beach-towel, wrapped round me by my mum who cuddled me back to life.

I was about seven or eight years old when I was really badly sunburned, requiring frequent applications of calamine lotion, which dried hard and white but did relieve the symptoms somewhat. It certainly taught me how dangerous and unfriendly the sun is so far as my skin is concerned and I now treat it with great respect. Mum always said that she and I had a layer missing; I think she was referring to our skin. It could explain the freckles and rashes I get instead of a tan. My sunbathing is now restricted to lying on a comfortable lounger, under a brolly, protected by a windbreak, sipping a cool drink and watching people getting wet and frying themselves – not often though; my fun is in shopping and seeing the sights.

Between our house and the next one at Felpham was an open lattice fence running the length of the front garden, with a three-inch wide coping spanning the top. I was killing time one afternoon before going out to the cinema with a friend and her mother, when I foolishly decided to walk the tightrope along the fence, just as I had seen my big brother John do. I missed my footing, fell off and hit my head on the concrete path. I probably knocked myself out, but nobody was around at the time, so when I came to I simply checked I was all in one piece and decided to keep quiet about it. This was partly because I knew I'd be told off for walking on the fence and partly because I hated fuss; I didn't want my mother or grandmother flying into a panic and whisking me off to the doctor. I went to the cinema as planned, but halfway through the film I had to rush out to the Ladies' to throw up. When I came back I confessed to my friend's mother, Auntie Mac, what had happened. She realized that I must have been concussed and I was ignominiously taken home to endure the very fuss I'd tried to avoid. I was always reluctant to admit to being unwell, I still am in fact, and I tend not to go to the doctor if I can possibly avoid it, but I have at least given up walking along the tops of fences.

We made many friends during our annual holidays. John got himself a job mucking out at the local stables, which in return gave him free rides. I took lessons every year until I was twelve, when my pony stumbled on a gravel road and I shot over his head into a puddle and grazed my face. When I arrived home, I remember standing on a chair in the bathroom to see in the mirror while I tried to clean myself up so there wouldn't be a fuss. When I was discovered trying to remove bits of gravel from my face, I was rightly hauled off to the doctor and given an injection for tetanus together with appropriate healing ointments. Perhaps I felt guilty for not riding my pony properly or just didn't want to trouble anyone with my problems.

Every year the veteran summer show impresario Clarkson Rose brought his revue *Twinkle* to the Pier Theatre in Bognor Regis. It was only twenty minutes by car along the coast and we made a point of seeing the show. It was always called *Twinkle*, whatever its composition, and it was still being performed at seaside resorts into the 1960s; it even made it onto television. The stalwarts of the show were Clarkson Rose, Olive Fox and Gracie Fields' brother Tommy Fields, but the star turn for me was the very funny and talented Kathleen West. She was tall and thin and appeared to be made of elastic, executing vertical high kicks as she sang.

When *Twinkle* left town, touring plays, amateur companies and talent shows took over. I had met Sheila Cornford and we got together an act called 'June and Sheila', both wearing top hat and tails. I sported a dickie, which was a false dress-shirt front, and at the matinée, during our tap dance, it flew up and remained lodged under my chin, exposing my vest. The audience was mainly children and my attempts to control my dickie, twirl my cane and prevent my hat from falling off, while at the same time trying to keep the dance going, caused howls of delight from the kids. I suggested repeating the process at the evening performance, but Sheila wasn't too keen. 'June and Sheila' went their separate ways, bringing to an end the only partnership of my entire career in which my name came first.

Bognor was a favourite resort of Mr F. R. Littler and his wife, Agnes, parents of the well-known impresarios Emile, Prince and Blanche. Mum became friendly with Mrs Littler after they met in a local café. I met them several times and was once invited to tea where I was introduced to the founding father of the dynasty. F. R. Littler was an imposing figure in a cape and fedora, rather like the man in the Sandeman's advert. Muff and I were hoping they would immediately recognize my potential and put me under contract. Inexplicably, I wasn't snapped up there and then – perhaps word had got out about my disaster with the dickie – however, I was promised introductions to the right people when I was a bit older. Years later, I worked for Emile in *Love From Judy*, but sadly his parents were no longer around to witness the event.

Our only other vague theatrical connection was through our family doctor. Dr Hunter was the guardian of Jack Buchanan, a much-admired light comedian and musical comedy star. They both came to Calderwood once and Jack was treated to a resumé of my latest theatrical activities. He oozed charm, was good looking and, to my thirteen-year-old eyes, was everything a leading man should be. I obviously impressed him, because twenty years later I was given a few lines to say on his radio show.

My life up until then had been fairly comfortable and uneventful, my time filled partly by school, friends and family, and mainly by dancing classes, elocution lessons and amateur performances in preparation for the career I assumed I would follow. Apart from Hollywood films, nothing beyond our small Streatham world seemed to have much importance. But on 3 September 1939, Dad, Muff, Gran and I gathered anxiously round the radio, like the rest of the country, waiting for an important announcement from the prime minister. I could tell by the look on their faces that my family were anticipating bad news. When the moment came and we were informed that, for the second time in twenty years, Britain was at war with Germany, my first reaction was to hug everyone. I felt numb, as I really had no idea what to expect, but I was aware that Mum, Dad and Gran would be reliving their own experiences of the First World War. The silence was broken by the wail of an air-raid siren. I'd heard the sound often in practice, but I shivered at the thought that this time it could be for real. Before we had time to reach the shelter of the cellar the all-clear sounded and as we made our way back to the kitchen, I thought of John, who had joined the army and was already with his regiment, and wondered if he would soon be sent into battle. My thoughts were interrupted by Dad saying, 'That's it then. You three had better go down to Sussex.'

So instead of heading for the bright lights of the West End or Broadway, the 'Little Genius' found herself bound for Bognor. And we know what King George V said about that!

Chapter Two

LICENSED TO ACT

'GERMANS INVADED HOLLAND – THE SO-AND-SOS!' I WROTE IN my teenage diary on 10 May 1940, and a fortnight later, 'Germans in Boulogne – bad. Played cricket.' I was in Sussex, by the sea, but it didn't really alarm me that the enemy was just across the Channel. Surely the barbed wire on the beach would deter invaders?

Dad must have thought otherwise as we returned to Palace Road. The promised air raids hadn't yet started, so I was pleased to be back in London and able to pick up the social life that had been so rudely interrupted by the 'so-and-sos'. I resumed dancing lessons and classes with Miss Massey and, apart from having to carry a gas mask around, life continued much as before.

I was fourteen years old and part of a group of girls and boys too young to go to war but old enough to arouse our interest. We enjoyed our usual activities of picnics on Wimbledon Common, bike rides into the country, tennis and, of course, visits to the theatre and cinema. There was no more skating, though, because Streatham Ice Rink had been turned into a mortuary for the duration.

The war was really brought home to me as, one by one, the boys in our group – the two Johns, Bill and Ken – were called up and joined the Army, Navy or Air Force. They were no longer available to accompany us on our various outings and we missed them. I eagerly waited for one of the Johns to come home on leave; he looked gorgeous in his uniform and was rather shy, though he regained his confidence once we were seated in the back row of the Gaumont cinema. The age of sexual liberation lay decades in the future and teenage affairs were still a rarity, so this kind of minor skirmishing in the 'one and nines' was considered frightfully daring at the time; it was certainly excitement enough for this Streatham girl.

Luckily, all the boys survived the war and, in due course, they married and had their own families. Some moved to different parts of the country and we gradually drifted apart and have seldom been in touch since those early days.

My brother John had lied about his age and joined the 2nd Battalion of the Queen Victoria Rifles, Territorial Army, in the spring of 1939, just before his seventeenth birthday. It was a motorbike regiment, which was the main appeal, and in August he was told to report to headquarters in Grosvenor Square with his bike and a mac! During his training, Mum received a very worrying letter saying he'd 'had a bit of an accident with an explosive device' but was 'fine'. He had, in fact, been temporarily blinded and deafened, but fortunately he made a complete recovery. Later in the war he was commissioned into the King's Royal Rifle Corps, and at the final parade, he and his fellow newly trained officers were told by their commanding officer, 'God help the men you are about to command.' Just the encouragement you need when you are about to face the enemy.

Dad's work in communications ensured he remained a civilian, but he became an air-raid warden and added many fire-watching nights to his daily routine. It was a worrying time for my parents, and I was no help as, through my own stupidity, I became seriously ill.

On a hot summer's day in 1940, I and a couple of girlfriends decided to go for a swim in an open-air pool that was part of a local block of flats. I ignored my mum's warning, 'Be careful. The pool probably hasn't been cleaned recently,' and took the plunge. I was undoubtedly showing off to the others as I executed a spectacular dive into the deep end. It's quite a good idea to keep your mouth shut under water, but I didn't and surfaced with the taste of green algae in my mouth, only to see my friends staring in astonishment. They had noticed that the water was stagnant and weren't at all impressed by my plunge into its murky depths.

The next day I had a sore throat, and the day after I was rushed into the Bolingbroke Hospital in Clapham with diphtheria. Flat on my back in a ward full of fellow sufferers, I was ordered to lie absolutely still, without a pillow, shifting only enough to have a syringe the size of a small fire-extinguisher stuck in my bottom. To say it was uncomfortable would be an understatement. The fact that the Blitz was just getting underway at the time did nothing to ease my state of mind. Whatever it was they pumped into me was effective enough for me not to have to undergo a tracheotomy, but there I stayed, unable to see anyone except our family doctor for twelve days. I once caught a brief glimpse through a window of my parents waving from the car park, but apart from that the nearest thing I had to a visitor was the Luftwaffe. When the planes came rumbling over, which they seemed to do almost every evening, we were all wheeled out to spend the rest of the night in the corridor, not knowing whether our families had survived the latest attacks. Every day, Mum and Dad drove to the hospital to make sure it was still standing.

It was my first time away from home, I was fourteen years old, there was a war on and I was miserably homesick. We didn't even have a radio to keep us in touch with what was going on outside. There had been a wireless, one of the nurses told me, but it had 'gone to the sailors'. The only thing that made the three weeks bearable was the delightful Dr Ellison. His rounds were by far the most enjoyable part of the day. He had a wonderful sense of humour and I still remember one of the terrible little rhymes he composed.

> Ellison is a noble man,
> He's just designed a new bedpan.
> You sit upon a ring of steel,
> And that is really all you feel.

He cheered up the ward no end and undoubtedly hastened my recovery. I improved steadily, and eventually the great day came when I was allowed a pillow. Then Dad brought a wireless into the ward, and when someone eventually found a plug for it, life didn't seem so bad.

I was the youngest person in the ward by some years, but I was quite friendly with the woman in the next bed, who had almost recovered from her bout of diphtheria. She seemed ancient to me – she was probably about twenty-eight! – and had got herself into a right old panic about the state of her hair. After a longish stay in hospital her roots had grown out, and she was about to be reunited with her husband who, she said, didn't know she wasn't a natural blonde. This chap must have been either very naive or extremely polite, not least because the dyes and tints available in those days were not what you'd call subtle, but I did as she asked and sloshed peroxide all over her head, turning her tresses an unconvincing canary yellow. She seemed delighted with the results and left the hospital confident that her marriage had been saved.

After three weeks they let me out and I went to spend a couple of glorious months on a farm in Sherford in Devon with my best friend Mog. It was a regular holiday haunt of Mog's family and was the most beautiful old Georgian farmhouse, owned by a farmer who was really called Farmer Giles. He had two sons, Peter and Charlie, and a daughter, Judy, who was being courted by a handsome RAF officer. Mog and I were both dotty about him; he looked so gorgeous in his uniform. We were paying guests and spent harvest time riding on the tractor mudguards – a highly dangerous activity but great fun – cycling into Kingsbridge and doing up one of the farm cottages ready for a batch of evacuees. While London suffered terribly from day and night air raids, we enjoyed a rural idyll. Once, when we were out in the fields, a German plane flew low overhead. Charlie told us to duck as bombs had been jettisoned in the area. We threw ourselves flat on the ground until the enemy had passed, but apart from that, the war barely made its presence felt.

At a later stage in the war, however, the nearby beach at Slapton Sands was the setting for the calamitous rehearsal for the D-Day landings, in which nearly a thousand American soldiers lost their lives. It was kept secret until after the war. Prior to the exercise, Mog was due to stay with the Gileses, and told me she was most upset when she received a curt message saying it wasn't possible, together with a parcel containing a pair of her old boots. There was no explanation and Mog couldn't think what she had done to offend her friends. It wasn't until the following year that Farmer Giles explained to her how the Americans had sealed off the whole area, requisitioned all the accommodation, including the farm, and imposed an order of secrecy on all the inhabitants. In due course they got their farm back, and Mog and I returned for another stay towards the end of the war. My husband Tim and I paid a visit to the farm a few years ago and were delighted to find it still in the family, and being run by the son of Judy and her handsome RAF officer Philip.

When I was invited to take part in *Holiday Memories* for BBC TV in 1997, the first place I thought of was Devon, and the person essential to the programme was my friend Mog. She agreed, and Tim, Mog and I set off to drive to Sherford and meet the crew. Judy's son Robert and his wife Heather kindly said we could stay with them at the farm. So there we were, fifty years on from our original visit.

Robert and Heather had made improvements to the interior of the house, but the kitchen was basically the same; it even had the bell that Farmer Giles would activate from his bedroom if he thought we were getting too noisy or were up too late! We saw Robert's parents, our friends Judy and Philip, shopped in Salcombe, visited the museum in Kingsbridge, had a picnic on the beach at Portlemouth – the best fish and chips at Torcross – and took the ferry from Dartmouth to Kingswear. Mog took to the filming like a duck to water and Tim loved every minute of it, visiting everywhere with us and retracing the steps of our youth.

The sharp-eyed among you will have noticed there wasn't a great deal of schooling going on when I was a teenager. The reason was that shortly after the outbreak of war, Streatham Hill High was evacuated to Brighton, and boarding at Brighton would have meant missing dancing lessons and Miss Massey's invaluable tuition. Once the raids started, my parents' concern for my safety prevailed and I was sent to Sussex again. I attended St Michael's school in Bognor as a day girl and took dancing lessons locally. However, no sooner had I enrolled at St Michael's than it, too, was evacuated to Penzance – just as I was due to swot for my School Certificate, the equivalent of modern GCSEs.

My education was sketchy, but it wasn't all my fault because the schools kept leaving *me*. In any case, I was rather bored by school. My interests and energies were directed towards my extracurricular activities. By the time I was thirty I had begun to realize how little I knew, and was ready, willing and more able to listen and absorb the knowledge that had gone in one ear and out of the other in my youth. My career was already under way, so any thoughts of catching up on my education remained on the back burner. Adult education is now so popular and widely available that it appears I'm not the only one who would have appreciated studying later in life.

In an endeavour to give me some sort of training for a 'proper' job, Dad suggested a secretarial course. He didn't really believe anyone could make a living in the theatre and wanted me to have an extra string to my bow.

The Blitz was approaching its height in December 1940, so Mum and I were packed off to Huddersfield as Dad thought we'd be safer up North. He had a friend there who ran Kaye's College, and I was taken on to learn typing and bookkeeping.

As we would be in Huddersfield for some months, the decision was taken not to impose on Uncle Ron and Auntie Mary's hospitality, so we were installed in an hotel. Just as well, as Muff and Auntie Mary had a totally different outlook on life. Mary looked down on amateur dramatics and Muff could never understand Mary's penchant for housework. They had little in common apart from being married to brothers. Mary spoke her mind and insisted on doing all her own cleaning and washing. One washday I was helping her with the laundry, watching her grow hotter and hotter as she moved the washing round the machine with wooden tongs, having rubbed all the collars and cuffs on her scrubbing board and then forced everything through the mangle, turning it by hand. I eventually asked her why she didn't send it all to the laundry. She turned her bright-red face to me and said, 'Oh no, June, we do things properly in Yorkshire, you know!' indicating that only a pampered southerner would suggest such an outrageous idea.

Auntie Mary's direct approach made me laugh. We often visited her and Uncle Ron and their children, Richard and Verena. We were invited for coffee, tea or dinner and were made extremely welcome. We enjoyed those evenings round the piano; a truce was declared between sisters-in-law and controversial subjects were carefully avoided. As years went by, I noticed that Mary and Mum became more tolerant of each other, having decided that their differences were unimportant and that they could be friends.

We stayed in Huddersfield until the summer, by which time I was becoming fairly proficient at shorthand and typing, as well as picking up other invaluable skills, such as bookkeeping and the correct way to address a bishop or a baronet. I made reasonable progress, and in May I was awarded my first, and only, academic honour: the form book prize.

Poor Muff was bored stiff stranded in a 'foreign country' with no theatricals to keep her going, and she couldn't wait to get home. While I was occupied at college, and enjoying the experience, she had nothing to do but take tea or coffee with Dad's even more distant relatives, who were not really on her wavelength, either. So in the summer of 1941 we returned to London for good.

I completed my secretarial studies at Pitman's College on Brixton Hill and achieved a shorthand speed of 130 wpm and a typing speed of 80 wpm – sadly down to about 10 now. Sorry Dad.

Mum and I renewed our association with the Comedy Club and the Belfrie Players, whom we'd joined the previous year. The Belfries, as they were called, were an amateur touring company who were particularly active during the war. We went to prisons, fire stations, anywhere that would have us. The company was founded by Teresa Balfour, a small, round lady of uncertain age, who always directed the shows and usually played the leading roles, regardless of her suitability. Muff and I appeared frequently with the Belfries, and there was one memorable performance we gave in 1940 under rather hazardous conditions. The play was Noël Coward's *Hay Fever*, with Muff playing the lead, for once, and myself slightly miscast as the sophisticated vamp, Myra Arundel, and also helping out with the stage management. We were due to perform in a hut next to an anti-aircraft battery in Hyde Park. The site was quite a local landmark, not far from Speakers' Corner, and was often alluded to in the press as it was manned by Winston Churchill's daughter, Mary. We got about halfway through the first act when the air-raid warning sounded. By Act 2, the German bombers had been spotted and the huge guns sprang into action, firing furiously. There are countless instances of shows going on during air raids but probably not too many performances of *Hay Fever* took place with a fully operational ack-ack battery blasting away in the wings: 'You can see as far as Marlow on a clear day' – CRASH! 'It's awfully nice, Cookham' – BOOM! We soldiered on until all the characters were onstage playing the parlour game, In the Manner of the Word. The noise was deafening and Mother enquired of those remnants of the audience who hadn't been called to their posts if there was really much point in continuing. The mood of the hall was that there wasn't, since they couldn't hear a word anyway, so we gave up and raced home through the unlit streets with the accelerator of Mother's Austin Seven pressed hard to the floor and the speedometer needle nudging forty!

In the spring of 1942, Miss Massey suggested that I should audition for the Royal Academy of Dramatic Art. I was coached by her in my Shakespeare excerpt – Puck again from *A Midsummer Night's Dream*. In due course I presented myself at RADA in my best two-piece, specially purchased from Pratt's of Streatham with Dad's clothing coupons. During my rendering of 'Now the hungry lion roars,/ And the wolf behowls the moon', I heard a strange rattle coming from the box at the back of the stalls. I found out later that it was the principal, Sir Kenneth Barnes, holding a teacup and saucer in his rather unsteady hand. Not quite as bad as an anti-aircraft gun, but disconcerting nevertheless. Incidentally, the sound of rattling crockery was something all actors, not just students, had to learn to contend with in those days, for this was the heyday of the matinée tea, an unusually disruptive custom whereby theatregoers were able to order and consume a full tray of tea, scones and cakes without stirring from the comfort of their seats. It was supposedly served in the interval, but often lingered through the second and third acts. Rex Harrison was once giving a performance when someone in the front row placed their laden tray on the front of the stage. He strolled elegantly towards it, poured himself a cup of tea and scoffed their cakes.

Shortly after my audition, Sir Kenneth Barnes offered me a place starting in the autumn of 1942. It probably had less to do with my ability and more to do with the exceptional circumstances of the war. I doubt if many were turned away.

There were several of my fellow students who were to make quite a mark on the profession: Richard Attenborough, Miriam Karlin, Patricia Lawrence, Bryan Forbes and Pete Murray to name a few. 'Lord Dickie' and I were not in the same year, but we were once paired up to sing a carol at a concert at Whitefield's Tabernacle in Tottenham Court Road. Shortly afterwards, in what was, I hope, an unrelated incident, the hall was flattened by a bomb. RADA, too, was hit during the early part of the war and fire-watching duty was part of the student routine. It was mainly the boys who did this, although Bryan and Pete were only too happy to take any interested girls up onto the roof for a couple of hours' 'fire-watching instruction' – that's what they said it was, but I never found out because, rather disappointingly, they never invited me.

It was at about this time that I met my first serious boyfriend. I was seventeen and he was thirteen years older. Amateur dramatics brought us together and I was flattered by his attention. He introduced me to the bright lights of London – theatres, restaurants and nightclubs. He wooed me with flowers and presents and swept me off my feet. He was there for me at the start of my career, which he keenly followed, and when I was away on tour, we exchanged long newsy letters and missed each other dreadfully. I thought we were in love and our romance flourished for three years. I was devastated when I received his letter informing me that he was getting married – to a girl he'd met through me!

My devastation didn't last long, though. I soon convinced myself that he was not the man for me, and I didn't want to get married any-way. Well, certainly not yet. I am a fatalist. In the words of a Doris Day song, I believe 'Whatever Will Be Will Be'. Life is too short to spend time regretting the past, the future is more important. Rejection is always hard to take, but few people die of a broken heart.

I didn't attend the wedding.

In spite of the various dangers and deprivations, being a student in London during the war was actually quite exciting. All the shortages seem much worse in retrospect than they did at the time, and when you're in a group of people of your own age, you make the best of it. Many of the students had part-time evening work to help them pay their way. We used to gather in Taylor's Café in Goodge Street, where we'd linger for hours over just one cup of coffee, putting the world to rights and discussing who was in what play and how much better we could have played their parts.

To someone whose role models were Judy Garland and Eve Arden rather than Ellen Terry and Sybil Thorndyke, the RADA approach seemed somewhat solemn, and the choice of plays we worked on was a bit heavy for my taste. There was a little tome in circulation at the time called *The RADA Graduates' Keepsake and Counsellor*. I quote:

> It is unfortunately possible for women without skill, talent, training or vocation as players to use the stage to advertise their real profession, with the connivance of managers whose theatres are not temples of the drama but houses of drink and disorder . . . Note also that drugs more potent and rapidly destructive than alcohol have been discovered. In spite of the most stringent laws they are offered for sale by secret agents.

My grandfather could have written it! The great stage and film actor George Arliss, who was later to present us with our diplomas, made a brief but severe personal contribution to the booklet:

> Lack of moral fibre is responsible for the snuffing out of many a histrionic genius. Do not allow yourself to drift into excesses . . .

Sound advice, no doubt, but to a crowd of drama students, many of whom couldn't wait to drift into excesses, it didn't seem much use. However, the practical training we received at RADA was excellent. Among the staff, then, was Iris Warren, a brilliant voice teacher who was adored by all, and who went on to become voice coach at Stratford. There was also Molly Terrain, who was quite fierce and could reduce you to tears, and we were taught mime by Rose Bruford, who later founded a drama school of her own. At the end of the first term I was surprised and delighted to be awarded a scholarship. Dad was even more delighted. Generous as he was, he wasn't averse to saving a few quid, and the RADA fees weren't exactly cheap.

John Gielgud came to speak to us, and we even had a visit from Queen Elizabeth, now the Queen Mother. My diary has few words about this momentous event. I've been told that Her Majesty tripped over a cleaner's bucket in a corridor, but the only entry is, 'Queen came to public show, had tea, talked to various people and cast grins around.' Our beloved Queen Mum has been casting her grins and charming souls in all parts of the world ever since.

Another teacher who, if not quite regal, was, to quote Mrs Malaprop, 'the very pineapple' of urbane sophistication, was Hubert Gregg. He had notched up a string of successes playing elegant romantic leads and gave us, of all things, our first kissing and embracing lesson. I think the females outnumbered the male students by about fifteen to one at the time, however, consummate professional that he was, Hubert made up for the shortfall by giving expert, one-to-one tuition to each of the girls in turn. Now that's what I call dedication to your art!

The shortage of men meant that we often had to play the boys' parts, and it followed that competition for the female leading roles was fairly stiff and I usually ended up playing character parts – male character parts, too, as often as not. I was the second gravedigger in *Hamlet* and Peter Quince in *A Midsummer Night's Dream*, which was a bitter disappointment because I rather fancied myself as Puck. I wore a bald wig, known as a 'bladder', and a false beard for Quince, although the beard itched so badly that I got rid of it after the first performance. We toured the *Dream* around local schools, performing at the somewhat untheatrical hour of ten in the morning. If you've never tried forcing your head into a cold, clammy bladder at 9.30 a.m., then don't, it's not nice.

The rough yokel accent I adopted for Peter Quince resulted in the appearance of a nodule on my vocal chords, and I was forbidden to speak for two weeks to allow it to clear up. My family talk in amazement of this fourteen-day period of silence, unable to believe it really happened. I got through several notebooks, scribbling out messages and requests. Dad took me to Blackpool to recuperate in the crisp, northern fresh air.

When we came to do *Major Barbara* I was dreading the cast list being pinned up on the noticeboard. What Shavian lowlife character was I going to be lumbered with now? The good news was I was going to play a woman at last, the bad news was that the part was the old tramp, Rummy Mitchens. I adopted a crouch, tatty clothes and a dirty face, and for this I was awarded a half share in the Character Prize, which was duly presented to me by George Arliss – the one who was so worried about us drifting into excesses.

All the time I was at RADA I continued, against the rules and without the knowledge or consent of those in charge, to work with the Belfrie Players. I played some fairly unsuitable roles, but it was great experience. Also, and this was no small consideration at the time, in return for our services we were fed after we'd finished the entertainment. I noted in my diary that, after a performance of *Hay Fever* at a fire station, we were given, wonder of wonders, 'a slice of lemon' with our fish.

Dividing my time between RADA and the Belfries did, however, involve quite a bit of travelling and a lot of late nights. We mainly used public transport or shared cars. When I was seventeen, Dad arranged some driving lessons for me. I duly applied for, and got, my provisional licence, which after six months became a full one. So I am of the age group who never had to take a driving test. On the day I received my full licence, I drove Mother's maroon Austin Seven – ELU 117 – very slowly into a tree. Touch wood I haven't done anything similar since.

At RADA, I continued to be given the character parts. When I played the Nurse in *Romeo and Juliet*, I was especially nervous, because no less a personage than Miss Massey was coming to cast her critical eye over the production. I had played the part once already under her direction, and so it was with some trepidation that I made my way to the front of house after the performance, anticipating a word of approval. I found her in the foyer with little Melrose as ever at her side.

'You did it exactly as you did it before,' she said rather crossly. 'You haven't improved at all.' My confidence took a sharp dive.

One of the directors must have spotted in me some potential as a classical actress, because he cast me as a nun in a heart-rending piece, set in a convent, called *The Kingdom of God*. It was my first experience of playing a really serious heroine and I was useless. I did my best to play the part as he wanted, but I was convinced the audience would start laughing at any moment. I had always hated the idea of taking myself too seriously and, as a result, I developed a kind of aversion to heavy, serious roles; it was a lack of self-confidence really. Fifty odd years later, I have gained enough assurance to accept straight parts in shows like *Common as Muck*, *Family Money*, the film *Jude* and Catherine Cookson's *The Secret*, and, as Muff used to say after a performance, 'I think I've got away with it.'

Some male comedians have said that they avoided being bullied at school by making their schoolmates laugh in the playground. I drifted into comedy because I believed that, since the audience was going to laugh at me anyway, I might as well be in things that were *meant* to be laughed at. I've always much preferred to make people smile than to bring on the waterworks or make them clutch their heads in despair. Miss Massey and Miss Nancy had both indicated that they thought my career would 'take off' when I reached forty. Would I really have to wait that long?

One of the other teachers at RADA was the producer David Horne. I always enjoyed working with him because he knew exactly what he was doing and what he wanted from his cast. Ex-Eton and Grenadier Guards, David was a splendid actor of the old school and, as well as teaching us students, he was appearing in *Pink String and Sealing Wax* at the Duke of York Theatre. Whenever he made any money from films or shows, he'd plough it back into his own company, which he ran with his wife, Anne Farrer. David asked if I would like to join a tour he was setting up the following year, and he suggested that, while waiting for the launch of his new season, I should join the *Pink String* company to replace the departing assistant stage manager and understudy. I was thrilled. For a wage of £3 a week *and* work in the West End, I didn't need to be asked twice. On the grounds that I was still a student, David got me a work permit, which exempted me from being called up, and I was free to embark on my first professional engagement. As it said on the permit, I was now 'Whitfield J. EMBC 2763', licensed to act.

Chapter Three

FORCED TO TOUR

IN REALITY, MY WEST END DÉBUT AMOUNTED TO SETTING THE props, running up and down the stairs to give the actors their calls and occasionally, under close supervision, I was permitted to press the button to cue the curtain. Not the most glittering of starts, perhaps, but in the London blackout in 1944, not even leading ladies were permitted to have their names up in lights. In due course, I was promoted to being 'on the book', that is, following the script from the prompt corner and giving the lighting and effects cues. It's a position of some responsibility, and concentration is needed so as not to unleash a burst of thunder and lightning when the doorbell is supposed to ring, or vice versa. I watched the actors, longing for the day when I would be out there in front of an audience, instead of following the script under dim light in the prompt cover.

In common with other shows, ours was badly affected by the intensification of the German air raids, a campaign that now included the dreaded doodlebugs. If ever there was a legitimate reason for poor business, this was it. At the height of the bombing we played to houses of under a hundred.

When St Martin-in-the-Fields received a direct hit, we felt the shock waves rock the Duke of York a quarter of a mile up St

Martin's Lane. But the show must go on, as they say, and it did. The scene in progress at the time of the explosion was the end of a formal meal, with a typically stiff-backed Victorian family seated round the table. At each performance, after the meal, David Horne, who was playing the strict father, stood up and belched loudly, banging the table with a spoon to cover the indelicate moment, after which Iris Hoey – Mother – stood up and said grace. On the night of the bomb, after the terrifying noise, her next line of dialogue was, 'For what we have received, may the Lord make us truly thankful.' There was a silence, followed by an eruption of relieved laughter that rivalled the noise of the bomb.

The raids made the journey to and from Streatham occasionally hazardous and, one night, the car broke down as Muff was driving me to work. An alert sounded, and since there didn't appear to be any trams or buses running, she flagged down a lone motorist crawling along the high road in near darkness.

'My daughter has to get to the Duke of York Theatre for a very important play,' said Muff imperiously. The driver had a sense of drama and responded enthusiastically to our plight, no doubt imagining some distraught manager holding the curtain for my arrival. With the raid now in full swing, the driver told us to get in the car and keep our heads down; we gratefully obeyed while he sped us towards the West End. We arrived at the theatre in a fairly be-draggled state, but in good time for me to attend to my very important role – setting the props and calling the 'half'.

The doodlebugs hit the suburbs rather worse than central London, and we weren't spared in Streatham. Three landed just off the high road within 500 yards of our house, one each in Barcombe Avenue, Downton Avenue and Telford Avenue. Muff had, by now, converted our cellar into an air-raid shelter, containing four bunk beds, one of which I helped to build from old orange boxes, and a range of other luxuries, including a standard lamp, a radio, a table and a kettle. It was christened the dugout and was really quite cosy and comfortable, but if a raid didn't start until late at night, there was a certain reluctance to leave the warmth of one's bed, grab a torch and hurry down the dark stairs to safety. During one particularly heavy raid, when Dad was on warden duty, Mother and Gran repeatedly called me down, but I stubbornly remained in my room, reasoning that the house had been through four years of bombs and was likely to survive one more night. I heard the drone of an approaching doodlebug – I found them the most frightening bombs, as when their buzzing cut out it meant they were on their way down – and heard its engine stop. My heart stopped with it and I slid a little further under the bedclothes and waited. There was a flash and an explosion, and all the air seemed to be sucked out of the room. Tentatively, I poked my head out, and was relieved to see that the walls were still standing and the house was still intact. Then I was out of bed, down the stairs and into the dugout in ten seconds flat. The bomb partially destroyed the church at the end of our road, a quarter of a mile away. Only a few weeks earlier, I had run for cover into the porch of the church after I heard another buzz bomb cut its engine. That one fell further afield and I continued my short journey home somewhat shakily.

On the night that Christchurch was hit, Dad was out fire-watching. More bombs were dropping in the vicinity and we were worried stiff that he might have been near one of them. I was so relieved when I heard his key in the door, but he brought us the sad news that members of three families we knew by sight had lost their lives. It was a typical result of a bombing raid: the partial destruction of a house killing only some of the inhabitants, and leaving the survivors to deal with the consequences for the rest of their lives. Counselling had not been invented, and those left behind had to rely on their own resources, and the help and support of friends, the vicar and their family doctor.

The war years were intensely busy for my father. He drove himself very hard at the Dictograph offices where he was now managing director and, at home, if he wasn't on ARP duty he would toil long into the night. I remember my mother often calling downstairs, 'Jack, are you ever coming to bed?'

'I'll be up in a minute,' he'd say, then carry on working on papers spread out on the dining table. He was always in his office at Croydon by nine and was invariably the last to leave the building in the evening. His conscientiousness was legendary at Dictograph, possibly because he had come into the business as the boss's son and was determined to prove himself in his own right. Whatever the reason, he was a good boss, knew all his employees by name and was interested in their lives. He was greatly respected, and his Yorkshire sayings like 'You never get owt for nowt' and 'Look after the pennies and the pounds will look after themselves' were well known by his colleagues. He taught us to treat people as we would like to be treated and to never buy anything we couldn't afford. I think he would have hated credit cards. He was meticulous about keeping his own accounts, and at the end of every day he would sit down and work out exactly what he'd spent – every penny. Sometimes I would help him. It drove him mad if he couldn't get his sums to tally – 'It's just this last ha'penny,' he'd say, peering at the figures through his spectacles. I have inherited some of his cautiousness where money is concerned. I like to have a record of where it's come from and, more importantly, where it's gone. Nowadays, we'd call my father a workaholic, but he always had time for his family, and the obvious pride he took in my efforts as an actress was a wonderful encouragement to me.

In the autumn of 1944, David Horne finally got the backing he needed to set up his long-promised tour, and I joined the company to play as cast and help with the stage management. Prior to the rehearsal period, I was sent out, as was the lot of ASMs in those days, prop-hunting and hiring, or borrowing furniture from local retailers or anyone who could be persuaded to loan items in return for a pair of complimentary tickets and an acknowledgement in the pro-gramme. A regular port of call was the Old Times Furnishing Company, where you could get anything from a chaise longue to a stuffed bird, and I spent many hours searching through the various rooms for a particular prop. Nowadays everything is either bought or custom built for each production, but in those days badgering a shop-keeper into loaning or hiring out his stock was an essential part of the job.

I was given my first professional acting role in the opening play of the touring repertoire. David cast me as the fey character, Margaret, in J. M. Barrie's *Dear Brutus* and, more importantly, he gave me the confidence to think I could do it. David was a brilliant director and gradually managed to coax an adequate performance out of me. There are certain directors, David was one and Noël Coward was another, who are such magnificent actors themselves that in rehearsal they always play the parts much better than the people they are directing. Some actors find this method discouraging; I found it helpful, and it got me through what might otherwise have been a traumatic début. I have not the slightest doubt however that David would have been a far more effective Margaret than me. We opened at the old Q Theatre in West London – another playhouse that is long gone – and my parents were in loyal attendance on the first night. Their appearance always made me more than usually nervous, but there was never the slightest chance of persuading them to come later in the run. Our actress daughter Suzy has banned Tim and me from her first nights, so I have lost this particular battle of wills twice in my life.

The second play of the tour was W. Somerset Maugham's comedy *The Land of Promise*. David cast me as an eighty-year-old woman – I was nineteen at the time – and asked me to understudy three other parts with a combined age of about 180. He finished his note to me with the words, 'Do hope this will interest you as I would hate to be without one of my bundles of mischief.' I wasn't too sure how to approach playing an eighty-year-old. It was a very small part and there was no-one else available in the company, so I had to do the best I could. I was, after all, hardly in a position to say no!

When you are nineteen, you can approach ancient character parts in two ways: either plaster your face with purple shadows and dark lines, or wear no make-up at all and hope the result will be mistaken for aged pallor. I chose the latter, and added a stoop and a squeaky voice to complete the characterization. After a couple of weeks' rehearsal we were on the road. Fortunately for the theatregoers of Hammersmith and Hull, my appearance in the play was brief, and I was never required to go on as any of the other three crones I was understudying.

I had, by now, acquired an agent. Gordon Harbord had seen me in one of the public shows at RADA. When I was at the Duke of York, his offices were practically next door, so I took the opportunity to go and see him, and he took me on. Gordon was a shrewd Yorkshire businessman, like my father, and had produced a number of successful West End shows. He'd had a brief acting career before realizing that his talents lay elsewhere, and he knew the business inside out. He was helpful to me from the outset, and as soon as the tour finished, he got me straight into another one, this time a triple bill of one-act thrillers entitled *Appointment with Fear*, and advertised on the poster as 'An evening of suspense and thrills (but with nothing horrific).' The venture was intended to capitalize on the success of the radio series of the same name. The unmistakable voice of Valentine Dyall was played over the front of house speakers at the beginning of the first play and at the end of the final one. The evening finished with the Man in Black bidding the audience good night before lapsing into his familiar maniacal laugh.

The star of *Appointment with Fear* was the enchanting Dame Irene Vanbrugh. Over the course of the next year and a half I was to get to know her and her companion/secretary, Ursula Bradley, who, after Irene died, started a drama school of her own. Dame Irene formed a link with some of the Olympian figures in the theatre at the end of the previous century. She had been married to the great Irish playwright Dion Boucicault, and had created the role of Gwendolen Fairfax in the original production of *The Importance of Being Earnest*. Her sister Violet had been a distinguished actress and her brother was the RADA Principal, Sir Kenneth Barnes – he of the trembling teacup. At the age of seventy-two, she exuded patrician grace and had the gift of appearing utterly natural onstage. She had never been a great beauty – she was a little too sharp-featured for that – but she had an engaging smile, a remarkable stage presence and excellent timing. She had a habit of flicking a glance towards the upper boxes before delivering a line, and invariably getting a laugh. It was an education to watch her work from the wings.

As an acting ASM, my position in the pecking order was a lowly one. The author didn't consider the character I played worthy of a name, and so I was simply listed in the programme as 'The Girl'. I was discovered in a cupboard by a German baddy, dragged out and slapped across the face. This brought me out in a rash after the first week, and since I didn't fancy a painful smack in the chops in the same spot every night for the next three months, I came to an agreement with Frederick Horrey, the actor playing my brutal tormentor. We cut it down to a good slap on Mondays and Saturdays, and then he pulled his punches for the rest of the week.

Appointment with Fear was my introduction to the realities of a long tour – the digs, the damp sheets and, oh, those dreaded train calls. The cast and crew of a touring company used to meet at a given time at the station on Sundays as they moved from town to town. We were checked in by the company manager, as he had to make sure we were all there, apart from the lucky ones who were going by car. Travelling by rail on Sundays during the war was tedious and often bitterly cold. There was no heating – or just enough to burn the back of your legs – no refreshments and the carriages were inclined to be grubby. However short the distance between towns, we always seemed to cover the length and breadth of the country, invariably changing trains at Crewe. We passed the time playing cards and sharing sandwiches and drinks hastily assembled before leaving home. I may not have had much opportunity to progress as an actress during the tour, but my card-playing skills improved by leaps and bounds.

As the tour rumbled towards completion, news of the war became steadily better until, during our week in Preston, we heard on the radio that all hostilities in Europe had ceased. I noted in my diary on 8 May 1945, 'The European war is over. Felt very depressed. Lunch with Dame Irene. Felt better.' Why was I depressed? I also wrote the next day, 'Still crowds of people standing about staring at each other.' Maybe we all needed a few days for the news to sink in; maybe it was because we were in Preston.

It was in marked contrast to the wild rejoicing a few months later when the war in the Far East ended. I was staying in Devon with the Giles family, recovering from having my tonsils out; I always seem to be recovering from things in Devon. We danced on the quay at Kingsbridge to express our joy and relief at the end of six years of raids and bombs. No depression that time! The holiday had to be cut short when I received a call to return to London and join Dame Irene in her next venture, this time as stage manager.

There was no part for me, but a stage manager earned ten bob or so more than an assistant stage manager, so I didn't hesitate to accept. Nowadays stage management is a profession in its own right, but then it was often a stepping stone to becoming established as an actor and gaining the then-mandatory Equity card, which I had already acquired during *Pink String and Sealing Wax*. The job requires an ability to stay calm and compile a great many lists. I quite enjoyed it. I still have the foolscap sheet on which I typed all the cast's phone numbers, with those wonderful period prefixes: 'Paddington 2988' – that was Dame Irene; a 'Primrose' number for Olaf Pooley; Lois Maxwell, the original Moneypenny, was 'Gulliver', and Ursula Howells was 'Prospect'.

The play was *Fit for Heroes*, a light comedy about aristocrats falling on hard times, and it was directed by Henry Kendall – his were 'Sloane' and 'Temple Bar' prefixes; you could tell where people lived in the days before we all became just numbers. *Fit for Heroes* had a successful try-out at the Embassy in Swiss Cottage and it was decided to bring it into the West End. However, the producer Anthony Hawtrey couldn't find an available theatre. At the last minute, the Whitehall became vacant and Hawtrey took the unusual step of bringing in *Fit for Heroes* with another play he couldn't find a home for, running that play at six o'clock and ours at eight thirty. Transport services were still limited at the time, and the audience for *Fit for Heroes* had difficulty getting home at such a late hour. It killed us stone dead.

There is nothing worse than playing to poor houses. Actors and directors get very frustrated. After the show had opened, a rehearsal was called. The cast was assembled for 'notes' and there was a heated discussion onstage between the director and Raymond Lovell. Dame Irene, sensing the argument would continue for some time and wishing to distance herself from it, retreated into the wings and said to me quietly, 'Juney, I shall be in my dressing room. Let me know when I'm wanted.' We closed on 29 December 1945, leaving the theatre for the exclusive use of the other play. It was called *Worm's Eye View* and it ran for five years.

The Lancashire comedy *The Cure for Love* was approaching the end of its run at the Westminster Theatre and the management was planning to send it out on the road. It was a topical tale of a soldier returning to his home town and forsaking his fiancée for an evacuee. Dora Bryan had made a name for herself playing the brassy fiancée Janie Jenkins – catchphrase: 'I've got his ring' – but she couldn't do the tour and they were looking for a replacement. My agent, Gordon Harbord, did a good selling job on me and got me an audition. I gave a reading at the Westminster, and after a chilly thank-you from the august figure of H. K. Ayliff, the play's director, I was offered the part. What made the breakthrough such an important one for me was that Wilfred Pickles was playing the leading role. He was then at the height of his fame, and anything he took on attracted an enormous amount of attention.

My performance at rehearsal seemed to be acceptable, but I was still very inexperienced professionally and had never played a comedy role in front of a large audience. On the first night I was very nervous and the butterflies were flitting round my stomach. I kept telling myself, don't be silly, you know the words. Now get on and do it, and I did. I sailed through my performance. Unfortunately, I also sailed through quite a few of Wilfred's laughs. There was one particular scene where I was sitting on his lap, reminding him that I'd got his ring, when I suddenly felt Wilfred's knee jabbing into my back and his urgent remonstration out of the corner of his mouth, 'Wait for the laff. Wait for the laff.' Wilfred said nothing to me afterwards, but the director H. K. Ayliff came storming round to my dressing room and reduced me to tears, telling me I had played it like a student.

'But I *am* a student,' I wailed, because I wasn't that long out of RADA.

It was my first lesson in timing. I soon learned to wait for Wilfred's laughs, and with his help I even managed to pick up a few of my own. He was a good teacher and it was an enjoyable education. Audiences vary from performance to performance and, with a comedy, if the first expected laugh doesn't come, the actors know they're in for a rough night.

Strictly speaking, Wilfred was too old for the part, but he was a very fine actor, a fact often overlooked when his name comes up, and his popularity was such that if the boxes weren't full on Monday night we thought it was a bad week. The tour was initially intended to last ten weeks, but we ended up doing ten months.

1946 was the first year of the radio phenomenon that was *Have a Go*. Wherever we went on tour, the BBC would arrange to record an edition of the programme on the Sunday, either in the theatre where we were playing or in a hall near by. Ginny Lovell, who played the evacuee from London, and I attended some of the recordings, squeezing into the packed auditorium among hundreds of locals eager to take part in this good-natured game show. Imagine *Who Wants to Be a Millionaire* with five fewer noughts and double the audience. We were handed printed cards bearing lyrics of the show's theme song, and on cue we'd all join in to the piano accompaniment of Violet Carson, who later achieved fame as Ena Sharples in *Coronation Street* with her trademark hairnet.

Then Wilfred would appear at the microphone and deliver his opening catchphrase, ''Ow do, 'ow are yer?' to thunderous applause. Seated at a table stage right, holding the gong and the contestants' questions, was Wilfred's wife/assistant/manager/boss, the ever-present Mabel. It was Mabel who had planned Wilfred's career from the start, she who had persuaded him to try his hand at acting professionally, she who had convinced him that radio offered him his best chance, and she who now presided over his triumph. Next to Mabel was a PA, and moving busily about during the recording was the producer Barney Colehan – 'Give 'im the money, Barney'.

After ''Ow do, 'ow are yer?' Wilfred would chat to the first contestant, always asking, ''Ow old are yer?' and if the answer was anything over sixty, Wilfred would look astonished and encourage the audience to give a big round of applause. The contestants had to give a brief résumé of their lives and answer a few questions; if they got a question right they won a small sum of money, but if they got it wrong, Mabel banged the gong and the audience groaned in disappointment.

At the end of the show, Violet Carson played the theme tune again and we all sang:

> That's the show, Joe. You've been and had a go.
> You didn't lose owt, it cost you nowt,
> You've won yourself some dough.
> So listen in next week again to hear another show.
> So long, Joe. You've had a go!

Have a Go ran until the late Sixties, and at its height commanded a listening audience of over 20 million. Mabel employed two secretaries to deal with the fan mail alone.

Amid the stilted, plummy tones of the majority of the BBC's output in the late Thirties and early Forties, Wilfred's voice and unaffected ordinariness were like a breath of fresh air, but he had plenty of detractors, and *Have a Go* drew the same kind of protests we hear now when critics talk of 'dumbing down'.

Wilfred first came to prominence when he was brought down from BBC Northern Region in Manchester to read the national news. Believe it or not, at a time when the war was going badly for the allies, Wilfred's flat 'a' was of sufficient national importance to be reported on the front pages. The minister of information, Brendan Bracken, was personally responsible for Wilfred's appointment. He felt that a more homely voice would be reassuring to listeners and might help to raise morale. Wilfred's head of department also revealed to him the astonishing fact that Bracken feared a Nazi infiltration of Broadcasting House, and believed that it would be harder for the Germans to imitate Wilfred's accent than that of, say, Stuart Hibberd or Alvar Lidell. I would have enjoyed hearing a uniformed SS announcer struggling to emulate Wilfred's characteristic 'good neet'.

Wilfred's Yorkshire ordinariness wasn't at all put on, but he and Mabel were very good at PR. His photograph was printed on his cheques, with the result that landlords, restaurateurs and hoteliers up and down the country would keep them as souvenirs rather than cash

them. I'm sure that's not what he was anticipating when he ordered
the cheques, but it must have saved him a few quid. I must admit I
never saw any evidence of his supposed meanness; quite the reverse,
he was always very generous.

He had to put up with a certain amount of youthful high spirits
from the younger members of the cast, such as myself and Ginny
Lovell. The giggling started at Norwich when, during the first act,
the safety curtain started to come down. The descent of the 'iron' is
always a slow process because it's so heavily counterweighted, and
although we carried on for some time, it was impossible to ignore the
absurdity of the situation. When it reached the tops of our heads, we
ducked down in order to remain visible, but then we completely lost
control. Fortunately, the audience thought it was equally funny, and
when someone found a way to get the iron up again, it received a
sympathetic round of applause. The corpsing bug reappeared a little
later in the tour, and Wilfred got a bit ratty about it, but I'm afraid it
continued. Then, one night, after a particularly disgraceful outburst
in Liverpool, the company manager informed Ginny and me that
Wilfred wanted to see us in his room at the Adelphi Hotel after the
performance. That wiped the smiles off our faces and we trudged
over, convinced we were going to get the sack.

The hotel door was opened by Basil, the company manager, who
beckoned us into the dimly lit room. There was Wilfred sitting at a
green baize table wearing a green eye-shade, and next to him Mabel
was shuffling a deck of cards. Wilfred invited us to come and take our
places at the table. We played a few hands of pontoon, waiting for the
axe to fall, but nothing was said. At last Ginny and I plucked up the
courage to apologize for our childishness.

'It's all right,' he said, 'you won't do it again.' And we didn't.

We did, however, play a great many more games of cards. There were
card schools on the train, at the digs and in the dressing rooms. Wilfred
used to play solo, poker, pontoon, anything, even bridge, which I've long
since forgotten. I still have a cheque dated 14 December 1946, made out
to Wilfred for five pounds, which I lost playing pontoon with him
and Mabel. Wilfred returned the cheque and wrote on the back, 'Buy
yourself something nice for Christmas and give up sticking on sixteen.'

Wilfred had a lot to answer for. He not only encouraged my gambling but introduced me to the doubtful pleasures of smoking. I inhaled my first du Maurier halfway through the tour and didn't kick the habit until thirty years later.

The chief preoccupation of touring life in those days, as it is now, was always the quest for comfortable digs. Ginny and I stayed in some wonderful digs, but also one or two that were only good for one thing, and that was to provide material for theatrical anecdotes. Landlady stories are legion, but I did have one or two memorable encounters. In Nottingham we had a fire in our room; very cosy we thought, but unfortunately it was a coal fire, with just enough warmth to bring a horde of bugs out of hibernation and into our beds. We complained to our gorgon of a landlady and, after inspecting the invaders, she swore we'd brought them with us and asked us to leave. We couldn't wait. Then there was the cheery soul who, when I brought some friends back for a drink after the show and found my bottle of sherry somewhat diminished, replied to my enquiry with, 'Oh yes, I had some people round. You don't mind, do you?'

The tour of *The Cure for Love* came to an end, and I was glad to return to the warmth of home and the comfort of my own bed at 5 Palace Road. But this wasn't to last for long as my parents planned to move house. Rather than move to a smaller house, which would have been the logical step to take, we took up residence at 52 Cadogan Place, SW1. It made no sense at all, particularly for poor Dad, who now had an even longer drive to his office in Croydon, and the house was far too big for us. Brother John and I had a floor each! I loved it, of course. I had to climb three flights of stairs to get to my bedroom which was twice the size of the one I'd left behind at Calderwood. I even had my own sitting room and bathroom. I was definitely in no hurry to leave home. I suspect that Mum thought a Knightsbridge address might help my career – it was certainly nearer theatreland, although my next job was *Pink String and Sealing Wax* at Penge rep!

Sadly, Grandad and Uncle Billy had passed away in the last couple of years and Auntie Bea had gone back to Northamptonshire, so we were now only five. Our housekeeper, Mrs Suter, came with us and moved into the basement. Gran had a room on the ground floor, the first floor was taken up by a large L-shaped drawing room, Mum and Dad were on the second, I was above them and John was at the top.

John was now demobbed and working at the Foreign Office. He was also busy indulging his chief passion in life: golf. I remember Gran saying to him, as he set off on a blustery afternoon, 'Oh, John, surely you're not going to play today. The wind will blow your balls all over the place.'

My performance in *Pink String and Sealing Wax* at Penge led to an offer of *Pink String and Sealing Wax* at Palmer's Green. The Intimate at Palmer's Green offered a mixed repertoire of adventurous and commercial plays and was well-supported by the locals. It lived up to its name as, backstage, it was very intimate indeed, with only three dressing rooms, a tiny proscenium and no wing space whatsoever, which made scene changes virtually impossible. The theatre was run by a gifted and resourceful director, Ronnie Kerr. Legend has it that Ronnie once overcame the scene-changing difficulties in *The Merchant of Venice* by running all the Belmont scenes in the first half and then all the Venetian scenes in Act 2, using the interval to strike and reset. More than one critic thought it cast a fascinating new light on the play. I liked working for Ronnie in *Pink String* and enjoyed playing the part I'd so often followed in the prompt corner night after night at the Duke of York, and to be performing it without bombs dropping around us was a bonus.

It was at the Intimate that, some years later, I committed the cardinal actors' sin. It happened when I was in a play called *Women of Twilight*. The management switched the matinée time from five thirty to two thirty but, for some reason, I had a memory lapse and, at curtain-up time, I was to be found gaily having tea in the Arts Theatre with a girlfriend. She asked me what I was up to and I answered, 'Well, I'm doing this play at the . . . Oh sh—!'

I jumped into the car and drove at breakneck speed across London to the theatre. I hurtled into the dressing room and heard the producer Anthony Hawtrey informing the audience that, 'Miss

Whitfield has now recovered from her indisposition and will resume her role in the second act.' I was mortified for days about my inexcusable behaviour and was convinced that my short career was over, but luckily I was forgiven.

When the run of *Pink String* ended, Ronnie asked me to be in his next production, an ambitious project he was hoping to bring into the West End after a short tour and a run at the Lyric, Hammersmith. It was the première of Sean O'Casey's *Oak Leaves and Lavender*.

I confess I didn't really understand the play. It was set in a Cornish manor house during the Battle of Britain, but the action was interrupted by the appearance of ghostly ancestors, and there was a certain amount of soap-box-style dialogue, including lines like 'Woe unto any nation making war on the Soviet Union – she will slash open the snout, and tear out the guts of any power crossing her borders!' Not exactly a laugh a minute. However, it had a good cast, including Dickie Attenborough's wife, Sheila Sim, and Robert Urquhart.

O'Casey came up from his home in Devon to attend rehearsals. Dour-faced, with white wispy hair and thick, steel-rimmed spectacles, this giant of the theatre was pleasant enough, but he could be severe when crossed. Playing a small part in the show was an actor who was himself to become a distinguished writer, John Whiting. During a rehearsal he grumbled about having to stand still throughout a long scene with nothing to do.

'Shakespeare's characters stood still for hours,' replied Sean tersely.

I played a land girl and also a seller of lavender, whose disembodied voice was heard singing a song during the prologue. Lavender, as is explained in the play, is an omen of death in Cornish mythology, and it certainly did the trick on this occasion. Some of the critics liked the production, but it closed quietly after its scheduled run at Hammersmith, and I returned to that peculiar state of actors' limbo which some call 'resting' but everyone knows means 'out of work'.

*

I have never planned anything in my career, not now and certainly not then. I loved being in the theatre, but I wasn't especially ambitious, and apart from ringing my agent to see what was going on, I didn't do a great deal about pushing myself. Of course I was keen to attend whatever interviews and auditions he arranged, but I never chased after particular parts. It was long before the term 'networking' was invented. But whether it was laziness or fatalism, it didn't seem to place me at a disadvantage. I always had the feeling that something would turn up, and sure enough it always did. The following week a telegram arrived from Broadcasting House:

CAN YOU BROADCAST 8 JULY 8–8.30 P.M.
INCLUSIVE FEE FIVE GUINEAS.

The title of the programme – just in case you missed it – was *Focus on Nursing*. I had one line, something about there being too many patients and not enough staff, which I was asked to deliver in a Devonshire accent. One of the scenes needed the noise of a baby cry- ing, but the sound effects disc had gone missing, and so, during rehearsals, the producer asked me to 'read in' for it. I would willingly have played an entire children's ward, plus the ambulances that brought them, if required. My bawling was considered to be up to broadcasting standards, and so I acquired a second role.

A month later there was another telegram. This time I was asked to be in a hard-hitting drama documentary about the pernicious effects of popular music on the nation's youth. It was called *London's Dance Bands*. I still have the script with my lines marked out, and it rather resembles one of Harry Enfield's period sketches:

MUM: Come on, eat up your food, girl.
ME: Sorry, I'm off to the Palais.
DAD: Again?

Gritty stuff, and it netted me another five guineas. Riches indeed. There was great excitement a few weeks later when Dad took us on a business trip to Dublin. Muff and I planned to stock up on the things that were unavailable in Britain, where goods were still rationed, if not quite so strictly as they had been during the war. Dad and I had developed a mutually convenient arrangement over the previous few years whereby he gave me his clothing coupons and I gave him my sweet ration. It worked well, but one was always looking for ways of supplementing the allowance, and we'd heard that the Irish shops were groaning with goodies. We sailed to Belfast, then caught a train down to Dublin, having to pass through two sets of customs. After a day's sightseeing on the Sunday, we looked forward to a shopping spree on the Monday – I was keen to buy some fleecy-lined boots. What we'd overlooked was that it was a bank holiday and everything was shut. We wandered around window-shopping, noting the shops we'd attack the next morning before we had to leave. We had tickets for the theatre in the evening, but a blizzard forced us to turn back. Still, we managed to stuff ourselves with steak and chops and bacon and eggs, which were an almost unattainable luxury at home. We had just an hour to spend in our targeted shops the following morning, and using my BBC five guineas I purchased my boots. I was in such a hurry that I failed to notice they were half a size too small, so they languished unused for years in my wardrobe. Come to think of it, my wardrobe contains a great many injudicious holiday buys.

The closest thing I had to a career plan was a strong desire to keep working. Although I wasn't aware of it at the time, this is not a bad way to approach life in the theatre, because the more work you do the more contacts you build up and the greater your chances of re-employment, as I was now about to discover. Wilfred Pickles had signed a two-year deal with the man who was known as the pantomime king of the North, Francis Laidler. Wilfred was to play Buttons at the Bradford Alhambra in the 1947/48 season, and then take the show to Leeds the following winter. My agent received a call from Laidler's office asking me to play Cinderella. So my association with Wilfred, which began with me treading on his laughs, then degenerated when I kept getting the giggles during his serious moments, was now at the stage where he was recommending me for a title role. He must have thought it was a case of better the devil you know!

As we are about to spend some time in the world of pumpkins, dames and fairy godmothers, I might be allowed one or two blimpish observations on the state of pantomime. I know there are still good traditional shows – Roy Hudd has been responsible for some wonderful pantos – but many recent offerings leave a lot to be desired. Sports personalities and TV presenters do not necessarily have the skills to perform in pantomime, but that doesn't stop them topping the bill – not always to the benefit of the show. I wonder how the English rugby team would like it if they had to carry an actor in the scrum. I go along with Roy Hudd, who would much rather have performers who really understand pantomime and know how to handle it.

Pantomime in the late Forties was done on a lavish scale and it was very big business indeed, especially in the provincial cities. Leeds might have three pantomimes running at the same time and all doing a roaring trade. Laidler pantos were among the most glittering. They contained the familiar ingredients – comedians, speciality acts, chorus, a troop of 'babes' etc. – great care was taken over the sets and costumes and there was a full complement of musicians in the pit. Everything in a Laidler panto was planned down to the last sequin, with nothing left to chance. I treasure a letter from him enclosing seven clothing coupons for Cinderella's silver ballroom shoes, to be purchased before rehearsals so I could 'break them in' in time. One felt like a small but vital functionary in some vast entertainment empire.

I had a couple of numbers, a solo and a soppy duet with Fay Lenore, my Prince Charming. It began:

> My love is only for you my darling,
> For you, just you.
> My day begins as it ends, as always,
> With you, just you . . .

It was not one of my finest efforts, but Fay was an excellent

Wedding day for my mum and dad, John Whitfield and Bertha Flett.

LEFT: 'Executive Dad'.

BELOW LEFT: Dad as Charlie's Aunt.

BELOW RIGHT: My glamorous mum.

ABOVE: Auntie Bea, Grandad and Granny Flett.

LEFT: Brother John reporting for duty.

RIGHT: John and fiancée, Rosemary (Bud).

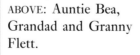

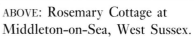

ABOVE: Rosemary Cottage at
Middleton-on-Sea, West Sussex.

BELOW: Shivering at Felpham
with Muff and John.

ABOVE: The family home, Calderwood,
now a block of flats, once a home for
unmarried mothers.

BELOW: A reluctant beach babe.

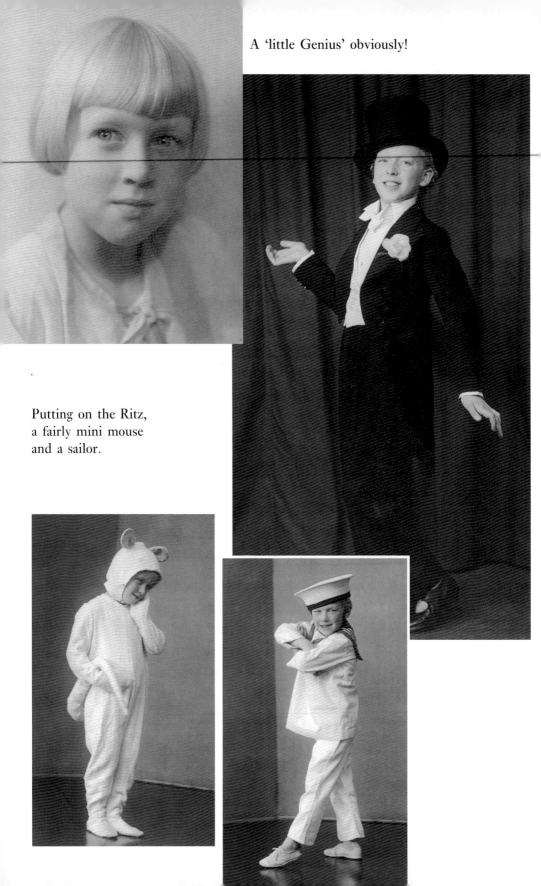

A 'little Genius' obviously!

Putting on the Ritz,
a fairly mini mouse
and a sailor.

ABOVE: As Puck for Miss Massey with assorted fairies.

LEFT: 'Something nasty in the woodshed'.

RIGHT: A Christmas special.

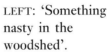

RIGHT: 'A boy' – it must be serious, the vicar has arrived.

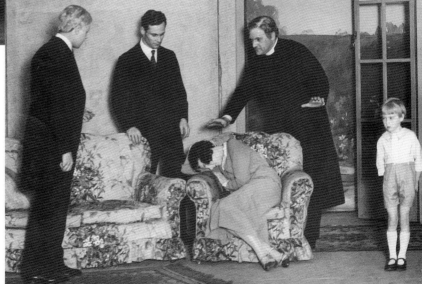

LEFT: *Pink String and Sealing Wax* at Penge.

BELOW: *Appointment with Fear*: 'the girl' with Lewis Stringer.

ABOVE: Panto publicity with Wilfred Pickles – 'Will that fly reach the top of the window?'

LEFT: *Cinderella*, Bradford Alhambra, 1946.

FAR LEFT: *Ace of Clubs* party with Noël Coward, 'the Master'.

BELOW: *Ace of Clubs* – me left front, hoping to keep my hat on.

ABOVE: *Penny Plain* revue, left to right: Elisabeth Welch, Rose Hill, Delia Williams, Moyra Fraser, Marjorie Dunkels, me and Joyce Grenfell.

RIGHT: *Love From Judy*, the dream ballet.

BELOW: Me as Sally McBride.

BELOW RIGHT: *South Pacific*, leading fellow 'nurses' showing off the fake tan.

Love From Judy – the opening number, 'Mardi-Gras'.

principal boy, who steered me through and took the high notes where necessary. We performed it on radio, live from the Bradford Royal Infirmary on Christmas Day as part of *Wilfred Pickles' Christmas Party*, no doubt baffling the children as we weren't in costume. As often as not nowadays in pantomime the principal boy *is* a boy, the theory being that children won't accept a girl dressed as a boy singing love songs to another girl. The way things are going, we may end up with the principal girl being played by a boy serenading another boy – back to Shakespeare's day! There have been many famous female principal boys – Dorothy Ward, Evelyn Laye, Hy Hazell – and I must say I prefer the traditional approach; it is Fairyland after all.

I shared digs with Dandini – June Campany – and we shivered together through the very severe winter of 1947. One week Max Bygraves was staying in the same digs. He'd been on a bill with Judy Garland at the Palladium and we must have driven him barmy asking him all about her. What's she like to work with? Is she as marvellous onstage as she is on film? etc. I think he was rather upset that we hadn't asked about his own performance and he finally lost patience: 'What are you, lesbians or something?'

The rest of the panto cast comprised the Tiller Girls, Marion Dawson and Richard Milner as the ugly sisters, Bert Rich as the Baron, the Barbour Brothers on stilts, Kirby's Flying Ballet – 'with sensational auditorium flights' – the Little Sunbeams and four ponies to pull Cinderella's carriage – later reduced to three, as one of them got pregnant and had to leave before the end of the run (the ponies, not the Sunbeams) – this is not an unknown occurrence in a long-running pantomime, but it's the only time I've known it happen to the ponies.

Wilfred was not very keen on the ponies to begin with. He was afraid they might do what every little boy in the audience was praying they would do right in the middle of the stage and, preferably, during a love song. He asked for a dustpan and brush to be on permanent standby in the wings, just in case. A week into the run, the inevitable happened. Wilfred fetched the dustpan and got an enormous laugh when he cleared up the mess. The next few shows passed without incident, but the memory of the laugh preyed on

Wilfred's mind. It's agony for a comedian to see a laugh go begging, so he consulted the property master and asked if it was possible for some false pony dung to be made. The prop man rose to the challenge and produced a not very convincing combination of canvas, glue and latex, a sort of prototype Naughty Fido – Naughty Ned in this case. It was one of the Tiller Girls' delightful task to conceal these things and drop them on the stage behind the ponies as they exited, pulling Cinders to the ball. You could see Wilfred's eyes lighting up in anticipation of the huge laugh he was going to get, but unfortunately the prop man's creations bounced on impact and bobbled to the front of the stage in a most undunglike fashion, finally coming to rest in the footlights – yes, we had them in those days. Wilfred went to work with the dustpan and brush, but the audience hadn't the faintest idea what he was up to and, although it caused a confused giggle, Wilfred came to the conclusion that he had to leave it to the ponies to get their own belly laugh. He was reprimanded by Francis Laidler, but the dustpan and brush was still always at the ready.

No show starring Wilfred would have been complete without a special appearance by Mabel. It was clear to everyone, with the possible exception of Wilfred, that her abilities as a performer were somewhat limited, nevertheless a character called Margery was created for her, and a short scene was written into the script. The set-up was that Margery would go into a shop and ask Buttons, who was serving, for some material to match her skirt. She'd turn out front to admire something on an invisible shelf and then Wilfred, who was wielding some scissors, presented her with the matching material. As she turned upstage to face him, the audience was treated to a view of Mabel's bloomers, as Wilfred had cut the material from the back of her dress. Hearty laughter all round, proving that, in panto, the old gags are the best.

Once offstage, Mabel's power was considerable, and she hardly ever let Wilfred out of her sight. She wouldn't even allow the dressers to help him with his quick changes. This seemed excessively cautious, since it was highly unlikely that Wilfred would run off with one of the wardrobe girls, but she wasn't taking any chances. She insisted on attending to what is always a very quick change for the lead comic after his final spot with the song sheet and the kids from the audience. Mabel yanked off Wilfred's Buttons trousers to reveal his gold spangled finale pantaloons underneath. But one night she did it with such force that she broke her little finger. No sympathy, of course, just cruel laughter from everyone who thought she should have left the job to a professional. Poor Mabel. She was the power behind the throne and very protective of Wilfred.

At the end of the run, Mabel and Wilfred threw a big party at the Great Northern Hotel in Bradford. 'Cocktails at 7 – oo 'eck' said the printed invitation. 'Hangovers by John Haig and Alka Seltzer. Ambulances at 12. RSVP. Let's know if th'art coomin.' It certainly was 'a bit of a do' thrown by the kind and generous Pickles.

It was quite a shock to leave a Laidler show, where everything was done with great care and efficiency, and go to work for a manager well-known in the touring world, not just for the tattiness of his sets and costumes, but also for his erratic date schedules, with weeks off in mid-tour and venues ranging from the cavernous to the cramped. James Shirvell was putting out a tour of *The Desert Song*, as he had been doing since the early Thirties, and was to continue to do into the late Fifties. I went to see him and was offered a part in the chorus at eight pounds a week.

'Oh no, sorry,' I said, 'I've been getting more than that,' and turned to leave.

'You can have ten if you understudy the leading lady.'

'Done,' I said.

He didn't ask if I was capable of doing it, and little did I know what I was letting myself in for.

When the tour reached Glasgow, Mary Moreland fell victim to the infamous Glasgow throat, and on the Monday night I took over. Mary's costume didn't fit me, so the wardrobe mistress delved into a mouldy old basket of clothes, kept for such an emergency, but hardly ever opened, and produced an unpleasantly damp specimen which had probably been worn by Edith Day in the original production. There was barely time to air it before the show.

Although I had several understudy rehearsals and had learned the score, my voice wasn't really up to the role. My entrance was through double doors at the top of a flight of steps. I was terrified, and I stood shaking, waiting for my cue to enter thinking, What *do* I think I'm doing? I can't do this. Then I was on, walking unsteadily down the flight of stairs, saluting and singing:

> Girls, girls, girls, here are Cavaliers,
> Handsome cavaliers. Aren't they fine . . .

Soon the song climbs to high 'C' and stays there for what seemed like about half an hour, which for a bass-baritone like me is a daunting prospect. I would like to take this opportunity to apologize to the people of Glasgow and anyone unfortunate enough to have paid for a ticket that night. The critic of the local paper wrote, 'June Whitfield, after a shaky start, proved herself to be as capable an artist as she was a charming heroine. Hardly a Hollywood case of the understudy's dream coming true for Miss Whitfield has played the part before.' Written over this clipping, in my hand, it says, 'Furious, untrue', I'd barely learned the part, never mind played it before.

The tour had its lighter moments, however. I remember a week when we coincided with Monsewer Eddie Gray, who was playing at the Variety Theatre. He was staying in the same digs and it was almost impossible to eat a meal he was so funny. He was famous for his cod French and kept us all in fits. It was a good week.

Then there were the Riffs. The Riffs, for those who may not know *The Desert Song*, are rough and ready tribesmen, followers of the Red Shadow. Our chorus boys were charming, but not exactly what you'd call butch. On more than one occasion, they received severe reprimands from the management, and instructions to desist from making eyes at members of the audience in the front row. I wouldn't have missed their flirtatious antics or their sibilant rendition of the Riffs song.

After the tour and a few weeks in rep, it was time for me to head back up north to Leeds for another three months of *Cinderella* at the Theatre Royal. It was quite common for pantomimes to run from

Christmas to Easter in those days, and Laidler once ran *Humpty Dumpty* at Leeds until 26 May! We didn't do quite as long as that, but at the end of the Bradford run the local paper ran a photo of the chorus sunbathing on the roof of the theatre. Doing the same thing for months at a time, you tend to search for ways to break the monotony. I remember feeling particularly desperate at one matinée. There were some rowdy and unruly children running up and down the aisles, not listening to, or watching, anything, except the slapstick scenes, and there was the usual smell of oranges wafting onto the stage, no doubt handed out by mums hoping to keep the kids quiet. Cinderella – me – was by the fire feeling sorry for herself as the ugly sisters had gone to the ball, and I had to say:

> Alas, poor me, left lonely and forlorn,
> To sit and wait till they return at dawn.

For my own amusement, I said:

> Alas, poor me, left lonely and forlorn,
> Whilst all the others to the ball have gorn.

There was no reaction at all, except a faint offstage snigger. It was really rather sad that not a soul noticed.

Over the course of the two seasons we gave around 400 performances of *Cinderella*, doing twelve shows a week and only dropping a couple of matinées during the final month. One certainly earned one's twelve pounds.

Wilfred later regretted taking on such a heavy commitment. He had agreed to it against Mabel's advice and it was the first and last time he took a professional decision without her approval. He had done it, he said, because he felt that performing to children was a good way of building up an audience for the future. Panto is an endurance test. Wilfred was very tired after the Leeds run. I don't think he did another, and it was 1982 before my next, when I 'graduated' to Fairy.

*

I had worked pretty solidly since leaving RADA. I was twenty-four and had seen little of the world, except for the backstages of the majority of the country's theatres. In some respects that gave me a broader education in the ways of the world than most twenty-four-year-olds receive, but it was confined to the theatre. Apart from my unsuccessful shopping trip to Dublin, I hadn't travelled at all, and Dad decided that, as a belated coming-of-age present, I should have a trip to America.

In the summer of 1949, I sailed from Southampton on the *Queen Mary*, bound for New York. When the Comedy Channel in America launched the third series of *Absolutely Fabulous*, they flew us first class on Concorde – a wonderful experience if someone else is picking up the bill – but nothing could possibly match the splendour, the glamour and the unalloyed luxury of that first voyage on the *Queen Mary*. Thanks to Dad's generosity I was in a first-class cabin, and was kitted out with a different evening dress for each night of the voyage. We were supplied with a booklet containing the names of all the other passengers. I was told in awed tones by a steward that I would be seated at the same table as Mrs Pleydell-Bouverie. As the voyage progressed, people seemed impressed by my social coup. 'I see you're at Mrs Pleydell-Bouverie's table,' they'd say. 'Oh yes,' I'd reply, though the name meant absolutely nothing to me. I didn't know she belonged to such a prominent American family. She was very pleasant, but we were never on intimate terms.

Dad had arranged for me to stay in Vermont with some business associates of his who had also become friends, Joan and Gordon Boyce. Gordon was attached to a university, and had founded an organization called the Experiment in International Living. They arranged for students from one country to live with a family in another, and the movement attracted quite a bit of attention in the Forties and Fifties. Gordon and Joan were so hospitable and made me very welcome. There seemed to be endless parties and 'drinks with . . .' and we spent some time at their log cabin on an island in the St Lawrence River; when a flag was flown on a neighbouring island, it meant Martini time. It was my first encounter with this dangerous cocktail and our outboard dinghy weaved a bit on the way back.

The log cabin's 'powder room' was a wooden shed some yards away from the house – all well and good, until you were inside and had shut the door. The inside of the door was a favourite spot for spiders and, oh, they were large – probably harmless but quite enough to frighten Miss Muffet away. Tricky at times. I solved the problem by leaving the door wide open and whistling.

Coming from austerity-gripped Britain, America was a land of plenty, and when I went to stay in Connecticut with Joan's sister and her husband, the Snodgrasses, I set eyes, for the first time, on a deep freeze. My hostess, Ione, had just acquired this novelty, and I remember the whole kitchen being filled with food to be frozen. Bread, beef, chicken, fish, pies, vegetables – in it all went, carefully wrapped and labelled as instructed. It took the best part of a day to load it. I wonder if they ever got through it.

I was taken to see all the usual sights – Empire State, Statue of Liberty, racing at Saratoga and so on. I went to a rodeo at Binghamton and saw the original productions of *South Pacific* and *Kiss Me Kate*, which I adored. I saw Uta Hagen in *A Streetcar Named Desire* and the Rockettes at Radio City. We also went to one of the other radio studios in New York to see a variety show being recorded. At the start of the proceedings, they asked for volunteers from the audience to enter a Queen of Song for the Day talent contest, and I was persuaded – not too difficult a job – to take part. We had to sing 'Take Me Out to the Ball Game', which I'd never heard before, but it's not a very complicated tune, so I soon picked it up. The Queen of Song's prize was a Polaroid camera, which I have to this day. Unfortunately it became obsolete about forty-five years ago, so it isn't a lot of use.

While I was staying with the Snodgrasses, I was invited by some friends of theirs, a father and son, to go sailing on Long Island Sound. I thought it would be fun, which it should have been, but the pair of them started arguing as soon as we cast off. A squall blew up and they couldn't agree on how best to handle the situation. The matter was eventually taken out of their hands when the squall suddenly developed into a hurricane which capsized or sank every boat in the vicinity. As we went over, they kept saying, 'Stick with the ship. Stick with the ship.' Being unfamiliar with sail-speak, I didn't know what they were talking about, nor did I have a great deal of confidence in them, so I dived off, thinking I would come up and hang onto the boat. Unfortunately, my dive took me right under the mast, which, with its sail attached, was now lying flat on the water. I banged my head on it, took a watery deep breath and, thinking my last moment had come, swam with all my might. Miraculously, I surfaced at the end of the mast. I clung on to it for dear life, looking like a bedraggled fairy on an overturned Christmas tree. Slowly I began to pull my way, hand over hand, back towards the hull, which was on its side and being lashed by the waves.

'I was just coming to look for you,' shouted the son, sitting comfortably, having 'stuck with the ship'.

Thanks a lot, I thought. Too late. I was shocked, shivering but relieved to still be of this world. So there we stayed, barely afloat, with the hurricane howling and whipping up the sea. Meanwhile, on the shore, Ione and Bill Snodgrass were going frantic with worry over the fate of Jack Whitfield's daughter from England.

We waved at a few boats that were still the right way up, but they just waved back and sailed on. For several hours we hung on, getting steadily lower in the water. Eventually, the coastguard came and fished us out, but it took a while because over a hundred other boats had tipped over. It was a wonder that only seven people were drowned. At the height of the storm, the strong winds had bent palm trees on the shore, and the Snodgrasses were very pleased to see me in one piece. We dined out on the story for some time.

Luckily I'd left my passport and cash at the house, but I had taken a small bag with me, containing lipstick, powder and my diary – silly girl – which sadly was lost, and so who knows what secrets lie at the bottom of Long Island Sound. No doubt a catalogue of 'drinks with . . .'

So the 1940s ended, for me, as they had started in a murky Streatham swimming pool: with a ducking. I came back to England on the *Queen Elizabeth* in the autumn, hoping to get my career going again using the method I'd employed successfully before, namely waiting for the phone to ring. After a slightly longer period than usual it did. The call was well worth waiting for; it was an audition at the Cambridge Theatre for Noël Coward.

Chapter Four

LIFE UPON THE WICKED STAGE

I HAD NO IDEA WHAT THE COMPETITION WAS LIKE BUT IT WAS CLEAR from the hordes of hopefuls thronging the Palace Theatre that there was a lot of it. The queue ran from the stage door, along the dressing-room corridor, into the wings and round the back of the set, finishing up on the far side of the stage. By the look of it there was a wait of several hours. It occurred to me that if I surreptitiously went underneath the stage and up the steps on the other side, I'd merge with the head of the queue. If you can get on at the beginning of an audition, while those who do the choosing still have fresh minds, I think you stand a better chance. There is an argument for going on at the very end, when they're absolutely desperate, but it's not so good to appear in the middle, when one face tends to merge with the next.

After five minutes or so the stage manager, having checked that my name was on the list, ushered me on stage to audition for the man who was rightly known as the Master. Gladys Calthrop, Noël Coward's designer, used to write little notes next to the names to help remind him which one was which: 'Biblical type – big tits' was what she allegedly wrote of one aspirant. Not me obviously, as no-one could say I had pronounced religious convictions.

I sang 'Wonderful Guy' from *South Pacific*, which I'd recently seen on Broadway, and when I'd finished I was asked to descend into the gloom of the stalls to meet Noël Coward.

'Where did you get that number from? It hasn't been released here yet.'

'I brought it with me from America,' I said, which seemed to satisfy him.

'Well done,' he said, and went on to explain a little about the show which was set in a London nightclub. 'Can you do a South London accent?'

'I hope so,' I replied. 'I was born in Streatham.'

He grinned at me. 'We'll let you know.'

I left, thrilled to have actually spoken to the great man, and rushed home to tell Muff all about it. We were jumping up and down with excitement. I knew there was no guarantee that I would be in the show, but I kept my fingers crossed. Coward's diary entry for 30 March 1950 shows that I was right not to get too carried away:

> A gruelling day of auditions. Saw hundreds, picked a few possibles. Really felt worn out by the end of it and oppressed by the thought of those legions of unattractive men and women thinking they were gifted enough to entitle them to appear on the stage. Caught the nine o'clock ferry to Paris.

Unattractive and deluded we may have been, but he had to cast *some* of us. I was recalled for a second singing audition, followed by a reading, and at the end of the afternoon I was told to report for rehearsals in a fortnight's time. I was over the moon. Thanks to that 'wonderful guy' I was in.

The show was *Ace of Clubs*, starring Pat Kirkwood and Graham Payn. It was a light-hearted gangster story, set in a Soho dive. I was cast as Sunny Claire, one of the floorshow girls. We were not called 'chorus' but 'small part players', as we each had the odd line to deliver. Also in the cast were Vivien Merchant, who hadn't much to do except sit at a table, and Jean Carson, who played the part of a singer called Baby Belgrave. I understudied Jean and went on for her, just as I was to do a couple of years later in *Love From Judy*. I also understudied Pat, but luckily never had to take her place as she was extremely sophisticated and glamorous.

Some of the floorshow songs gave Coward an opportunity to send up the nightclub entertainment of the time. In one number, we all shimmied on wearing very short shorts and bras with balloons round our waists singing 'Would You Like to Stick a Pin in My Balloon, Daddy?' It was gratifying to read in his diaries years later that he had appreciated our efforts at satire. Everyone tried hard to earn his approval. He had triumphed in every branch of the theatre – writing, composing, directing and performing – and there was probably no-one who commanded greater respect in the profession.

He was living proof of the saying that genius is 10 per cent inspiration and 90 per cent perspiration. The writing of *Ace of Clubs* had spanned more than a year. Coward started with a few numbers and not much idea what to do with them, so he set them aside to work on other projects. Then, in March 1949, he spent an evening listening to Ivor Novello playing through the score of *King's Rhapsody*. It seems that hearing his old friend and rival's new work spurred him into action as, a few days later, he began to apply himself to *Ace of Clubs*. Initially, he called the show *Over the Garden Wall*, then changed the title with each new draft. It became *Hoi Polloi*, and then *Come Out to Play*, before he finally settled on *Ace of Clubs*. He had great difficulty finding a producer for the show. Successive managements expressed interest out of deference to his reputation, only to develop cold feet when they read the script and remembered that his two previous musicals had not been successful. It must have been a humiliating process for him, but he was determined not to be defeated. In the end, he got it put on by agreeing to waive his royalties until such time as the show went into profit, and by guaranteeing two thirds of the production costs himself, thus breaking one of the cardinal rules of show business: never invest in your own work. At last, with the reluctant backing of the impresario Tom Arnold, he was able to go into production, and began holding those tiresome auditions at the Palace Theatre, on the set, as it happened, of *King's Rhapsody*.

Coward had tremendous faith in the show, and with good cause, as it had some excellent numbers, like 'Sail Away', 'I Like America', 'My Kind of Man' and 'Chase Me, Charlie'. It also had a delightfully silly plot, involving a parcel of stolen jewels and a love story between a sailor and a singer. The singer was given a pair of falsies by her girl-friends in the chorus as a birthday present; the parcels got switched, the singer got the rocks and the thieves ended up with the boobs. All harmless fun, and a great show to take part in. There's something magical about being in a musical, and I shall never forget the excitement I felt before every performance when I heard, 'Overture and beginners, please,' and the orchestra struck up.

We rehearsed for a month in Manchester and, apart from a troublesome set that prolonged the dress rehearsal until five thirty in the morning, things went as smoothly as they ever can with the birth of a new musical. There were no public previews then, and it is extraordinary how performers can summon up the energy for a first night when they've had hardly any sleep the night before after a long and tiring day. You feel at your lowest – no energy and convinced that you'll get it all wrong. It's then that Dr Theatre looks in, and once the first night curtain goes up the adrenalin kicks in, your energy and enthusiasm return and, with any luck, you give a good performance. The second night might suffer a bit, but if you're young and healthy you soon recover.

The Master remained perfectly calm and composed throughout this often fraught period. He really was a consummate man of the theatre and he knew everyone's job inside out; whether you were a stage manager, an electrician or an actor, he always seemed to be one step ahead of you, and you had to be on your toes when dealing with him. When I asked him if it would be all right to wear a fringe in the show, he replied, 'Good idea. It'll hide that vast expanse of forehead.' He once told one of the other girls, Liz Kearns, that she must look at Graham Payn while he sang 'Sail Away', instead of facing out front. She had long blond hair hanging down over one eye, Veronica Lake-style, and she said, 'But Noël, if I do that, the audience won't see my face.' She knew as soon as she'd spoken that she'd left an open goal. There was an expectant hush in the assembled company then, smiling slightly, he said, 'That will only serve to hide the wrong expression on it.' From then on, her gaze was directed towards Graham. If you were on the receiving end of one of the Master's celebrated put-downs it was, to say the least, an uncomfortable experience, although he was always right and caused great amusement to those who were not his targets.

There was a similar occasion when Sylvia Cecil was rehearsing a rather sentimental number called 'Nothing Can Last For Ever', and Pat Kirkwood, who had to be onstage with her at the time, asked, 'Noël, what do I do while Sylvia's singing this song?'

'We're going to bring on a pink wheelbarrow,' he said, 'and you're going to wheel it up and down.'

Pat got the message and remained motionless during Sylvia's song.

A few months later, Noël came to watch the show, which was then running at the Cambridge Theatre. Pat had developed a very tiny gesture of support, as though to indicate she was listening to Sylvia. It was the merest flicker of the hand, and not remotely distracting. Coward called a rehearsal to tighten up the show and, doing an exaggerated pantomime of Pat's gesture, asked, 'What is this Uriah Heep-like doubling-up you're doing? When did that creep in?'

Quick as a flash, Pat said, 'Well, you never did give me that pink wheelbarrow.'

The opening in Manchester was a success. Coward was delighted with the show and especially pleased with the performance of his devoted long-term partner, Graham Payn, in the male lead. Graham was an excellent dancer with a reasonably good singing voice and, in some measure, the show was a vehicle for him. Coward naturally felt protective – he used to call him Little Lad – and was determined the show would succeed, as much for Graham's sake as his own. After the first night in Manchester he wrote in his diary:

Quite obviously a smash success. Terrific ovation. Graham nearly stopped the show twice with 'Sailor' and 'America'. He became, before the first act was half over, a star. I am fairly bursting with pride and satisfaction.

Coward gave us a party at the Midland Hotel. He played the piano and sang for us, and we all joined in. His spirits were high, and after a meeting about the show's immediate prospects with his producer, Tom Arnold, he wrote:

Apparently I can have any theatre I want. Am I gloating? Yes, dear diary, I am gloating like hell.

The London first night at the Cambridge was the most glamorous event. The theatre had been specially decorated in pink for the occasion, with a canopy outside the foyer. Coward had reserved a hundred seats for his friends, who formed what the *Evening Standard* described as 'a wall of white shirts and diamonds', and that was just the fellers! The Attenboroughs were there, the paper reported breathlessly, also C. B. Cochran, Leslie Henson, Cesar Romero, Beatrice Lillie, Emlyn Williams, Irene Dunne and Ava Gardner. Frank Sinatra punched a photographer – a ritual without which no glittering occasion could expect to be taken seriously.

Even allowing for first-night excitement, the audience response was overwhelmingly favourable, although there was a bit of a rumpus in the gallery when a small group of first-nighters booed Coward as he walked onstage to make his curtain speech in front of the cast. He smoothed his hair and pretended to stifle a yawn while the hecklers quietened down. He thanked the company, then made a slightly defensive speech, perhaps betraying his fear of what the critics might be about to write: 'What I have written has no significance, carries no message and is simply intended to provide an entertaining evening in the theatre.'

They didn't savage it exactly, but the consensus was that the simplicity of the love story was at odds with the sharp satire of the numbers, and that he was somehow 'writing down' to the audience. The advance bookings were not bad but, with his vast experience, Coward sensed it was not going to be quite the hit he had hoped. A fortnight after *Ace of Clubs* opened, he flew back to Jamaica to lick his wounds. A few days after his arrival at Blue Harbour, he wrote to his secretary, Cole Lesley, in London:

I am furious about *Ace of Clubs* not being a real smash and I have come to the conclusion that if they don't care for first-rate music, lyrics, dialogue and performance they can stuff it up their collective arses and go and see *King's Rhapsody* till *les vaches se rentrent*.

Meanwhile, the show settled into what seemed to us to be a successful run, and we continued to have the time of our lives. After the performance we would go to the Buxton Club in Shaftesbury Avenue or the Café de Paris to see the brilliant cabaret stars of the time.

We were also caught up in the craze for the card game canasta. Noël and Graham had been introduced to it the previous year and were fanatical about it, as was the majority of fashionable society. Coward described in his diary an evening at the American embassy, when he partnered Princess Margaret against some formidable opposition, including the Queen Mother – then Queen – and won. Cole Lesley wrote in his biography of Coward that they even had a little folding baize-topped table, which they would set up on railway-station platforms, so they could play while waiting for trains. I was taught to play by Myles Eason, an *Ace of Clubs* cast member, a witty, funny fellow and a very good friend. A group of us would regularly get together after the show, usually at Myles's flat in Jermyn Street and occasionally at my home or the studio at Gerald Road, which Graham shared with Noël and Cole. After a bite to eat, we would play canasta till the early hours. I wonder now how we got by on so little sleep and marvel at our youthful stamina.

Most exciting were the parties at the Gerald Road studio, which was, in fact, a large, elegantly furnished room in the top half of a house just off Eaton Square. It occupied most of one floor and had a raised dais at one end, on which sat two grand pianos. It was a stage really, with a big picture window behind. I think I was invited because I was in the show and friendly with Graham. Working for the Master gave one temporary membership of his family and an occasional glimpse of 'the stars at play'. There was always splendid food and drink, as you would expect at any good party, but at Gerald Road there was impromptu five-star entertainment thrown in.

Where else could you see Noël Coward and Kay Thompson playing two pianos and singing together while, sitting around on the floor, were the likes of Bea Lillie, Frances Day and Florence Desmond? I had never been in such rarefied company and it was really all very heady.

Then there was 'The Game'. This was a form of charades that later became the TV show *Give Us a Clue*. Those who have played it will know that, as the evening progresses and the drink flows, what begins as a polite parlour game usually degenerates into an unseemly display of rude gestures and frenzied shouting. The Coward household's version was no different. When it was your turn, you would be given a slip of paper on which was written a phrase or saying; it was either terribly erudite or filthy, and often both. Then you had to act it out for everyone else to guess. Cole Lesley recalled one boisterous session at the studio involving Joyce Carey, the Oliviers and the Millses: 'Margaret Lockwood, exquisitely pretty, viciously kicking from time to time, and Joycie enquiring of her, ever so gently, "Darling, could it by any chance be 'Take a flying **** at a galloping mule'?"'

There were two other Coward residences, both in Kent: Goldenhurst, a large seventeenth-century house at Aldington, and White Cliffs, a more modest place on the coast at St Margaret's Bay. I spent several weekends at both houses, but chiefly at White Cliffs. Graham would drive me and Myles down after the show late on Saturday night, and we would sustain ourselves during the journey with tasters of pink gin from a flask. We'd laze about on the Sunday, being given more lovely things to eat and drink, playing canasta or, at Goldenhurst, croquet. The library shelves were stacked with Noël's books and records, and we did our best to work our way through them. On Monday afternoon, Graham would drive us back to London in time for the evening performance.

I was still living at home, which by now was a flat in Kensington Court. After *Ace of Clubs* had been running for a while, I threw a party for a few of my fellow actors after the show. On the appointed evening, Graham waylaid me in the wings and said, rather tentatively, that the Master would quite like to pop along later and would it be all right? 'Would it be all right?' I couldn't believe it. I hadn't had the nerve to invite him initially, but was thrilled at the prospect of his coming. Noël arrived with Joyce Carey and Cole, and stayed for the whole evening. He charmed my mother to pieces before sitting down at our baby grand and instigating a general sing-song. The Master, in our home, playing our piano! We didn't get rid of the piano for years; once Uncle Ron had gone there was no-one in the family who could play, yet my husband Tim and I transferred it from house to house until, eventually, we sold it to a piano dealer because it took up too much room. There is probably someone playing it now who has no idea that Noël Coward once tinkled its ivories.

A cast recording was made of *Ace of Clubs*, which has probably sunk without trace, but some of us were disappointed that our little sextet, 'In a Boat on a Lake with My Darling', was omitted from the album, so the six of us decided to hire a studio and record it ourselves. When we'd finished, the engineer floored us by asking what we wanted to put on the 'B' side. We had forgotten about records having two sides. He said he had something that might interest us if we cared to hear it. We did. It was the 'balls' record. He had pirated it from an innocent children's radio broadcast. It began with a female presenter saying, 'Now children, we're going to play a hiding and finding game. We're going to pretend you have some balls and you are going to hide them, and then the music will tell you where they are.' The piano then tinkled in the treble and she continued with flawless enunciation, 'Now your balls are on the ceiling and I hope you've all jumped up and got them.' Then the piano grumbled in the bass, 'Now your balls have dropped to the floor so you must bend down and pick them up . . .' and so on. The lady presenter was mortified when it was pointed out that her script could be misinterpreted. I think she should have received a generous royalty payment for all the laughter she created. I lent my record to someone and it was never returned, so if anyone's memory is jogged, I'd love to have it back.

After exactly six months, the life of *Ace of Clubs* drew peacefully to its close. This would probably have been considered a respectable enough run if the author had been anyone but Coward. As it was, the show was branded a flop. The Wimbledon Studio Theatre revived it a couple of years ago and it stood up extremely well, so perhaps its time will come again. This period is generally regarded as being the absolute low point of Coward's great career. I must say that, for a man who was supposedly on the rocks, he was remarkably lively and cheerful. In fact, he was on the brink of an extraordinary revival.

I mentioned earlier that during the *Ace of Clubs* run Myles, Graham, Cole and I were habitués of the Café de Paris, where we saw some of the best cabaret performers around: Elisabeth Welch, Marlene Dietrich, Liberace, Frances Day, Florence Desmond and Bea Lillie – who one night forgot the lyric of a new number, said, 'What the hell,' and did one of her old ones instead, much to the amusement of everyone. But it was Coward's friend, Kay Thompson, who made the greatest impression: tall, angular, a wonderful dancer, pianist and singer, with a rapid-fire delivery that Kenneth Tynan likened to Morse code. She was backed by the four Williams Brothers, one of whom, Andy, was to become an even bigger star in his own right. After seeing several of Kay's performances at the Café de Paris, Coward was persuaded to have a go himself, and we attended his first performance. He was an instant success. Kenneth Tynan described him 'romping fastidiously, padding down those celebrated stairs on black suede-clad feet and baring his teeth as if unveiling some grotesque monument before giving us "I'll See You Again" and all the other bat's wing melodies of his youth'. A year later he went to Las Vegas and became the most successful cabaret artist of the decade, earning $35,000 a week in 1951!

My own career in cabaret began, and ended, at about the same time. It was at the Studio Club in Knightsbridge. I think it was Graham who persuaded me to have a go. I sang 'Chase Me, Charlie' and a not very entertaining number about the Festival of Britain, which was in progress at the time.

I wasn't asked back, and they didn't give me $35,000. So instead of Las Vegas I was obliged to return to the unemployed actors' cab rank and switch on my 'for hire' light. Emile Littler had asked me to do *Cinderella* at the People's Palace in Mile End, but since he only offered me half the salary I'd been getting in Leeds with Wilfred Pickles the previous winter, I felt justified in turning it down. I was beginning to wonder whether or not I'd done the right thing when the call came for me to make my first foray into the exciting new world of television.

Television in 1951 was well out of its infancy, but still a little on the gawky side, with awkward pauses between programmes, frequent mishaps of the kind that fill up those 'blooper' shows, and an awful lot of the test card. A television set could cost up to seventy-five pounds in those days, which was a lot of money, and there were only just over a million sets in the country. I had seen very little television myself, because for so long my evenings had been spent in theatres. My parents owned a set before the war; it was housed in an enormous wooden cabinet with a wireless and gramophone built in. The screen was tiny – eleven inches, I think. I was short-sighted, even then, so if I stood near enough to see I blocked everyone else's view. I had one or two squints at it, then gave up.

There was still a lingering snootiness about television in some quarters of the acting profession, and a feeling that it would always be the poor relation of radio and theatre. I was more than happy to 'lower my standards' and make the trek out to Lime Grove. My first television appearance was in *The Passing Show*, a musical nostalgia series which drew on the history of popular music in the first half of the twentieth century. There were five ninety-minute editions – one for each decade – and I was in the first, which covered the Edwardian period. I was in eight numbers, with seven rapid costume changes in between. As it was a live transmission there was no time to go to our dressing rooms, so the changes were made in the studio, in an area not in use at the time. Nicholas Parsons was in the show, and while I was singing 'I Wouldn't Leave My Little Wooden Hut for You', a piece of scenery came crashing down, revealing him standing in his underpants – a bonus for the viewers. The series was a notoriously complicated one technically – there were over a hundred sets for some of the programmes – and there are grey-haired technicians around now who shudder at the memory of it. The evil genius who devised this endurance test was the stalwart BBC producer Michael

Mills. His deep-set eyes and Mephistophelean beard earned him the nickname Dark Satanic Mills, but he was an energetic and irrepressible man who presided over many excellent musical extravaganzas over the years.

Within a few years television would produce a host of good comedy shows, but its comedy output up until then had been fairly limited. There weren't too many comics to be seen on the small screen in the early days. When variety theatres were booming a comedian could tour the same act year after year, but once seen on TV by a few million people he would have to find new material to present to his theatre audiences, so most established comics kept well away. Comedy on the wireless was subject to the BBC's stringent self-censorship regulations, and in the theatre the Lord Chamberlain's office laid down the rules. The kind of comedy that might be termed 'sophisticated' or 'satirical' found its natural home in intimate revue, an art form which flourished either side of the war but came to an end soon after the innovative *Beyond the Fringe* – an absolute delight which introduced us to Peter Cook, Dudley Moore, Alan Bennett and Jonathan Miller.

Intimate revue had some superb practitioners; the likes of Henry Kendall, Hermione Gingold, Hermione Baddeley and Cyril Ritchard, and later Maggie Smith, Kenneth Williams and Dora Bryan, were all very popular. Unfortunately, the big theatrical managements seem to have decided there is no longer a demand for such shows, although Sheridan Morley successfully presented a revue quite recently. So perhaps it will return to the West End and delight theatregoers as it did in its heyday.

One of the great practitioners of the art was the producer/director Laurier Lister. He forged a highly successful partnership with Joyce Grenfell in 1947, with the revue *Tuppence Coloured*, which, after a disastrous try-out, enjoyed a long run at the Globe under H. M. Tennent's banner. Laurier subsequently fell out with Binkie Beaumont's partner, John Perry, and in 1951, when he and Joyce had enough material for a follow-up, he decided to present the show himself.

With my trusty sheet music for 'Wonderful Guy', I auditioned and was accepted by Laurier for the new revue, which was to be called *Penny Plain.* There was a lot of trial and error in staging a new revue, and the content and running order changed almost daily during the pre-London tour. By the time we arrived at the St Martin's Theatre I was in a variety of sketches and ensembles. Laurier had the knack of cajoling and badgering people to work for him by writing them complimentary letters, and he persuaded the likes of Donald Swann, Herbert Farjeon, Alan Melville and Richard Addinsell to contribute material to supplement Joyce's monologues for very modest fees.

Joyce was, of course, the queen of this particular kind of entertainment. Her brilliantly sharp, yet sympathetic character-izations have endured to this day. Maureen Lipman had a great success reviving many of Joyce's songs and monologues in her show *ReJoyce!* One of my favourites is 'Stately as a Galleon', the song about the two well-endowed matrons who partner each other for olde tyme dancing, another is Joyce's spoof of a WI talk on useful and acceptable gifts, such as 'Modernistic waste-paper baskets made from disused biscuit tins – make love to your grocer and wheedle him into giving them to you.' Grocer? Whatever happened to him?

Joyce cut a distinctive figure onstage – tall, aristocratic and often encased in a strikingly coloured taffeta gown made by her friend Victor Stiebel. She was not the first woman to do character comedy in monologue form – she was always keen to acknowledge her debt to Ruth Draper – nor did she have the broad appeal of Beryl Reid and Joan Turner, but what she did was truly original, at a time when female comics were not very numerous and were often viewed with suspicion.

It was not really the thing, certainly as far as men were concerned, for women to be funny. Many young actresses thought the same and aspired only to be the heroine or innocent victim. I never minded making a fool of myself if it was in the interests of getting a laugh, which increased my chances of employment in comedy shows no end.

Also in the cast of *Penny Plain* were Elisabeth Welch, whom I understudied but luckily never had to go on for, and Max Adrian, who delivered point numbers with great aplomb and was also Laurier Lister's partner, and a sharp foil to the other's somewhat restrained formality. Liz was unique, blessed with great charm, and she was also pretty hot at canasta. It was a happy company, and I still have the little sketch Joyce sent me with a penny stamp affixed to wish me 'more than a pennyworth of luck' on the first night.

The show opened to good reviews and was warmly received by audiences, but it struggled at the box office. Some of Joyce's recently published correspondence reveals that she accepted £330 from a friend in order to pay the cast. Imagine being able to cover the wage bill of a West End show with just £330! I think a few of us chipped in to keep it going in one way or another. I have a letter from Laurier regretting that I would not be able to recover my 'investment' – probably a cut in salary – but hoping I would be able to 'recoup at some point in the future'. Some hope! It seems strange that Joyce's popularity was not enough to fill the theatre, and still more so that she had to rely on the kindness of friends to subsidize the show. For all her blue-blooded connections – she was related to the Astors – she and her devoted husband Reggie lived quite modestly in a maisonette above a toy and confectionery shop in the King's Road, with the noise of the traffic rattling the windows. They loved it. I was once invited to tea and, yes, there were cucumber sandwiches, and Joyce and Reggie were charming and entertaining hosts.

Like *Ace of Clubs*, *Penny Plain* managed to stagger on for six months, although I had to leave before the end of the run because another nodule appeared on my vocal cords. A further two weeks of silence was ordered, and out came the notepads and pencils again. *Penny Plain* went on tour the following year, and its fortunes revived to the extent that it returned briefly to London. I had moved on by then, although I did rejoin the show for a week while two of the cast were off.

I kept in touch with Laurier over the next few years, and in 1955 he asked me to take part in his revue *From Here and There* at the Royal Court. This was to be an Anglo-American cast, with twelve performers, six from either side of the pond. For some reason Laurier cast me on the American team, which confused me rather.

But I did have far more to do than in *Penny Plain*, so much, in fact, that I didn't have time to get up the sixty-odd stairs to the dressing room and made all my costume changes under the stage. Among the characters I played was a child star, lamenting her declining popularity at the age of four, and a Marilyn Monroe number in which she thanked all the men who had helped her, but insisted that her true love was Oscar. One of the lyrics went, 'With an eighty-foot vestibule and a platinum swimming pool, what does a lady need with love?' The dress I wore for that song was a beautifully made, spangled sheath, with a fish tail. It took about ten fittings and hours of standing still, which reminded me of the costume-fitting sessions with Gran for my dancing displays.

The three other principals in the cast of *From Here and There* were Betty Marsden – who was so good in *Round the Horne*; she was a brilliant comedienne who could also bring a tear to your eye – a dancer called Richard Tone, with whom I did a cod ballet routine, and an American, James McColl, who did Noël Coward and Maurice Chevalier impressions, but was often 'indisposed' – as indisposed as a newt in fact – and was eventually replaced. He failed to turn up one day and, at very short notice, his place was taken by Johnny Heawood, our choreographer, who was a vast improvement.

The show was a modest success and ran till the autumn of 1955. Was I therefore among the last to deliver a wholly frivolous, non-significant, apolitical line on the stage of the Royal Court? Within months the theatre was taken over by the English Stage Company, and they were not best known for their intimate revues.

In the summer of 1951, while I was still in *Penny Plain*, it was announced that *South Pacific* was finally to be put on in London, and that auditions were to be held at Drury Lane. I went along and sang, guess what? 'Wonderful Guy'. It did the trick again. Four days later I was asked to come back and present myself in a swimsuit and, after I had been inspected to see that I had enough things in the right places, I was offered a part in the chorus and third understudy to Mary Martin. I couldn't wait to be part of a full-scale musical at Drury Lane and I joined the company to start rehearsals for what was already one of the most successful American musicals of all time.

'All you girls must have a South Pacific tan,' we were told. 'You've all got to go on the sunbeds.'

To the Americans we were a pasty-looking lot, and something had to be done to brown us up. Bearing in mind my mother's theory that she and I had a layer of skin missing, I didn't want to risk getting fried under a sun lamp, so I opted for tan from a bottle. Some of the other girls followed suit, and we'd spend ages in the dressing room, slapping the stuff on and helping each other cover the parts we couldn't reach – a laborious process and not a pleasant one as, in 1951, bottled fake tan had a rather sickly pong.

Mary Martin had played Nellie Forbush, the heroine of *South Pacific*, 900 times in New York, and seeing her in the London production you would have thought that every performance was her first. She was magnificent, and we girls knew we were in the presence of a real star; a joy to watch and listen to, and a lesson to us all.

The original show was co-written and produced by Joshua Logan, and the London production had to be an absolute carbon copy of the Broadway version, gesture for gesture, word for word. If a particular character had blond hair in New York, then she had to have blond hair in London. It was restaged by Jerome White, who was meticulous – he had been an assistant director in America, and no doubt had his instructions. In rehearsal he once told Hartley Power, an actor of many years' experience, 'OK, Hartley, you need to take a beat before that line,' simply because the original actor had paused there. We waited to see how Hartley would react, but he did as he was told, as did the rest of us. In the end the show proved to be almost as successful as it had been on Broadway, so it was hard to argue with the way it was directed.

The first night was unforgettable. We were all onstage for the curtain call and witnessed the tumultuous applause and standing ovation for Mary, who gave encore after encore and absolutely tore the place up. It brought a lump to my throat. The audience obviously adored her and made sure she knew how they felt; that's what makes a star – the audience! I was proud to be part of that evening. I still have the good-luck card that she sent me: 'June, darling, now *don't* be afraid! just *knock* yourself out and remember. There's *Always* to-morrow night.' Yet Mary always worked as if there *wasn't* a tomorrow night, even after 900 performances.

Some of the reviews were a bit sniffy, which was a pity as we waited up half the night for them, but it made not a jot of difference to the tremendous popularity of the show. After the first night the full company was called for a post-mortem, and we gathered in the stalls. Josh Logan looked grim-faced onstage and Oscar Hammerstein was deep in conversation with Mary Martin. The trouble, it seemed, was that the audience hadn't laughed when Ray Walston as Luther Billis said, 'It ain't worth a red cent,' and we were asked why. There were forty-odd English actors and actresses who could have told them. For one thing, Ray's American accent wasn't all that easy to understand, and those who heard what he said had no idea what a red cent was; 'Red scent? What does it smell like?' But no-one was brave enough to speak up.

Also in the chorus were Joyce Blair, June Charlier, Louie Ramsay – now married to George Baker – Deidre de Peyer and, later on, Millicent Martin. We had a reunion lunch some years ago, which was a very enjoyable affair, and there's another one threatened. The male chorus was quite a nursery for talent, too, boasting as it did at different times Sean Connery, Ivor Emmanuel and an absolutely gorgeous young man called Larry Hagman, whom all the girls used to drool over. I had a couple of dates with Larry, as did most of the others, but eventually we lost out to the beautiful Swedish designer Maj Axelsen to whom he has now been married for forty-six years. Larry was Mary Martin's son – at least he was in those days. After he became world famous as J. R. in *Dallas*, Mary Martin became known as Larry Hagman's mother. They both returned in 1980 for a *Royal Variety Show* in which I also took part and was able to renew our acquaintance. He forgot the words to the number he was doing and ground to an agonizing halt, poor man. Mary marched on in her *South Pacific* outfit and rescued the situation by belting out 'Honey Bun' from the musical. Well, what's a mother for?

After the curtain came down on the evening performance at Drury Lane, I had to scrub off my bottle tan, jump into the Austin and drive to the Watergate Theatre off Leicester Square, where I was appearing in a late-night Sandy Wilson revue called *See You Later*. It was a smaller scale show than *Penny Plain*, but very popular and considerably more wicked. It featured a hilarious version of 'The Desert Song' and a cruel Joyce Grenfell send-up called 'I'm Rather Keen on Life'. Dulcie Gray was in it, and we clashed elbows during many quick changes in a minute shoebox of a dressing room. I had taken over in the show from Yvonne Marsh and much appreciated Dulcie's help and sensible advice.

Did I say 'drive' just now? Yes folks, those were the days when you could take your car into central London and actually park outside, or near, your destination. They were also the days before the drink-driving law and we often drove home after having had a couple of 'drinks with . . .'

It was also the age of smog, that sulphurous, impenetrable mass that could bring the city to a complete standstill. Joyce Blair and myself found ourselves in the thick of it one night coming home after the late show at the Watergate. It was a genuine pea-souper, so dense that you could only see a few feet ahead. Joyce offered to walk in front of the car with a torch all the way back to Kensington. My left foot went numb from balancing the clutch at four miles an hour. Joyce was a heroine and we ended up with a line of cars following us. We arrived home exhausted and grimy with smog, but at least I'd managed to avoid running Joyce over.

After my last performance in *South Pacific*, I came out of the theatre to find that my car had disappeared from where I'd parked it in Drury Lane. I went back into the stage door keeper's office and was looking for the number of the police station when Mary Martin and her husband Richard Halliday came past and asked what the trouble was. I told them, and they insisted on taking me to the police station in their chauffeur-driven limousine to report the missing vehicle, then they drove me all the way home, which was a pretty decent gesture as Mary must have been exhausted after two performances. ELU 117 was recovered the next day, undamaged; someone had taken it for a joy-ride. I was so pleased to see it again and we resumed our partnership for another two or three years.

I had been given grudging permission to leave *South Pacific* by the management, 'providing a replacement could be found'. All they had to do was get a short blonde who could sing and dance and was capable of saying 'What's the matter, knucklehead?' in the middle of 'I'm Gonna Wash That Man Right Outa My Hair'. Somehow they managed to find such a rarity and I was free to leave. I'd been offered a part in a controversial new play called *Women of Twilight*, which was about to transfer from London to Broadway. Maria Charles had come out of the show and my old RADA chum Miriam Karlin, who was playing one of the leads, suggested me as a replacement for Maria. It was a small part – just a couple of scenes – and not a memorable role, but it was the trip to America that appealed. It would be a chance to renew friendships made on my previous visit and to catch up with the composer Hugh Martin, whom I'd met during *Penny Plain*, and who was working with Jack Gray on the score of a new show, *Love From Judy*.

I nearly didn't go to America because, when I received my contract, I noticed that Jack Hylton, who was co-presenting *Women of Twilight*, expected me to pay him 10 per cent of my salary in agent's commission. Hylton's representative, Brian Michie, explained that it was only fair as the Hylton management had got me the job. 'Oh no they hadn't.' It was through Miriam not Hylton that I'd been cast, and I thought it was unacceptable. Messages went back and forth and I eventually received a note saying the matter was so serious I would have to talk to Mr Hylton himself. I checked with the director, Anthony Hawtrey, who was kind enough to back me up, then replied that I would be more than happy to talk to the great man as soon as possible. Time ticked away and nothing happened until, the day before we were due to sail, I received a letter informing me that Mr Hylton was prepared 'on this occasion' to waive his commission. I appreciated the change of heart and hoped that, in future, the Hylton management might think again about taking 10 per cent when they'd done nothing to earn it.

I boarded the *Queen Mary* in a somewhat delicate state. I'd been at the Café de Paris the previous night, seeing Kay Thompson's final cabaret performance, then afterwards I'd gone to Noël Coward's studio for a party, which lasted until five thirty in the morning. I hoped the sea would be calm. Once on board I soon revived, and it wasn't long before we girls set about getting ourselves invited into the first-class areas of the ship, such as the Verandah Grill, and generally enjoying the voyage.

Just before I sailed I received a cable from Hugh Martin, asking me to come to the Palace Theatre on the evening we docked in New York. He was playing the piano for Judy Garland, who was giving her final performance of the season. I was to see the show and afterwards he would introduce me. I was thrilled at the prospect, as I'd idolized her since I was a child. Hugh had known Judy Garland for many years; he wrote the famous 'Trolley Song' for the film *Meet Me in St Louis*, for which he received an Oscar nomination, and he was a familiar name on Broadway.

After being spellbound by Judy's talent, I met Hugh backstage and we chatted and caught up on gossip while waiting for the brilliant girl to join us at the after-show party. We waited and we waited, but still no sign. When she finally appeared it was clear what had taken her so long. She looked wonderful and had dozens of little bows tied in her hair – a good hour's work for her attendant hairdresser. Hugh introduced us and, since it was her last night, I volunteered the information that I'd just seen Kay Thompson's final performance at the Café de Paris. Judy asked me how Kay's show had gone; they were friends and Kay often acted as her singing teacher. I enthusiastically replied that she'd gone like 'a bomb'. Judy Garland's face dropped, thinking I'd meant she'd bombed, and that I was somehow relishing her downfall. 'Oh no!' she said. 'That's terrible.' I tried to explain, but the damage was done and Judy moved off to talk to someone else before I had a chance to gush about her performance and tell her she'd been my idol for years. It was proof that English and American are sometimes two separate languages, and it was also a pretty inauspicious start to my stay.

The controversy surrounding the play *Women of Twilight* was due to its sensational subject matter: unmarried mothers and baby-farming. London audiences had found it perfectly acceptable and the expectation was that it would go down equally well with sophisticated New York theatregoers. That couldn't have been more wide of the mark. Things got off to a bad start when we arrived at the Plymouth Theater to find it being picketed by the scenic artists' union. They objected to us bringing our own set, rather than paying them to build one for us. A few weeks earlier, Laurence Olivier and Vivien Leigh had turned up, also with their own scenery, for *Caesar and Cleopatra*, and so we were the last straw as far as the scenic artists were concerned. The theatre unions were far stronger than our own, and American Equity insisted on two of our cast, Linda King and Marjorie Clark, changing their names because they were the same as those of two American actresses. Linda and Marjorie acquiesced but the management held firm over the set, and we opened on time, with the audience having to cross a picket line. It was hardly the ideal first-night atmosphere.

As far as the critics were concerned the picket line was the most entertaining part of the evening. 'Repulsive, slatternly, trite!' ran one headline, 'One of the most deplorable plays ever presented on Broadway' said another. 'Overwrought, clumsy, maudlin, mawkish, silly and generally unbelievable' – that was the *New York Post*. The best notice we got said it was 'an inept unsavoury offering. However, all the subordinate actresses are excellent. In fact, I have the feeling that they are only subordinate because of the limits of their parts.'

One can laugh at it now, but it wasn't very pleasant at the time, and my friend Miriam took it rather badly. She was furious about the notices. We shared an apartment on the seventh floor, and one night, after a poorly attended show, she was in quite a state. She threw open the window, saying she was going to throw herself out and end it all.

'Well, either jump or shut it because there's a hell of a draught,' I said.

Luckily she roared with laughter and stopped being a drama queen. Mim, to her credit, went on every radio programme stoutly defending the play. One interviewer said the show was doomed because its subject was the illegal sale of illegitimate babies, a practice that simply did not exist in America.

'Well, you obviously go about with your eyes shut, then,' said Miriam, 'because it's everywhere.' Now, of course, surrogate motherhood and the sale of unwanted babies are a legitimate trade.

Despite Miriam's sterling efforts, the notice went up on the second day and the show closed on Saturday, after only five performances. The pickets remained outside every night, and by the end of the week they almost outnumbered the audience.

Critics and pickets aside, I found the brief run rather enjoyable. My character only appeared in one scene at the beginning and one at the end, which left me with a good hour to kill in between. As my role was fairly insignificant and could be assumed in about three seconds flat before my entrance, I looked for ways to pass the time. I discovered that if I went out of a side door of the Plymouth Theatre, across a yard and through another door, I was backstage at the Broadhurst, where *Pal Joey* was playing. By lurking in the wings and taking care not to get in anyone's way, I managed to see a sizeable chunk of that incomparable show, with Vivienne Segal and Harold Lang working together so splendidly. It wasn't easy to drag myself away from 'Bewitched, Bothered and Bewildered' and 'I Could Write a Book', and trudge back to the rather depressing *Women of Twilight*.

I stayed on after the play closed and saw some of the other hit musicals which were on Broadway at the time, like *Guys and Dolls*, *Paint Your Wagon* and *Call Me Madam* with Ethel Merman. I also witnessed the sad spectacle of Gertrude Lawrence, with not many months to live, struggling to nurse her ailing voice through the songs of *The King and I*.

The visit was a chance to catch up on friendships I'd made on my previous trip, three years earlier. I went to stay with the Boyces again at their beautiful house in Vermont, a lovely old place nestling in the trees, with deer nibbling the grass a stone's throw from the windows. One evening, the Boyces took me to a very smart restaurant up in the hills, where I ate lobster, and I was slightly taken aback when the waitress asked me, 'Do you care for an extra plate for your claws?' Not long after my 'went like a bomb' faux pas, the language difficulty cropped up again when I asked Gordon, my host, 'Would you mind knocking me up at seven thirty tomorrow morning?' He roared with laughter and, seeing my puzzled expression, explained that it wouldn't be a very good idea as, in America, 'knocking up' doesn't necessarily mean a wake-up call.

Hugh Martin asked me if I'd like to stay and work on the score of his new musical in order to demonstrate it with Jack Gray, the lyric writer, who was also a singer. *Love From Judy* was an adaptation of Jean Webster's novel *Daddy Long Legs*, about an orphan girl who falls for her guardian. There was a possibility for me to play one of Judy's fellow students. I was thrilled to be in on the birth of a new show, to hear the numbers as Hugh wrote them, to be coached by him and Jack and to be the first to sing Hugh's great score. I made arrangements to stay on and then spent several very happy weeks learning the score and having a whale of a time in New York. We'd work for two or three hours in the afternoon, then hit the town in the evenings, either to see a show or a film, or to eat at places like Sardi's and the Algonquin. Once we took a trip into Chinatown and I had my first brush with chopsticks. We went to the opera and ballet, as well as the theatre, and we heard Victoria de Los Angeles singing Mimi – her tiny hand may have been frozen, but the rest of her was pretty well lagged against the cold. They took me to the Stork Club and to the jazz clubs of Harlem to hear the likes of Thelonious Monk and Count Basie. In the daytime we performed the *Love From Judy* numbers to various producers, but there were no takers. Eric Maschwitz, who had written the show's story, outline and dialogue – commonly referred to as the 'book' – suggested that Emile Littler might be interested in putting it on, so Jack and Hugh decided to try their luck in London, and at the end of April we all set sail for England.

On the voyage home I learned that Noël Coward was also on board, in first class, of course, so I sent a message up to him, saying that I was down in steerage with a couple of chaps who would very much like to meet him. He came through to the second-class section of the Mermaid Bar. When I introduced them, Jack was a little off-hand, but after Noël had sized him up and said, 'Oh, I see, you're a who-does-he-think-he-is type,' they all got on extremely well. Noël admired Hugh's work and happily chatted to us for several hours. He went through the pitfalls of mounting a show in London, particularly with the Littler organization – Emile Littler had yawned while Coward played through the score of *Ace of Clubs*, so he was a little sore about it. He also invited us all to Goldenhurst for the weekend to perform the score for him, and so, a few weeks later, we did just that. He made some further helpful suggestions to Hugh and Jack and, to my immense delight, said I was 'a find'. We played croquet and, after dinner, the Master sat at the piano and sang a number he'd just written for the *Lyric Revue*. It was called 'There are Bad Times Just Around the Corner', and we must have been among the first to hear it.

After that initial meeting on the boat, Hugh and Jack kept in contact with Coward over the years and even became involved in a collaboration of sorts when they turned his wartime hit, *Blithe Spirit*, into a musical. The idea for the project originally came from my mother. Hugh and Jack often came for dinner, and Muff adored their company, and they hers. One evening, when the talk was, as usual, about the theatre, she mentioned to Hugh that the story of the author who was henpecked by both his living and dead wives would be an ideal subject for a musical. After many late-night discussions, Jack and Hugh went to work on the score. Coward vacillated over giving his consent, but was eventually won over when he heard the numbers. *High Spirits* had a successful run on Broadway, with Bea Lillie as a wildly over-the-top Madame Arcati, and it came to the West End the following year with Cicely Courtneidge.

The day came for us to present *Love From Judy* to Emile Littler. Before a group of unsmiling, expensively suited moneybags, we launched into our now-familiar routine. There was no reaction at the end, of course, apart from a thank you, not even a 'we'll let you know', and we were ushered out wondering whether we'd wasted our time once again.

Hugh and Jack had been working on the show for a year and a half, and were relieved when Littler finally confirmed that he would present it at the Saville Theatre. He already had Jean Carson in mind for Judy, but he was happy for me to play the part of Judy's room-mate, Sally McBride. Six weeks later we started rehearsals.

On the first morning, Hugh, Jack and I were asked to perform the score once again, this time to the rest of the cast. We had done it several times by now and just about knew it by heart, but it was still rather frightening having to sing all the numbers with the show's company sitting right in front of us. After we finished, rehearsals began in earnest.

I really enjoy rehearsing a play or a musical, working with fellow actors towards performance level. We all share the same hopes and misgivings and don't want to let ourselves or each other down. Then the opening night arrives and we nervously wish each other luck and cross our fingers, trying to calm the butterflies and the beating heart. People react in different ways; I'm inclined to pace up and down before a TV show, going over my lines and trying to think calm thoughts, then suddenly the show is over and there's nothing you can do about it, so that's the time to stop worrying. In the theatre there's always another chance.

Apart from the adults in *Love From Judy*, there were a further dozen or so 'orphans'. I remember a particular young, small, blonde orphan, who looked rather like me at that age. Her name was Barbara Deeks; she didn't become Barbara Windsor until a few years later. As the run progressed, the orphans grew up, and out, and were replaced as soon as they began to develop unwaiflike physical features, but Barbara stayed for eighteen months, with nary a bulge showing. A short time later I saw her in cabaret at the Pigalle Club and was amazed by her obvious maturity.

'My goodness, where did those come from?' I asked. 'How on earth did you manage to outlast all the other orphans for so long?'

'I used to bind 'em up, didn't I.' She giggled. Some Chinese ladies used to bind their feet up but *they* stayed small! Barbara was clearly talented. She's a good actress, singer and dancer, and has deservedly enjoyed a brilliant career ever since.

Love From Judy opened in Coventry, and I was thrilled to see my name up outside the theatre. But my pleasure was spoiled by the news that one of my numbers was to be cut; it was a song I was rather attached to called 'Get a Horse'. The story was set in 1900, and I used to sing it to Johnny Brandon, who was playing my brother, when he tried to crank his automobile into life. It was a terrific number, but they thought it was similar to one that Jean Carson had called 'Go and Get Your Old Banjo'. The show, it seemed, was just not big enough for the horse and the banjo, and since the entire cast had been taught to play the banjo in order to back Jean's number, it was less trouble to get rid of the horse. There was the usual tinkering with the show after the opening and, during our second week in Bournemouth, my hopes revived when I heard a rumour that the horse was to be reinstated. It did indeed come back, but as a sextet rather than a solo. By the time we got to Birmingham seven days later, the horse had bolted again, this time for good. I didn't mind too much because, by now, Hugh and Jack had written me another song, 'Dumb Dumb Dumb', which was a joy to do.

We made a record of the show and when it disappeared from all the catalogues I thought it had probably gone for ever, but I was pleased to see that, in 1998, a CD of the show's numbers was released, including 'Go and Get Your Old Banjo', 'Voodoo', 'Daddy Long Legs', 'Here We Are' and 'Dumb, Dumb, Dumb'.

After a four-week tour we opened at the Saville to mixed notices. One of them said I added 'a pertly gay touch of comedy', a phrase one is unlikely to find in a theatre review nowadays! But Kenneth Tynan, who alone had praised *South Pacific* when all his colleagues were so snooty, went overboard on our behalf:

This adaptation of Jean Webster's *Daddy Long Legs* frisked and yelled by a company of young newcomers is the neatest show of its kind I can remember. It sang (let us all pray) a requiem over the corpse of middle-aged musical comedy. What happened last night to Jean Carson, playing the New Orleans orphan sent to college by an elder benefactor, is without parallel in recent years. It happened once to Yvonne Printemps, to Gertrude Lawrence and to Mary Martin, and yesterday as we saw her stretching out small delighted fingers, feeling the support of her wings. She has the password, and so I think does June Whitfield, the pudgy blonde who plays her room mate.'

Pudgy indeed! A few days later, he went even further:

What of Jean Carson, the ice-cream redhead whose limpid voice is illuminating *Love From Judy*? She is an exciting pet and knows the password to theatrical Elysium. Never overlook June Whitfield, the *jolie laide* from the same show, who has the bounce and gumption of a young Courtneidge.

Oh dear, 'pudgy' *and* 'pretty ugly'. Ah well, but he did indicate 'talented', which softened the blow.

Jean Carson rightly became a star as a result of the show. She had come up through variety shows and pantomime and, though still only twenty-four, she was a seasoned professional by the time *Love From Judy* came along. She eventually went to America and had her own TV show, *Hey Jeannie*. I understudied Jean, just as I had done in *Ace of Clubs*. Judy was a very demanding role, and after a year and 500 performances, Jean, not surprisingly, collapsed and had to be carted off to recover. I took over, and after I had played Judy for a week, Emile Littler wrote to me expressing his approval and enclosing a five-pound note. It was very civil of him, although he added a cautious reminder that my understudying was, of course, included in my salary.

With my elevation to the leading role came a certain amount of press attention. Diary stories appeared in the papers regarding matters of such national importance as how I looked after my wig, what I thought about marriage and so on. Harry Foster, the agent, persuaded me to sign with him for a year, and I also entered into a recording contract with Philips. The producer Norman Newell booked me to make a couple of records, and Philips promoted me as 'the new British singing star'. My first number was a country and western song called 'Seven Lonely Days'. It had rather dire lyrics, but the reason it didn't get to number one may not have been entirely the fault of the lyricist, as the *Evening Standard* remarked on my surprising decision to sing a hill-billy song with an English accent! Worse was to come. The follow-up was a cover version of the song made famous by Marilyn Monroe, 'Diamonds are a Girl's Best Friend'. The *Standard*'s music reviewer, who'd had enough of me by now, observed that 'Miss Monroe knows the difference between diamonds and rhinestones, but I have a horrid feeling that June Whitfield doesn't yet.' I was probably trying to emulate Ethel Merman at full-throttle – obviously, it didn't work. The *Daily Sketch* commented kindly that, with experience, I might become 'a welcome home entertainer', but my career as a pop idol quickly waned, and Doris Day was no doubt able to breathe an enormous sigh of relief. You live and learn.

Meanwhile, I was finding that life as a West End leading lady, even if only a temporary one, very much agreed with me. It was hard work but hugely rewarding, and I thoroughly enjoyed it, but I also liked playing my role of Sally McBride, so it wasn't too traumatic when Jean returned and I was relegated to one of Judy's two room-mates. The other one was Audrey Freeman, who played Julia. Audrey and I shared a dressing room, and there was great excitement as she was being courted by David Tomlinson, who called in from time to time. It was a successful courtship as she later married him.

After the curtain came down at the Saville, there weren't too many nights when I toddled straight home to bed with a mug of cocoa. I'd more likely visit the Buxton or the Café de Paris with Cole and Graham. Noël Coward returned for another successful cabaret season – we saw him there several times – and, later on, Liz Welch and Hermione Gingold. Gingold was a brilliant cabaret performer, who knew how to use the Café de Paris' unique architectural features to maximum effect. She would appear at the top of one of the curving staircases which ran down to the stage, and would stand there waiting for the applause to subside. Then she would raise a finger to her lips and say in that wonderfully lascivious voice, 'Hush hush, whisper who dares, old Mother Gingold is coming downstairs.'

There were more parties at the Gerald Road Studio, weekends at Goldenhurst and, of course, endless canasta. The Master gave a memorable party at the studio on his fifty-second birthday, and another after the last night of Shaw's *The Apple Cart*, in which he had scored a big hit. All manner of people were there, including Ava Gardner and the equally glamorous pin-up from an earlier era, Ina Claire – 'merry as a grig', he wrote in his diary, which could as well have applied to anyone else there. Then there was a party which Mary Martin and her husband gave at their palatial Park Lane flat, where the Tynans and the Hitchcocks rubbed shoulders with the Oliviers and at which I stood gawping and hero-worshipping.

It was at about this time that Stanley Hall and his partner Noel McGregor, who together ran Wig Creations, started the star-studded New Year's Eve parties which became well known to everyone in the business. Stanley and Noel made wigs for leading film and stage actors here and in the US; whenever John Gielgud, Ralph Richardson or Margaret Lockwood required wigs or hair-pieces, they went to Wig Cs and many of them would attend the parties. Initially, the gathering took place at a flat off Baker Street, but it grew so quickly that the venue was switched to the Wig Creations studio. They used to keep the food warm, very successfully, in the wig ovens which were normally used in the process of wig making. Noel and Stanley were both non-drinkers, but they dispensed alcohol with lethal liberality. You could hardly move in the crush, but I wouldn't have missed it, and attended year after year, meeting friends and glimpsing the leading lights of the theatre, past and present – glimpsing because my height restricts my view in a crowd. I always seem to be surrounded by tall people! When my husband attended his first Wig Cs party he soon became acclimatized to the hello-darlings atmosphere. He was a great help as he could see who was there and point me in the right direction. It was, to say the least, a very social time. I must have got some sleep between 1950 and 1953, but it wasn't a priority.

One September morning, about a year into the run of *Love From Judy*, I answered a call that was to change my working life. Sometimes one can get a little carried away when describing these turning points in your career. I read in the paper recently of a well-known model being asked to describe how she felt when she first stepped onto a catwalk, and she replied breathlessly, 'Oh, it's hard to explain it. I mean, how did Louis Armstrong feel when he first set foot on the moon?' I can't claim to have experienced anything quite on that scale, nevertheless as phone calls go this was a very important one.

'It's Frank Muir here,' said a voice. 'And this is Denis Norden,' said another.

Chapter Five

MY RADIO TIMES

FRANK AND DENIS HAD A HABIT OF MAKING TELEPHONE CALLS together, with one or the other of them talking into an extension. As the three-way conversation progressed, I realized it wasn't two friends pulling my leg and that I'd better pay attention. They asked if I would be interested in auditioning for *Take It From Here*. They explained that they were looking for someone to replace Joy Nichols, the Australian actress and singer who, alongside Jimmy Edwards and Dick Bentley, had become a household name through the popularity of the show. I was on a long list of people recommended to them by two other writers I'd worked for in revue, Alec Grahame and Peter Myers. Frank later told me that when they were presented with a page full of unfamiliar names they picked mine out with a pin.

Take It From Here, better known as *TIFH* – to rhyme with 'life' – had been running for five years. I'd heard of it, of course, but having been so busy in the theatre I don't think I'd actually listened to it, still less been aware that it was heard by over half the country; it had the kind of audience figures TV executives can only dream of in these multi-channel days. Had I known, I might have been very nervous when I turned up for an audition at Aeolian Hall, the BBC Variety HQ in New Bond Street.

I met Frank and Denis, and the producer Charles Maxwell, an ex-lawyer with round-framed spectacles and a Scottish accent, whose brainchild the show had been. Frank and Denis stood six foot six and six foot three respectively, while Charles, though definitely the boss, was about my height. They made for an unusual group when they were stood next to one another. They asked me to read through some material, and I did various accents: American, French and 'Sloane' – if you say out loud the words 'air', then 'hair', then 'lair', and say them in quick succession, you get 'air–hair–lair', the official Sloane Ranger greeting.

The three of them were charming and courteous, and Frank laughed politely at my efforts. I didn't know until I read his autobiography just how difficult the search for Joy Nichols' replacement had proved to be. Apparently they'd been seeing people for weeks – a tribute to Joy's range of talents. They finally gave up on finding a single replacement and decided to book two, an actress and a singer. I had noticed that, waiting to follow me in, was a young woman who was already beginning to make a name for herself as a singer, Alma Cogan. They hired both of us; Alma would do the songs and I would do the sketches. The arrangement suited Alma and me very well, as Joy had been extremely popular in the show and it took the pressure off us when we started.

The BBC offer was ten guineas. 'Ten quid!' I exclaimed to my agent, when he told me the news. 'I was getting more than that in the chorus of *South Pacific*!' When he got me another fiver I graciously accepted. What I hadn't realized was that the fee was just for the initial broadcast; with the weekday repeats on the Light Programme, followed by the Home and Overseas Service, it came to forty-five guineas per programme. By holding out I might have lost the job. Ignorance was certainly bliss on that occasion.

A photocall was arranged for the new *Take It From Here* girls. I was rather looking forward to it, then I remembered those amazing frocks that Alma wore. I had better explain, for the benefit of the under-forties, that Alma was renowned for her wonderfully extravagant outfits, most of which she designed herself. They were often feathery or frilly, with voluminous petticoats to fill out the enormous skirts. Rather than try to compete, I decided to go in the opposite direction and present a more casual look. As a result of this brainwave, I arrived at the first recording in a turban, looking more like someone who had come to clean the studio than one of the 'exciting new discoveries'.

At the press call, we posed for the photographers with the rest of the team. The *Evening Standard*'s photo was captioned, 'The new *Take It From Here* girls signed their contracts in London today and got to know their new boyfriends.' Alma and I also appeared on the cover of *Illustrated* magazine – long since defunct – and so began one of the happiest periods of my working life.

As I read through the script of my first episode, I became aware that I had two problems. The first came in a sketch where I had to play the Mona Lisa; how do you find a way of expressing the stage direction 'she smiles enigmatically' in a way that registers on radio? I came up with a sort of gurgling noise, which seemed to satisfy Charles. The other problem was more tricky.

Frank and Denis had written a sketch inspired by their irritation with cosy radio and TV families like the Dales, the Archers, the Huggetts and the Lyons. The family they created was, of course, the thoroughly unpleasant and indolent Glums, and my difficulty was that I hadn't a clue how to play Ron Glum's fiancée, Eth.

The script was delivered on the Saturday before the recording, so I had just one day in which to find a voice for Eth. I did what many young people do when they find themselves in an awkward situation. I asked my mum.

Muff read the script and said, with her usual perceptiveness, 'Well, it's Mrs G, isn't it.'

I have often been asked if Eth was based on anyone in real life, and I've always given the evasive answer that it was someone my mother knew, which was true enough. At the time we had a daily who had a high-pitched voice and a terribly earnest way of speaking. She also kept a very tight grip on her grammar, as though terrified that it might suddenly let her down, revealing her to be impolite. She used the same whining tone whether it was to say 'nice day' or

'Granny's died'. I said to Muff, 'No-one will believe that voice.'

But mother knew best, and Eth was born, or rather reincarnated, on radio.

As the Glums became a more established feature of the show, I came across many Eths who would hold forth in pure Eth tones, 'Ooh, that *voice*! I know someone who talks just like that.'

'Really?' I would say. 'What a coincidence.'

We never recognize ourselves, do we?

It's interesting to read the script of that first sketch now and see how carefully the idea was introduced with a preamble from our announcer David Dunhill: 'Our family, the Glums, are very ordinary people. They might be you or you or you . . . All five of them are shifty, obstinate, argumentative and dim.' Notice he said five of them. To begin with, in addition to Pa Glum, Mother, Ron and Eth, there was a Gran Glum, played by Wallas Eaton, but she disappeared quite early on. Mother was played by Alma, and began as a speaking part before being pared down to an unintelligible offstage noise, which was a garbled version of 'what d'you want?' – it was a sort of 'Nnngiaaaooww!' sound. Pa Glum was, of course, played by Jimmy Edwards as a selfish, greedy tyrant – 'Quite a challenge,' Jim said.

'Muvver!' Pa would shout.

'Nnngiaaaooww!'

Then a Frank and Denis gem such as, 'Throw us down your tooth-brush. I've got some muck on me boots.'

The writers soon realized from the reactions to the first Glums sketches that their dysfunctional family was a winner, and central to the humour was Ron and Eth's hopelessly static relationship. 'They're goin' steady,' Pa Glum said. 'If they go any steadier they'll be motionless.' Frank and Denis could see that the state of being engaged was a fertile territory; they likened it to suspended animation, or like driving with one foot on the accelerator and the other on the brake.

Before long the Glums were occupying the second half of the pro-gramme in a self-contained, fifteen-minute segment of their own. Every sketch began with Eth whining, 'Ooh, Ron,' and in the first series the initial laugh came from Dick's dull-witted response, 'Yes,

Eth.' By the second or third series, 'Ooh, Ron,' was getting its own laugh, and Dick always generously waited, in so doing earning himself an even bigger laugh on his reply. It was the brilliance of Dick's Ron that provoked the bulk of the laughter for so many years. His flat delivery and Australian accent were somehow perfectly attuned to the words. His timing was immaculate and I learned a lot from him. He portrayed Ron's unerring instinct for misunderstanding brilliantly.

> ETH: Ooh, Ron, it's not natural for hot-blooded people like you and me to remain unmarried indefinitely. Oh, dear heart, if only you knew how much I yearn!
> RON: I do, Eth, and it's not enough for both of us to live on.

Or:

> ETH: Ooh, Ron, I do think you should try to get a job. It *is* four years since you last tried. And when we marry I want to feel secure.
> RON: (*uncomprehending, repeats dully*) Secure.
> ETH: Yes, Ron, secure. You do know what 'secure' means, beloved?
> RON: Of course I do, Eth. It's that metal spike that keeps the Sunday joint from unwinding.
> ETH: No, beloved, that's 'skewer'.

It was, of course, the scripts that made *TIFH* the great success it was over 325 episodes, thirteen seasons and eleven years. I've been fortunate to speak the words of some of our greatest comedy writers, but Frank and Denis, with their wonderful sense of humour and their sheer delight in the language, have never been surpassed, in my view. To say their lines was an unalloyed joy. Writers are not always given the praise they deserve, and I'd like to thank them all, as we actors couldn't do without them.

Most radio comedy writing up to the end of the war dealt purely with gags and catchphrases, many of them brilliant and memorable, but gags all the same. In the late-Forties, a new generation of writers emerged who had all served their time as gag writers, but who wanted to push forward into new territory; people like Spike Milligan, Eric Sykes, then later Galton and Simpson. Frank and Denis were not the first to rebel against the drudgery of gag writing, but they were the first to introduce a literary quality to their scripts. They gave the audience credit for having read the odd book. They believed that a reference to Beethoven or Picasso was not going to fly over their heads and have them reaching for the off switch. It was a principle for which they, and Charles Maxwell, had to fight very hard indeed. For this reason *TIFH* was quite a turning point in broadcast comedy, and was the seed that led to the more literate styles of *Beyond the Fringe* and *Monty Python*.

Muir and Norden were the alternative comedians of their day. They delighted in spotting examples of hackneyed stories and unconvincing writing, and it was an excruciating exchange of dialogue that brought them together. They had sloped off independently to the cinema one afternoon in 1947 and found themselves watching a period French drama where a man was drowning his sorrows because his girl has left him.

'Do not despair, copain,' said the barman. 'She will return.'

'No,' sighed our hero. 'Women are different than men.'

'Ah,' comes the reply, 'Monsieur is a philosopher.'

Frank and Denis simultaneously laughed out loud in the empty cinema, then each turned to see who the other was. They had, in fact, met at the Kavanagh agency earlier in the day, but it was here in the cinema that they hit it off.

Some of the most cherished and oft-repeated clichés in the language were originally identified and sent up in *TIFH*. 'Trouble at t'Mill' was the title of a running sketch that made fun of gritty northern books and films. The character 'Disgusted of Tunbridge Wells' was a Muir and Norden creation, as was a line always credited to the *Carry On* films: 'Infamy, infamy – they've all got it in for me.' It was originally in a *TIFH* script years before it was so memorably delivered by Kenneth Williams.

Another innovation was to incorporate the real lives of the performers into the show. Jim's drinking and waistline were often referred to, as were Dick's cigarette-advertising contract and his comparative senility – he was in his mid-forties. Jim said he'd tried to count the candles on Dick's birthday cake, but was driven back by the heat. Dick told the listeners that 'Horses take up much of Jim's time, and most of his drawing room.' 'Jim's always slipping into the vernacular,' said Dick. 'There's a lot of it about on a farm.'

Frank and Denis were fast workers. They sat down to write the script on Monday morning without an idea in their heads; on Thursday afternoon they would read it to the producer, Charles Maxwell, who would make what Frank and Denis said were infuriating, but usually correct, requests for alterations. They would rewrite on Friday, have a day off on Saturday, then at four o'clock on Sunday afternoon, we would gather at the Paris Cinema in Lower Regent Street to rehearse and record the show in front of an audience.

There was always an air of anticipation at the start of rehearsals. The success of the day depended in no small measure on the quality of Jimmy Edwards' lunch. Jim's performance could suffer just as much if he'd had too *little* to drink as when he'd had too much. He nearly always managed to get the balance exactly right. Jim was a great character who lived life to the full. He had a Falstaffian appetite, and one of his warm-up jokes was to pat his tummy and say, 'It's only puppy fat. I had a puppy for lunch.'

Dick, by contrast, was elegant and fastidious, although he could also tell the most filthy stories – the kind you laugh at, then realize that you oughtn't to. After some time spent hearing about Jim's equestrian exploits during the week, or Dick's Pekinese, Yulu, or our much-loved labrador, Sid, we would eventually get down to work and try out our various voices in the hope that Charles would approve. Jim had trouble with accents. He could do posh, Pa Glum and a non-specific country voice, and that was about it. Frank and Denis once wrote a Red Indian character for him purely for the pleasure of seeing him struggle with the accent. Dick, on the other hand, was as precise in his performance as he was immaculate in his attire. Frank and Denis sometimes contributed voices under the joint name of Herbert Mostyn – Herbert was Frank's middle name and Mostyn was Denis's. Denis was a more reluctant performer than Frank, but he was very effective as assorted workmen and agents of the law.

Then there was Wallas Eaton, known to us all as Woll. He played a variety of characters, including the landlord in the pub where Pa Glum drank. Woll was a landlord of sorts in real life; he had a lucrative sideline in property, out of which he did very well. He bought a house in Stockwell before it became yuppie-land. Is it now St Ockwell?

The Keynotes were our close-harmony quartet – every show seemed to have one then. They were led by Johnny Johnston, who later became the king of the advertising jingles and was responsible for such imperishables as 'Hands that do dishes can be soft as your face' and 'A Double Diamond works wonders'. His Mount Everest as a composer was to provide a catchy tune to go with 'Save, save, save with the Co-operative Permanent Building Society'. The tune of that one escapes me.

We also enjoyed a luxury that would be unthinkable for a half-hour comedy show nowadays – a full orchestra. The official name for this impressive group of musicians, which at times included such distinguished names as Eddie Calvert and Bert Weedon, was the Augmented BBC Revue Orchestra, conducted by Harry Rabinowitz. After the music rehearsal we would have a run-through of the whole show on mike and the band's reaction was always a good sounding board.

The run-through took us to opening time. Some of us would follow Jim round the corner for a drink at the Captain's Cabin. Dick didn't come with us, instead he preferred to sit quietly in the studio with a quarter bottle of champagne and a packet of smoked-salmon sandwiches, which Peta, his wife, had prepared.

Jim's fondness for a glass was famous. He used to say, 'I don't drink normally, I drink abnormally.' At one memorable *TIFH* recording he arrived half an hour late for rehearsals. He'd had lunch with Wynford Vaughan Thomas. They'd started on vodka, moved on to pink champagne followed by a good claret, then rounded off the meal with port and a brandy or two. By the time Jim pitched up at the Paris, his co-ordination between reading and speaking the script was somewhat out of synch. 'It doesn't make sense,' he kept saying. Charles Maxwell wasn't given to panic, but the show went out unedited in those days, and he was clearly very worried about the situation. After a totally useless run-through Jim announced, 'I'm just going round the corner to have a pint.'

Charles was in despair and it crossed our minds that we might have to cancel. But he needn't have worried, five minutes before we were due to start, Jim strode back refreshed, warmed up the audience as usual, and his performance was flawless. Years later when Jim wrote a memoir of his war service, the chapter dealing with his tour of duty in North America was headed 'Drink Canada Dry – I Did My Best'.

Before each recording, Charles Maxwell welcomed the audience and introduced Frank and Denis, who trotted out one or two tried-and-tested jokes of their own, then they in turn introduced Dick. Dick's warm-up routine never varied by so much as a syllable; it took the form of a letter, supposedly from his mother in Australia. 'A wonderful woman, my mother,' he'd begin. 'Eighty-six and not a grey hair on her head – completely bald.' Then he'd start to read the letter: '"Dear Sir or Madam" – she always did have a bad memory – "thank you for the money you sent. If we're ever in Lithuania we'll spend it. Your Uncle Charlie, the French polisher, had a nasty accident last week: he drove his car into the garage and died. Very sad, but he had a lovely finish. Must stop now, Granny wants the ball-point to do her eyebrows.' He did it 325 times, and although many of the same people sat in the audience week after week, the routine was always received with hearty laughter.

Jim's warm-up was more boisterous. The green cue light would flash for us to start the show and he'd take the bulb out and put it in his pocket. Then he'd drop his script, the loose pages flying every-where, and Frank would dash out of the studio to get a replacement. When he returned, gasping for breath, he would trip on the stage before safely delivering the proper script. Charles thought the routine was of dubious value as it tended to get the audience a little over-anxious. There was an audible sigh of relief when Jim replaced the light bulb, the orchestra struck up and the show began with the Keynotes singing:

Take it from here,
Don't go away when you can
Take it from here.
Why don't you stay and maybe
Join in the fun, now
The show has begun . . .

David Dunhill then introduced the cast, always managing to finish his words precisely before the final 'Take it from here'. Tricky to time, but David never faltered. Richard Clegg, our *News Huddlines* announcer, has the same immaculate timing, listing up to forty writers to music at the end of the programme.

Frank and Denis were there for every recording. I can see them now, Frank beaming and laughing along and Denis frowning and looking as though he expected disaster to strike. If we were over-running in the first half, they would leap up onto the stage and cross out bits of our scripts while Alma or the Keynotes were on. They were an integral part of the performance as well as two of the most delightful men and brilliant, witty writers.

I got to know Jim, Woll and Dick well, but never really socialized with Alma. She had become so busy, especially after her hit record 'Dreamboat', that she spent any free time in rehearsals autographing her photos. We did once share a dressing room at the Shepherd's Bush Theatre, and I asked her how she managed to achieve her wonderfully curvaceous figure onstage.

'Oh, I just give everything a shove,' she said and demonstrated. The effect was mighty impressive.

I was still on tour with *Love From Judy* during that first series of *TIFH*, and had to rush back to London from wherever we were play-ing on Saturday night. Johnny Brandon also had to get back, so we travelled together, usually catching the last London train, which stopped at every station on the way. Some of our journeys seemed endless, but we were young enough not to worry about the lack of sleep.

After Alma left the show to star in her own television series, Dick and I attempted to fill her spot with a duet and the Glums swelled to fill the second half of the show. That was the routine until 1960. Sometimes twenty-six in a series, sometimes sixteen, sometimes ten, then back up to twenty-six again. *TIFH* continued to command good listening figures throughout, until the last series, when Frank and Denis departed for television, handing over the writing to Barry Took and Eric Merriman. They were another two splendid writers, both much in demand in the Sixties. Eric wrote and presented a TV sketch show called *Mild and Bitter*, in which I took part, and Barry has also written and presented shows successfully for many years. Unfortunately, they became incompatible as co-writers and ended up writing the material separately. At the end of the thirteenth series the BBC decided to call a halt. In all, I did 153 episodes. It really was a great milestone in my career. At the end of each series we were con-tracted for the next one, providing a great sense of security, and I always looked forward to our Sunday recordings. *TIFH* became the longest running radio comedy show in history, a record which was broken first by *The Navy Lark* and then by *The News Huddlines* – more of that later. The BBC did release a couple of *TIFH* cassettes and a Glums audiotape. Some comedy shows do not improve with age but the scripts of Muir and Norden are timeless and still good for a laugh.

Frank and Denis's Glums sketches conjured up hilarious pictures in the mind's eye and stretched the imagination of the listener. This may have been why they never successfully made the transition to television. There were two attempts; the first was in Jimmy Edwards' *The Faces of Jim* series, in which Ronnie Barker played Ron to my Eth; and later, Patricia Brake teamed up with Ian Lavender. Their performances could hardly be faulted, although I must admit that, having created Eth, I hated the idea of someone else playing her. The fact that she was also doing it well made it even harder to take. The earlier television show featuring the Glums used the story where Pa Glum gets his toe stuck in a bath tap and Ron and Eth try to release him. Eth is only able to enter the bathroom once Pa Glum's modesty has been covered by Ron pouring several packets of gravy browning into the bath – 'Water so opaque it would get a "U" certificate from any censor in the country,' boasted Pa. On television, the sight of Jim in a bath of gravy browning was a slightly unedifying spectacle, and one couldn't help wondering why he didn't simply pull his toe out of the tap. But on radio you don't question things like that.

To round off these memories of *TIFH*, here's a favourite Ron and Eth story that never made it onto the air. The scene was the bedroom on their wedding night.

RON: I'm going to get undressed now, Eth. You're not to look.
[Eth was unpacking her case and held up her pretty new nightie.]
ETH: Ooh, Ron, isn't it lovely. All pink and crinkly.
RON: I told you not to look, Eth.

Love From Judy came to an end during that first series, and after twenty-six weeks of *TIFH*, I set off on a Mediterranean cruise with my parents; but before I headed for the sun, I was contracted to model some fashion accessories for a magazine. I imagined I would be draped in glamorous scarves or be seen packing my ultra-smart vanity case. I duly attended the photo shoot, but when I saw the fashion accessories I was expected to model it crossed my mind that the article might be appearing in the April the first edition:

After the show June is taking a cruise and her wardrobe will be mostly skirts, jeans and blouses. With them she will take some belts she has made. Dog leads make the nicest leather belts. Have you thought of hanging your initials from yours? And here's another gay idea for a belt, this time from the kitchen – a clothes line hung with key blanks.

It didn't get any better.

Don't you just love June's original little handbag? D'you recognize it? It's a lettuce-shaker, bought for a shilling.

Had this appeared at the height of the punk-rock craze I might well have become a fashion icon. Unfortunately it was still only 1954, so I just crossed my fingers and hoped no-one would see it.

I boarded the ship with several skirts, jeans and blouses, but none of the above accessories, and looked forward to ten days of doing nothing except spending time with my parents.

Dad needed a holiday a lot more than I did. He'd had a slight stroke four years earlier, but had carried on working as hard as ever. Muff had persuaded him to take a long holiday the previous summer at our cottage, 'Rosemary', at Middleton-on-Sea, and I had joined them there at weekends while *Love From Judy* was on in the West End. We convinced Dad that a cruise was what he needed to improve his health. My parents were fond of the sea, and Dictograph Telephones had close links with the shipping industry. The Royal Yacht *Britannia* – now ex-royal – had a Dictograph phone system as, later on, did the *QE2*. I suspect that one reason my mum was so fond of cruising was the opportunity it afforded to take part in the organized fancy-dress evenings. She took first prize on many occasions and I have photographs of her taken on board in an assortment of outfits, and also one of Dad in his *Charley's Aunt* drag. When they went on a cruise they took a trunk packed with costumes – there were plenty of porters about in those days.

We sailed on the *Arcadia*, which took us to Lisbon, Palermo, Naples and Capri, where we visited Gracie Fields' famous restaurant, Canzone del Mare. We met her briefly, as she liked to mingle with her guests. When we returned to Southampton, my mother persuaded Dad to stay on board for the next cruise as she felt it was doing him good. Off they went again, this time to Gibraltar, Cannes and Barcelona. I left them to it, as I had to get back to work, or at least to see if there was any.

In 1954, *TIFH* shared the *Daily Mail* award for the best radio show. The other winner was *The Archers*, a programme which *TIFH* regularly made fun of. At the same time, I began to be offered other jobs, jobs for which I didn't have to audition, and that was an important step forward.

I was booked to appear in several episodes of *Fast and Loose*, a new television sketch show, written by, and starring, two of the newer generation of writers and comedians, Bob Monkhouse and Denis Goodwin. They had been given their own series by Ronnie Waldman, the BBC head of light entertainment, while still quite young – Bob was only twenty-five – but they were already experienced comedy writers, having worked on shows like *Calling All Forces* and *The Forces Show*. *Fast and Loose* was transmitted live from the stage of the BBC Theatre on Shepherd's Bush Green. The theatre was converted a couple of years later to accommodate television equipment, but at the time it was just an old music hall, with a floor covering the orchestra pit and stalls for the cameras to move about on, and just two boom microphones, one onstage and the other clamped to the front of the circle. It was very basic in 1954. All the dressing rooms were named after BBC transmitters – I shared 'Derby' with Alma Cogan, while Bob and Dennis were in 'Bedminster'. We performed forty-five minutes of fast-paced comedy and musical numbers, live and without a break, to 11 million viewers.

Bob was, and is, astonishingly gifted. He could sing, dance, act and write as well as work as a solo stand-up. He was also terrific at physical routines, the kind of things he'd picked up from watching hundreds of silent film comedies. Denis Goodwin was a good writer, but a more limited performer than Bob, which caused a great deal of friction and eventually a very sad parting. Their difficulty at the time was that they were too popular. They had so much work that there simply weren't enough hours in the day to write all the shows they had been hired to do. After the first *Fast and Loose* programme, Bob collapsed and needed months off to recover, or so it was announced at the time. It wasn't until I read his autobiography some years ago that I learned how he and Denis had stage-managed Bob's break-down in order to give themselves more time to catch up with their writing commitments. It was a clever stunt. At the end of the first show, as the audience was applauding and the credits were rolling, Bob's eyes flickered, he buckled at the knees and fell to the floor.

'Good gracious! Did you see that?' the announcer Sylvia Peters is alleged to have said.

It worked a treat, and while Bob was 'recuperating', he and Denis were able to get down to work.

When I joined *Fast and Loose*, I was involved in most of the sketches, some of which were very long – ten minutes or more. There was one that Bob and Denis devised to provide an opportunity for Bob to display his brilliant slapstick skills. It was about a straight-laced Victorian family. Papa was played by Alexander Gauge – a memorable Friar Tuck in the *Robin Hood* series – Mama was Irene Handl – one of the funniest women ever – and I was the daughter, Charlotte, wooed by Bob as a disastrously clumsy character called Osbert. Osbert would come either to tea or dinner, and would end up accidentally wrecking the place in a manner that usually involved breaking a lot of crockery and spilling food and drink.

One week Osbert was taken on by Alexander Gauge as a clerk in his factory, and was invited home to tea in the front parlour, where there was a half glass door through which Bob entered. Just inside the door there was a hatstand; Bob had seen an old Ben Turpin routine, in which he gets caught up in a hatstand, and he planned to do the same, finishing with the hatstand breaking the glass door. It was a difficult trick to pull off on film, let alone on live television. Bob rehearsed it successfully several times, and on the night he did it absolutely perfectly. With his back to the door, he ended up with the bottom of the stand smack in the middle of the glass. It had shattered during rehearsal, but now, for some reason, it stubbornly refused to break. Bob turned round and took a run at it, but still the glass held firm. The audience started to laugh. Bob grabbed a walking stick and whacked the door. Nothing. Alex, Irene and I looked on with fixed, pained expressions until Bob lunged with all his might at the re-calcitrant glass, which finally shattered. Then he turned to the audience and said, 'I learned that one from beating the gong for Rank Films.' A great ad lib that drew loud appreciation from the audience. Afterwards, Bob was exhausted and understandably furious with the prop master, and he demanded an explanation. The chap said he thought it all looked a bit dangerous in rehearsal, so for the performance he had decided to replace the panel with shatter-proof glass!

We did a Christmas edition of the show in which there was a panto sketch. I was Cinderella and Alexander Gauge, if you can believe it, played Fairy Fabian of the Yard – Fabian was the Inspector Morse of the day. There was another Osbert sketch, again involving a lot of breakages and sloshing soup everywhere – getting a laugh is a messy job. We did the show on 22 December, then all dispersed for the Christmas holiday. I went to Sussex to join Mother and Dad for what was to be a time of unusual joy and sadness.

Dad was not at all well, and to ease our minds his doctor, Alistair Aitchison – known as Bobs – had suggested that we spend Christmas at a private hotel called Park House near his home in Midhurst, so that he could keep an eye on his patient. We took his advice and moved in just before Christmas.

Park House at Bepton was owned by Mike and Ione O'Brien, great friends of the Aitchison family. The hotel was, and is, quite delightful, and we were well looked after by Mike, Ione and the staff. In the small bar, where you helped yourself to drinks and made a note of your tipple, I was saying to Ione what a delightful man Dr Bobs was.

'Wait till you meet his brother,' she said.

So I was more than a little curious when Bobs invited me for a drink at the Bricklayers in Midhurst, where we would meet his brother Tim. We walked into the pub on Boxing Day morning and there, standing at the bar, was this handsome chap with a gorgeous smile and a lovely voice. He was with a group of friends and was talking, I think it's fairly safe to assume, about football. Bobs introduced us. Since I wasn't much interested in sport and Tim's visits to the theatre had been few and far between – although he was dimly aware of the existence of *Take It From Here* – it was not the most promising beginning. Certainly, the most likely outcome was not that we would spend the rest of our lives together, but since when have these things been governed by logic?

He invited me to a dance at the Middleton Sports Club the following evening and we saw a lot of each other in the next few months. Middleton Sports Club played a major role in our lives. The bar, run by 'Hutch', was a favourite meeting place. We still keep up with friends we met in those days. Although our interests were entirely different, we shared the same views and opinions about many things and found each other madly attractive, and one thing, as they say, led to another, and here we are forty-six years on. I've been in the public eye for some time now, but Tim and I have always tried to keep our private lives to ourselves, which is, I think, one reason our relationship has lasted so long.

Tim was a chartered surveyor and also loved his sport. He played county hockey and squash, represented his Cambridge college at tennis and captained the Sunday hockey team at Middleton Sports Club. As a cricketer he had been in the same Charterhouse eleven as Peter May, Simon Raven and Jim – now Lord – Prior, and he has the distinction of a mention in the cricketers' bible, *Wisden*. Over the next few months we drew close and spent more and more time together, with me trying to understand the finer points of hockey while freezing on the touchlines, and Tim trying to find something to say after watching his girlfriend camping about with sundry males in a revue for the fourteenth time.

I attended the hockey festival at Folkestone, where we first met Judith Chalmers, whose husband, Neil Durden-Smith, was a participant, and there were squash matches for the Jesters and the Bath Club Cup, which took place at various clubs around London. The players' wives and girlfriends would dutifully watch the games and join our men for a drink and a meal afterwards. A favourite venue after Saturday hockey was the Station Hotel in Richmond where there was live music and a friendly atmosphere – apparently the Rolling Stones played some of their early gigs there, but that was after our time.

Tim was gently initiated into the theatrical world by attending *TIFH* recordings, and he thoroughly enjoyed meeting everyone connected with the show. We socialized with Dick and Peta Bentley and had many jolly dinners at their place in St John's Wood. We also visited Jimmy Edwards at his house at Fittleworth in West Sussex.

Tim's father, Commander J. G. Aitchison RN OBE, was a very popular and amusing commentator at the home of polo, Cowdray Park at Midhurst, though he'd never actually been on a horse in his life. When Tim was playing cricket in 'The Ruins' at Cowdray, his father's voice could be heard booming over the public address system as he colourfully described the action on the adjacent polo ground. He was an impressive and slightly intimidating figure. I was strolling in the grounds of Ashfield House, the Aitchisons' family home, one time with the commander when he suddenly said to me, 'These, er, actor johnnies you work with . . . some of them are a bit . . . how's-your-father, aren't they?' I assured him that, from what I'd heard, actors were no more how's-your-father than sailors. The subject was then dropped.

Tim and I got engaged in 1955 – it was the done thing then – and because of *TIFH* the papers were full of 'Ooh, Ron! Look what's happened to Eth', and, 'What will Ron say?' Dick Bentley even received congratulations from those who'd got hold of the wrong end of the stick. Tim had to face photographers and journalists for the first time in his life; he endured it with good humour and emerged from the ordeal with flying colours, as he has done countless times during the last forty-five years.

A month before we were due to be married Dad had another stroke, and although the wedding invitations had gone out, we didn't feel like having a large celebration under the circumstances, so the invitations were followed by cancellation cards. We were married quietly a week before the original date at St Mark's, North Audley Street – I don't quite know why, as neither of us lived anywhere near it.

Our honeymoon was spent in Paris, where we saw the sights, visited the Tour d'Argent restaurant and went for a trip on a Bateau-Mouche. The weather wasn't brilliant in October and the magnificent view from the Tour d'Argent was obscured by fog. When I reminded Tim as I was writing this, hoping he'd jog my memory about the trip, he said, 'Oh yes, the Tour d'Argent. Marvellous view, wasn't it?' Still, we did agree that we went there! It was a while ago, so perhaps we can be forgiven for misremembering a few details.

On our return we discovered that my poor dad's health had deteriorated further. He couldn't speak or write, and yet I had the feeling that he knew what was happening and was desperately frustrated that he couldn't communicate with us. Mum was at her wits' end. She had consulted endless specialists and alternative forms of medicine in the vain hope of curing him, but to no avail. We were unaware of the Stroke Association, and have since learned that there are many people of all ages nowadays who recover from strokes; at the time we felt helpless and sad that we could do nothing. Dad went into hospital and then, when we were given to understand there was no hope, Muff brought him home, where he had twenty-four-hour nursing. He died at Christmas. I wrote in my diary, 'The end of a very nasty year – apart from Tim. 1955 can go.'

Muff was distraught and missed Dad dreadfully. My brother John had been helping her for the last year of Dad's life with the necessities of day-to-day living. She had never before needed to pay a bill or deal with rates and taxes but, aided by John and Tim, she soon learned to be self-sufficient. Tim found her a flat in Cranley Mews in Kensington, where she moved with Mrs Suter, who had been our housekeeper for many years. Tim and I weren't far away, her friends rallied round and her amateur dramatics kept her occupied for many years to come.

When Dad died my feelings were mixed. I was very sad that he had finally left us, but relieved that his suffering was over; he had been ill for so long. It was an additional sadness that, even though I was in my thirtieth year, we'd never really had what you might call a grown-up conversation.

I also regretted the fact that Tim never really knew him. He was already ill when they met. I know they would have got on well and liked each other, and he was much in our thoughts at our belated wedding reception, held six months after his death.

Chapter Six

ON THE BOX

WHENEVER I HEAR NOSTALGIC REMINISCENCES ABOUT THE DAYS of live television, I remember the time I was suspended on a wire some fifteen feet above the ground, dressed as a fairy and awaiting my cue to start a sketch with Arthur Askey. Just as I was being swung into position, the floor manager gesticulated frantically for me to slow down – not easily done on a wire – then he pointed at his watch and script to indicate that the show was under-running and that we were to reinstate a chunk of dialogue that had been cut at the dress rehearsal.

'Oh, we're putting that bit back, are we?' said Arthur once he'd worked out what was going on, then turning to the camera he said, 'You're lucky. You're getting an extra bit.' After a lot more mischievous ad libbing from him, which the audience and viewers loved, incidentally, we finally approached the end of the sketch, by which time we were over-running and getting frantic signals to speed up.

'Well, make up your mind,' said Arthur to the out-of-vision floor manager. Then back to the camera, 'He's hurrying us up now!' And we gabbled our way to the end of the sketch.

Those moments were not unusual in the early days of live

television. Everyone who experienced it can quote similar, and probably far more gruesome, instances of the white-knuckle ride that was TV comedy and drama prior to the advent of videotape editing. I have never been able to go along with those who want to turn the clock back and recreate the immediacy of live television. There was nothing magical about it for the performers. It may have been fun for the viewer – 'spot the mistake' was quite a good game. 'Did you notice the blank look on that actor's face when he stumbled over his lines?' Or, 'Did you watch that show where she had a shadow over her face most of the time? It was really funny.'

Some say that live TV is more exciting and gets better performances from the actors. I'm not so sure. Actors always do their best, whether they're onstage or in front of a camera, but the safety net of being able to re-record if you do happen to slip up is, I think, well worth having. The errors that you make can be saved for *It'll Be Alright on the Night* or *Auntie's Bloomers*.

There are some daytime shows and news programmes that have to be live, but mistakes seem less disruptive than in a sitcom or a drama. The technical elements of a TV show have multiplied tenfold since the far-off 1950s so, unlike live theatre where the actors are in charge, performers on television and in films are more than ever at the mercy of factors beyond their control.

Having said that, there were some performers who exploited the live situation to great effect, and none was more brilliant than big-hearted Arthur.

Despite his enormous radio success, Arthur Askey was more or less ignored by television until 1952. Things suddenly changed at the *BBC Christmas Party* that year when he was asked to step in at short notice as a replacement for one of the other acts. The *BBC Christmas Party*, which later became *Christmas Night With the Stars*, was an inexpensive way of making a seasonal programme. A dozen or so well-known performers were booked and paid to entertain an audience consisting of other not so well-known performers, who were *not* paid – in fact we were given three guineas each for our cab fare, and the note at the bottom of the invitation read 'drinks will be practical', i.e., not fake. It seems that at the 1952 event,

Terry-Thomas had a bit too much practical Christmas cheer and Arthur was asked to take over at the last minute. He did a few silly walks and stuck his face in the camera, saying, 'Count my freckles,' along with other spontaneous routines, and went down extremely well. Ronnie Waldman, the light entertainment chief, signed him up for a series, and Arthur's television career was launched. He was to continue with his own shows into the Sixties, but he said he did his best work in the mid-Fifties, 'before anyone noticed'.

I did several series with him, starting with *Before Your Very Eyes* in 1956. The show consisted of topical sketches in the first half, followed by a longer parody sketch, usually of a film, in part two. In this, Arthur appeared as a historical or fictional character, such as Sherlock Holmes or Beau Geste. When things went wrong, as they were inclined to, Arthur drew attention to them rather than trying to cover up. He made the camera follow him to the edge of the set saying, 'Isn't it funny how the desert finishes just here,' and when he was in the middle of a quick change, and knew he wasn't going to make it in time, he came on half dressed and said to us, 'Just do that again, would you. I'm not quite ready,' then, turning to the camera, 'I'll be with you in a minute, playmates.' When I was having trouble opening a door one time, he said, 'Don't worry. Arthur 'as key.'

Audiences loved these moments, but the management, who had been charmed by his antics to begin with, suddenly became concerned that Arthur was making fun of the important new medium of television and ordered him to tone it down.

Though already in his fifties when he started, Arthur was a pioneer of televised comedy. He was wonderfully natural in front of the camera and not remotely daunted by it. He spoke into the lens as if he were having an inconsequential chat with a friend. He said, 'I don't think about the millions watching, I just imagine two people sitting at home eating their dinner in front of the telly.' Excellent advice which I've tried to follow.

Working with Arthur was a delight. He was a charmer, as well as funny and modest. He called himself a 'silly little man', and when he was asked, 'What are you doing at the moment?' his reply was, 'Oh, the usual old rubbish.'

In one sketch, set in the Edwardian days, he was playing a pianist and I was his wife. He was at the piano and he looked at the music, saying, 'Paganini! Sorry, that's page nine. Would you turn over for me?' At rehearsal, just for fun, I did a cartwheel. It made him laugh and he said, 'We'll keep that in.' Luckily I remembered to wear my period frilly bloomers for the performance.

In another sketch I was Cleopatra – there were a lot of Cleopatra sketches in those days – and Arthur kept disappearing to look over the non-existent battlements. The first time he had water thrown at him, then came back to me, dripping, and continued our love scene. On his second trip to the battlements he returned covered in sand, which had stuck to his wet clothes. He always wore his glasses, and the inside of the lenses were thick with sand. You couldn't see his eyes, just sand. It was such a funny sight. His close-up caused the audience to laugh hysterically, and I'm afraid I did, too. He continued the dialogue, 'Cleopatra, my heart's a-flutter when I look at you.' He obviously had to keep his eyes shut, and my endeavours to turn him to face the right direction caused more laughter. 'Aye-aye,' he said, 'Cleopatra's got the needle.' I should think that show definitely over-ran.

Anyone who saw those shows of Arthur's will remember Sabrina. Arthur's idea was to have a glamorous blonde in the show; her magnificent figure came as an unexpected bonus and it bolstered the ratings no end. Her real name was Norma Sykes, but Arthur felt something more exotic was called for and rechristened her after the play *Sabrina Fair*, which was running at the time. To the crew, by the way, she was known as the Hunchfront of Lime Grove, and it was interesting how the fellas always found pressing reasons to go up into the lighting grid above the studio floor whenever she was on. She later had acting and singing lessons and did quite a polished cabaret act, but to begin with she behaved like the original dumb blonde. Arthur took her to open a church fête once, and when she was presented with a bouquet by the vicar she said, 'No thanks, I've got plenty of flowers at home.' Arthur felt she became slightly intoxicated by her success and I remember her breezing into rehearsals very late once. 'I'm *so* sorry,' she said. 'I had a late night and just *couldn't* wake up.'

'It's all right, dear,' said Arthur. 'On a wonderful day like this I wonder you bothered to turn up at all.' The tail, as Arthur said, had begun to wag the dog, and eventually she had to go. The parting was quite amicable and she and Arthur remained on good terms. When last heard of, she was married to a highly successful doctor and living in Beverly Hills.

Arthur was one of the few comedians who was as funny off screen as he was on. Dickie Henderson told the story of attending a memorial service with Arthur at St Martin-in-the-Fields. As everyone was seated waiting for it to start, a drunk staggered in and made his way up the aisle, going from one end of a packed pew to the other, trying to find a seat. Then he turned and made his way back along the next pew, disturbing another row of people before staggering out again. Arthur remarked, 'You see what happens when you book your tickets with Keith Prowse.'

Roy Hudd was in pantomime with Arthur at Wimbledon, and at one Wednesday matinée there were many fellow artists in the audience. There is always a moment in panto when the comic falls over and is asked, 'What are you doing down there?' to which the reply is, 'Getting up.'

Arthur was on the ground and Roy fed the line, 'What are you doing down there?' Before the audience could yell the answer, Arthur looked thoroughly affronted and said, 'I'm not giving away my best gags with all these pros in front.'

After Jack Hylton persuaded Arthur to leave the BBC and go to ITV, the show went through several changes of title and format. *Before Your Very Eyes* became *Living it Up*, which was an attempt to re-create the success of the radio show *Band Waggon* with Richard Murdoch, but it didn't quite come off, and the following year the show was reconceived as a series of one-off comedy dramas called *Arthur's Treasured Volumes*, the initial letters giving a plug to *ATV*. Each programme began with Arthur and his daughter Anthea discussing the plot of a book, then the picture dissolved and we were into the start of the story. In 1961 there was another rethink and *The Arthur Askey Show* was transformed into a sitcom set at the turn of the century, with Arthur and me playing husband and wife, and Patricia Hayes and Arthur Mullard as our neighbours. Arthur felt that Jack Hylton skimped on budgets and he wasn't entirely happy, so the following year he returned to the BBC.

I had great affection for Arthur. The first time I saw him was at one of Dad's Masonic dos when I was about eleven. I remember watching him sing 'The Bee Song', which became one of his trade marks, and I remained a fan from then on. Tim's first visit to a television studio was to see one of Arthur's shows, and Arthur, on learning that Tim was keen on football, gave us his tickets to the Cup Final. He was a dear, kind man and I feel privileged to have worked with him.

Arthur suffered a series of illnesses in his latter years, and he faced the final one with great bravery and his somewhat cynical sense of humour. He replied to the huge volume of get-well messages he received on hospital notepaper headed 'The Maternity Ward'. He certainly gave birth to an awful lot of laughter during his lifetime.

I had warned Tim that he shouldn't expect me to give up the theatre after we were married, which of course he didn't, but it soon occurred to me that it wasn't a very good idea for me to be leaving for work in the evenings just as he was coming home. I therefore decided to avoid working in the theatre if I could, unless something that I felt I absolutely had to do came along. Luck was on my side, and it just happened that the work I was offered was almost entirely in radio and television. Variety theatres were still booming in the Fifties, and with many of my potential rivals occupied in summer shows and pantos, it turned out to be rather a good strategy to be in London and available for any telly and radio that cropped up. As well as *TIFH* and the shows with Arthur and Bob Monkhouse, I made brief appearances in series such as *The Army Game* and *Dixon of Dock Green*, as well as a great many radio programmes and the occasional variety show.

In the first few weeks of ITV's existence I took part in a sketch show called *Here We Go* with Billy Dainty and Bruce Forsyth. It was recorded at Wood Green and received some pretty poor reviews. In one sketch we were all on roller skates; I was Lady Macbeth, Bruce

Before Your Very Eyes with Arthur Askey, 1957 – 'No thanks, I've already had a pint.' BFI

Take It From Here, 1953 – the Glums indeed: Jimmy Edwards, me, Alma Cogan, Dick Bentley, Denis Norden, Charles Maxwell and Frank Muir.
BBC

'All together now – take it from here!' BBC

The last *Intimate Revue* at the Royal Court Theatre, Sloane Square, before the serious mob took over.

Engaged to Tim
(no ring yet!).
Headlines: 'Ooh
Ron – look
what's happened
To Eth.'

Our small mock-Tudor in
Addison Avenue.

ABOVE: *The Straker Special* – a TV musical about a car, with Denis Quilley.

TOP RIGHT: *The Tony Hancock Show*, 1956 – vamping till ready? BFI

BELOW: Jimmy Edwards and Ronnie Barker – 'My daughter is not for sale.'

ABOVE: *The Seven Faces of Jim*, 1961 – 'The Face of Enthusiasm'.

The Seven Faces of Jim, 1961, with Jimmy and Richard Briers putting on a brave front.

Crowther's Crowd, 1963, with Ronnie Barker and Leslie Crowther – 'Tell us another one, do!' BBC

With Tommy Cooper, 1967. © Pearson Television

LEFT: 'The Blood Donor' with Tony Hancock and Frank Thornton – 'Blood is blood, Mr Hancock, all over the world. It is classified by groups and not by accident of birth.' 'I did not come here for a lecture on communism, Madam.' BBC

RIGHT: *The Benny Hill Show*, 1962 – 'Portrait of a Bridegroom'. BBC

BELOW: *The Benny Hill Show*, with Benny and Henry McGee. BBC

ABOVE: *Beggar My Neighbour*, 1966, with Pat Coombs, Reg Varney and Desmond Walter-Ellis.

LEFT: *The Stanley Baxter Show*, 1964, filmed in exotic Clacton-on-Sea. BBC

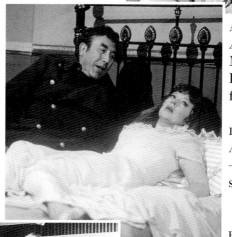

ABOVE: *Armchair Theatre*, 1968 – 'What's a Mother For?' – with Mona Washbourne and Joe Brown. © Pearson Television

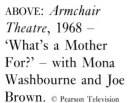

BELOW: *Father, Dear Father*, 1968, teaching Patrick Cargill to dance.

© Pearson Television

ABOVE: *A Tale of Two Microbes*, with Frank Muir as Basil and me as Desdemona Salmonella, for Unilever.

LEFT: *Frankie Howerd Meets the BeeGees*, 1968 – I seem to have swooned at the thought.

© Pearson Television

BELOW: *Steptoe and Son*, 1964. BBC

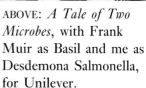

Susan Jane Aitchison.

played the Thane and Billy was Macduff. They were both totally at home on their wheels, whereas I had never roller skated and stood nervously waiting for my entrance. I was given a shove, which propelled me towards Bruce, who brought me to a shaky halt with his outstretched arm. Here is a sample of our Shakespearian dialogue.

JUNE: Together thou and I must kill the king.
BRUCE: 'Tis a thought methinks. During the banquet I'll slip a mickey finn into his goose.
JUNE: But, good My Lord, what if he will not take the mickey?
BRUCE: When he seest me in this kilt, he's bound to take the mickey!

I was going to say they don't write 'em like that any more, but I'm happy to say they do. That show was co-written by Dick Vosburgh, who is as prolific now as he was forty-five years ago. He recently had a success with his Hollywood send-up musical *A Saint She Ain't*. He has written for just about every comedian since the war, and Frank Muir told a lovely story about him, dating from around the time when he was at his busiest. He gave a party at his house, and some-one accidentally trod on his young daughter's hand. Dick went to comfort her saying, 'Who did it? Come on, tell me who it was and I'll . . . I'll *write for them!*'

The new ITV network decided, in its first year on air, to attempt what the BBC had hitherto resisted: to put the wildly successful Goons on television. Peter Sellers had tried for years and been ignored by a succession of BBC producers and department heads, who all believed that neither the Goon humour nor Peter's physical appearance were suitable for television. The new company, Associated Rediffusion, was prepared to risk it, and moreover to invest quite a lot of money in bringing the team to the viewing public. The first series was called *Idiot Weekly, Price 2d.*, the idea being that Peter Sellers, as the editor of a terrible Victorian magazine, linked the sketches as though they were a collection of articles. It was written by Spike Milligan, script-edited by Eric Sykes and, though a little less manic than *The Goon Show*, was still fairly chaotic. Sometimes Spike rewrote during transmission and people ended up working off different versions of the same script. *Idiot Weekly, Price 2d.* was also very expensive to produce; Peter, Spike and Eric were, by their own admission, getting huge fees – I think mine was the 2d. When Peter played Napoleon, someone was sent to Paris to copy designs for his costume. Those sorts of things don't happen nowadays. Peter certainly had clout.

The second series was called *A Show Called Fred*, and the one after that was *Son of Fred*. Fred was a name Peter and Spike were very attached to, and all the programmes made by the team were collectively known as *The Freds*. The final series was called *Yes, It's the Cathode-Ray Tube Show!*, or *YITCRTS!* 'Fred' had gone, because by then Spike had handed over the writing duties to Michael Bentine. There was no let-up in the lunacy though; if anything, Mike's ideas were even more outlandish than Spike's. I played a reporter interviewing Kenneth Connor, as the first man to circum-navigate the Earth on a standard British lawnmower. A ship interrupted the scene, then Ken ran me over with his mower. In the same show, Mike and I did a jungle sketch in which he shot several fierce animals that were attacking us, and then finally, at point-blank range, he shot me. I was rather nervous about this, but he assured me there was nothing to worry about as long as I kept still. That just made me even more apprehensive. I was told the gun only fired blanks, so I don't know what it was that thudded painfully into my back, but it gave me the fright of my life. I let out a shriek of alarm before slumping down dead. There was no acting required – I thought I *was*. I later discovered that what I'd felt was the blast. It was dangerous working with that lot.

The cast of *The Freds* changed from series to series as people went off to fulfil other commitments, but Peter was under contract and remained for all four runs, a little reluctantly perhaps, as he was well on the way to an established film career by then. He was a strange chap, very much aware of his increasing importance in the business, not easy to get to know, but not at all difficult to work with. He and I appeared in a radio show called *Curiouser and Curiouser*, a com-pilation of English and American humorous writing, and we worked together again in 1979, when he was making a record in Paris. Peter wanted to revive the character of Fred Kite, the shop steward from *I'm All Right Jack*. Fred had been knighted, but was still championing the workers and confronting the then leader of the Opposition, Margaret Thatcher. Peter had hoped that Janet Brown would be Maggie, but she wasn't available, so he asked me to provide the voice. It was some years before I impersonated her in the *News Huddlines*, so I had no idea how to do her, but I said yes as I was keen to work with Peter again, and Paris was an added attraction. I managed to get hold of a tape of Maggie, and practised her distinctive tones. I've always had an ability to mimic, so it wasn't too difficult. I can't explain how it happens; I hear the voice and it just comes out. Incidentally, I really miss her in the *Huddlines*; the current parliamentary ladies haven't nearly such recognizable voices.

I flew out to Paris in the morning, we recorded a sketch and a song, 'What About the Workers?' with Sir Fred and Maggie, and had a lot of fun doing it. But it didn't take very long and I was on a plane back to England the same afternoon. No time for even the merest squint at the shops, darling, just a quick break for lunch – baguette *pour moi* and caviar for Mr Sellers – then home.

The item was cut from the record, so I assumed the results weren't liked by Peter or the record company, and I forgot all about it – that is until I read Roger Lewis's recent biography of Peter Sellers. It seems that when Mrs T won the 1979 election, Peter wrote her a letter of congratulation. Then, just before the record was due for release, he received a charming letter of thanks from Downing Street. Fearing perhaps that satire might scupper his chances of further honours, he immediately put a block on 'What About the Workers?' The record company was furious because they felt they had a topical hit on their hands, but Peter wouldn't budge. He was, as I've said, a strange chap. Sadly, he didn't get his 'K'.

One of the most powerful people in television in the late-Fifties was Jack Hylton. He managed to strike a deal with Associated Rediffusion to provide a sizeable chunk of their light entertainment output. Hylton had bought a job lot of scripts from NBC in America. They were sketches that were originally performed by Sid Caesar and Imogene Coca, and were written by Caesar's legendary writing team, which included the likes of Larry Gelbart, Neil Simon, Mel Brooks and Woody Allen. The Australian actor Alan White and I were to be the English team. The plan was for the scripts to be anglicized, but by the time rehearsals started they had hardly been altered at all, so we spent most of the time changing dollars to pounds and 'purse' to 'handbag' etc. The result wasn't very funny, and sometimes, as with one particular courtroom sketch, mystifying. 'Unbelievably weak,' said the *Evening News*, and if it hadn't been for the Two Sippolos – 'music from unusual objects' – we would have been well and truly sunk. Sid and Imogene were brilliant in the sketches, but Alan and I obviously didn't have the right chemistry to make them work here.

So Hylton's judgement wasn't flawless by any means. Once, when I was working for him, he invited Tim and me out for an evening. He was accompanied by his current protégée, Rosalina Neri, who wore a splendid white feather boa which steadily moulted onto her protector's black dinner jacket as the evening progressed. The cabaret was a young unknown called Shirley Bassey. All of us round the table were knocked out by her, but not Mr Hylton. 'She won't last,' he pronounced. 'Lass can't hold a note.' I wonder what happened to her?

Fortunately, his correct judgements outnumbered his blunders. He was shrewd enough to pinch Tony Hancock from under the noses of the BBC. *Hancock's Half-Hour* was a big success on radio, but the BBC didn't develop it for television until 1956, by which time Jack Hylton had established a prior claim on the star's services for Associated Rediffusion. In the early Fifties, the senior management at the Beeb seemed to be stuck on the idea that, to appear on television, a comic had to have a 'telegenic' face. Because of this, they were slow to recognize the enormous potential of Peter Sellers and Arthur Askey, and it's possible that the same applied to Hancock. Whatever the reason, Hylton stole a march on them and a lot of legal wrangling ensued.

I appeared in the first series of *The Tony Hancock Show* for Rediffusion, along with John Vere and Tony's friend Clive Dunn, who gave his wonderful old dodderer character an early airing. The opening programme began with Tony kneeling before a giant photo of Jack Hylton and swearing an oath to keep the show clean and not reveal his salary. The dispute between Hylton and the BBC had been so well publicized that the viewers got the joke. We did a sketch set in a coffee bar, the Bar Depresso, where the plants ate the customers, except they didn't quite and the nylon threads guiding them were rather obvious, so the joke, like many others at the time, became a casualty of live transmission. When a stage-hand appeared in a sketch set in the Far East it was scarcely thought worthy of comment. We did a send-up of *A Streetcar Named Desire*, with me playing Vivien Leigh and Tony donning a torn T-shirt. Tony's Marlon Brando was absolutely hilarious. After I delivered about a page of passionate southern belle nonsense, he gave me a Hancock deeply hurt look and said, 'You've built that up a bit.' The show always ended with a dance number by a group called the Teenagers, which was then attempted by Tony and me. Routines in other shows included a Balinese dance, a somewhat bruising Apache duet, and a flamenco number in which he went off on a glorious choreographic ad lib while I swirled my skirts and clicked my castanets until he rejoined me.

Tony was very good at mime and slapstick, and he was brilliant in a nightclub sketch where he had to play all the characters from the doorman to the cloakroom attendant, the waiter, chef and gypsy fiddler, rushing about changing hats and various articles of clothing. He also performed the cabaret. I was the cigarette girl, and joined him in the floor show. This nightclub set-up later became the basis of the ill-fated *Hancock's*, for ABC in 1967.

There was a fruit machine on the set, and Tony and I had fun playing it in our breaks. The coins were the usual metal discs, and he handed me one of his winnings and magnanimously said I could keep it, so I did. I had it in my purse for many years, hoping that some of his genius might rub off on me. When I appeared in *The Morecambe and Wise Show* years later, I showed the disc to Eric, and when I explained how I'd come by it, he reached into his pocket and gave me a similar one with a hole in it. Now I have treasured mementoes of two of the funniest men who ever lived. I should have collected a set!

Tony was a great comic actor with that essential vulnerability, and his face was his fortune. Audiences knew that, despite the outward bravado, underneath he was as soft as butter, and they loved him for it. The character he played was so self-deluding and arrogant that you knew he was going to come a cropper, and it made you want to rescue him from himself. In real life he was his own worst enemy and he found life difficult to cope with.

He was great fun to work with, and if you did something he liked in rehearsal, he'd chuckle away, which is always encouraging. Even in the early days, though, he was very insecure, always worrying that the show wasn't funny enough, always fussing away at the script and trying to find ways of improving the performance. He was never satisfied, and after a transmission he would sit in his dressing room brooding over what had passed. Tim and I would often join him and his then wife Cecily for a few drinks, before going out for a meal, usually at the Balzac at the bottom of Wood Lane. There, he'd cheer up and go home in a better frame of mind. Cecily was delightful and, I suspect, had a pretty miserable time, as she acquired a drink problem of her own – if you can't beat 'em, join 'em. Tony was never satisfied or at ease with himself and depression eventually drove him to what most people presume was suicide. His death was a sad loss to the profession and to his friends.

It is a fact that many of our great comics have died from stress-related illnesses, but it's understandable, I think, as the responsibility for the success of a show rests entirely on their shoulders. If they are successful, the pressure to maintain the standard mounts, and if they fail, there's only one way to go, and that's down. I'm sure one of the reasons I've kept going so long is that I've never had to bear the sole responsibility for a show or had to deal with the pressure that involves; lack of ambition maybe, but at the time of writing I'm still here.

I appeared in five of the first six *Tony Hancock* shows for Jack Hylton, but I was unable to do the last programme because Tim and I had booked a holiday abroad before I knew about the show. I did, however, return for an episode in the second BBC series, in which

Tony visits an Alpine ski resort. I played a French girl who keeps going into his room by mistake – 'You can't grumble at service like this,' he says. Tony ends up having to share a room with Kenneth Williams, who plays a yodelling champion– 'I've got the biggest yodel in East Dulwich.' The script required Kenneth to play it as the familiar 'snide' character, complete with catchphrases like 'stop messin' about' and 'don't be like that'. Tony and Kenneth got on well together, and used to spend hours discussing religion and philosophy, but there was a certain amount of professional friction between the two in *Hancock's Half-Hour* due to the fact that Tony believed, as did the writers Galton and Simpson, that the show should be rooted in reality and not reliant on catchphrases or funny voices. But Kenneth's funny voices were very funny indeed and hugely appreciated by the audience, so Galton and Simpson tended to break their own rule in Kenneth's case, unable to deny themselves the big laughs he got. This irritated Tony rather. Not that he was envious of Kenneth, he was never insecure in that way, it was just that he thought the show shouldn't have to resort to 'tricks', as he called them. By the time I returned for the 1961 series, Kenneth had departed, as had the other regulars.

Kenny could be fairly outrageous offstage as well as on. Members of the *Carry On* team suffered his penchant for letting off stink bombs and depositing itching powder in uncomfortable places. I remember a party at Betty Marsden's house at about this time. Betty was doing the hostess rounds and said to Kenneth, 'Are you behaving yourself?'

'Is my cock hanging out?' he asked.

'Not yet,' said Betty.

'Well, I am, then.'

He enjoyed shocking people. During *Carry On* filming he would preside over a table in the dining room at Pinewood, and no biological function, human or animal, was considered a taboo topic for conversation. If you continued to eat your lunch you gained Kenny's respect. I worked with him on a number of occasions, including *Beyond Our Ken*, when I took over from Betty, who was off for a week. I even went through the ordeal of appearing with him on *Just a Minute.* I was hopeless at it, but when I was buzzed at my first attempt he was very supportive, saying, 'Go on! Give 'er a chance, she's new.' After several more buzzes it became, 'Oh no. Forget it, she's hopeless.' He was always friendly, and until I read his diaries I had no idea he suffered from depression. I first saw him in *Saint Joan*, playing the dauphin, before he became so well known. He gave a brilliant performance and maybe, like Tony, he resented the fact that he was known mainly for the *Carry On*s and comedy when he knew he was capable of serious work.

In 1956 I was offered a musical specially commissioned for television called *The Straker Special*. It was a romantic comedy built around the fortunes of a new British sports car, the Straker Special. I played the tomboy mechanic who fixes the car, settles a strike at the factory and finally secures its financial future by staging a triumphant launch at the Motor Show. Denis Quilley played the factory owner's son, who has no interest in cars and wants to be a composer – of musical comedies, funnily enough. I can't remember how Denis and I were united at the end, but I'm sure it was a deeply touching moment!

The fun and games were brought to a sudden halt when I came home from rehearsals one evening feeling a bit under the weather and, after dinner, had terrible stomach pains. Tim phoned brother Bobs, who diagnosed appendicitis and sent me off to hospital. I phoned Ken Carter, the director, to apologize for my bad timing, and the next day I had the offending organ removed. The surgeon's name was Cockett – and luckily he didn't. In fact, he gave me a 'cosmetic incision', invisible even in a bikini, I was told, not that I ever wore one. The staff at St Thomas's were marvellous and, as well as Mr Cockett, I was looked after by Sister Tancock and a consultant called Haycock – names to gladden the heart of a *Carry On* scriptwriter.

I was in hospital for about a week, then it was home and some cosseting from Tim, and no driving, lifting or otherwise putting at risk my neatly sewn cosmetic incision, and then back to work. They kindly rescheduled the *Straker Special* transmission, and we did it at the Hackney Empire a few months later. It must have been live because the *Evening Standard* cutting in my scrapbook says, 'The star of the show was the car, unfortunately its door didn't work and the girls had to climb over, to the detriment of their modesty, and once or twice we saw strange bodies moving across the screen.' I don't know, there's no pleasing these critics sometimes.

My third series of *TIFH* was due that winter, and I also took part in a new radio series starring Ted Ray, called *The Spice of Life*. It occupied a forty-five-minute slot, which I think is fifteen minutes too long, even for the most brilliant comedy show, but the BBC comedy chiefs were delighted with the first programme, and we were slotted in for a further twelve. I popped up as various debs, tarts and old bats, but my main spot was a regular double act with Ted, in which we played two wrinkly old girls in a laundrette, Mrs Pinny (Ted) and Mrs Drool (me). Mrs D. surfaces from time to time in *The News Huddlines*. We swapped stories about our aches and pains and hopeless husbands, with a good measure of, 'Ooooh yeeeees, Mrs Drool. Ooooh, Mrs Pinny, I knowww.'

Ted was a most charming chap and very easy to work with. He was also extremely funny offstage; his ready wit made him the first choice for just about every panel game made in the Fifties and Sixties, and he was a regular on *Does the Team Think?* for decades. Bob Monkhouse remembers doing a radio show with Ted and Diana Dors. The compère introduced Diana and said as an afterthought, 'So I hope you'll give her a nice warm friendly round.' Ted interrupted in a twinkling, 'After all, there's quite a lot of her that's warm and round and friendly.'

The Spice of Life hardly registered with the public, but it did nothing to dent Ted's tremendous popularity. I think he was reckoned to be the highest-paid comic in the country at one time, and he had his own monthly television show right through the second half of the Fifties. I was in a couple of his *It's Saturday Night* (With Ted Ray) shows; it was transmitted live from the Shepherd's Bush Theatre in the extreme heat of that 1959 summer. Ted and I did husband-and-wife sketches, and there was one in which we tried to give up smoking:

TED: Look at my hands, they're trembling. I won't be able to play the violin.
JUNE: ~~Might be an improvement.~~

And another in which I accused him of being unfaithful after he received a mysterious phone call:

TED: It was a wrong number. Someone wanting the maternity home. There's nothing in it.
JUNE: Nothing in it? What would you say if a man phoned me and asked for the maternity home?
TED: I would say it was a blooming miracle.

The show was notable for an early appearance of Ted's son, a shiny-faced Robin Ray, who popped up doing the intros to the pre-recorded film parodies.

The end of the Fifties saw the start of what was to become a unique comedy institution, the *Carry On* films – loved, hated, endlessly discussed by media historians, but mostly just fondly remembered and still enjoyed on TV. I did the second of them, *Carry On Nurse*, which started shooting in November 1958 on the kind of budget that wouldn't cover the cost of the caterers now. The first film in the sequence, *Carry On Sergeant*, had been a surprise success a few months earlier, but *Nurse* exceeded expectations and became the most popular British film of 1959, not that I can claim much credit for that. I played Leslie Phillips' girlfriend, Meg – she was described in the script as a 'Pitman's poppet' – and he was in hospital with a bunion, which ditched our plans for a saucy weekend. It wasn't quite as suggestive as the material later became, although Wilfrid Hyde-White did have a daffodil stuck in his bottom!

Nurse was directed, as were the other thirty *Carry On*s, by the late lamented Gerald Thomas. Gerry liked to work quickly, indeed he and the producer, Peter Rogers, assembled their regular company not only for their talents, but for their ability to get it right first time. They usually finished inside five or six weeks, which meant keeping up a very lively pace indeed. On the first day's shooting of one of the films, Barbara Windsor was on the set running through the lines of a scene she was about to film. Her character was supposed to be on the phone, and she held the receiver as she rattled through the words. When she finished Gerry called out, 'Splendid. Moving on.'

'Was that a take, then?' asked Barbara.

'Yes, excellent, onwards.'

'Oh ****!' she said. 'I was going to play it posh this time.'

On another occasion, Sid James had to walk down some stairs, but when he got halfway down he missed his footing, fell and knocked himself out. Gerry simply moved on to the next shot and edited out the fall later on. I don't think he once went over budget or beyond his allotted schedule.

There were two minor difficulties on *Nurse*. The first was that the chaps playing the patients had to spend the whole day in bed and, under the heat of the powerful arc lamps, they kept falling asleep. Kenneth Connor ruined at least one take by snoring. Kenneth Williams indignantly denied having nodded off until Gerry showed him a photograph of himself spark out and next to a handwritten notice saying, 'Spare a copper for an ex-actor, Guv.' The second problem was that when the film was released, Wilfrid Hyde-White objected to what he felt was the misrepresentation of his bottom. Although the cheeks in question were never actually glimpsed during the film, he took exception to Hattie Jacques' reaction shots, which were filmed on another occasion. He threatened legal action, and only backed down once he realized that the court case would be like a scene from a *Carry On* and would only boost the film's publicity.

Peter Rogers was a good producer, but not overly indulgent of his performers' egos or complaints. When one well-known member of the team felt he was being ill-served by the script, he demanded, 'I should have more funny lines. I'm a comedian.'

'Your secret is safe with me,' replied Rogers, and the actor was dropped from the next film.

Carry On Nurse wasn't my first film – I had appeared briefly as a dancer in *Quiet Weekend* in 1946, and even more fleetingly in *The Twenty Questions Murder Mystery* in 1949 – but it was my first featured role, and I rather hoped they might ask me back. And so they did – fourteen years later.

In the meantime it was back to one-off television and radio appearances, and the final series of *TIFH*. Frank and Denis had departed for television and *Round the Horne* had surfaced. I did wonder if there was room for both shows. There wasn't, and *TIFH* sailed off into the sunset. There's always a feeling of regret when an enjoyable and successful series comes to an end, but for Tim and me it was also the beginning of a new phase in our lives. Susan Jane Aitchison was about to be born.

Chapter Seven

A WORKING MUM

SUZY WAS DESTINED TO BECOME AN ACTRESS. SHE MADE HER first appearance as a small bulge in a sketch with Arthur Askey on *The Vera Lynn Show*, and she got her first laugh during the making of a special *Take It From Here* record. I was eight months pregnant at the time, and when I said my opening line, 'Ooh, Ron, d'you notice anything different about me?' the giggles from the audience meant that we had to do it again, after they had been politely requested to ignore Suzy's obvious presence.

In those days one wasn't so aware of the dangers of smoking and drinking during pregnancy, and I'm amazed that Suzy didn't emerge with a fag in one little hand and a gin in the other. She made a bolt for freedom a few weeks later, on one of the hottest afternoons of the summer. She was tiny, weighing under five pounds, but there was a splendid sister of Brunhilde-like aspect at the hospital, who said briskly, 'She's a full-term baby and will be treated as such.' Nowadays, I'm sure she'd be confined to an incubator but, thanks to Brunhilde, I was able to keep her with me. She has been an utter delight and a source of pride from that day to this. Definitely my greatest achievement – with a little help from her dad.

We engaged a marvellous nanny from New Zealand, Yolande

McDonald, who gave me basic baby-training and was as unflappable as she was invaluable. Unfortunately, she couldn't stay with us for more than a month and was replaced by a Swiss au pair who was temperamentally the complete opposite. Shortly after she arrived she came to us in a distressed state, saying that she had been arrested for non-payment of a train fare, and that it had all been a mistake due to her not understanding the system. We went along to court and spoke up in her defence. Much to our relief she was let off with a warning, but as we left court we noticed that she was laughing. Shortly afterwards, things started disappearing from around the house and we realized that we'd been had. She gave Suzy a christening spoon, but we felt rather uneasy about hanging on to it, wondering where it might have come from. As dodgy au pairs go, she went. She was replaced by Sybil, a frightfully well-connected German girl whose father was a consul, and on her second day he arrived in his chauffeur-driven Rolls to take her for tea at the Ritz. We liked her very much, but she developed mumps, which was rather alarming. I was working with Arthur Askey at the time and didn't want to infect the cast, so I asked Mother if I'd ever had mumps.

'I expect so, dear. You had most things,' she said.

Arthur was prepared to take the risk of working with me, and hospital visiting duties fell to Tim. Sybil was in an isolation ward and visitors had to scrub up on leaving the building. Tim dropped his signet ring into the paper-towel bin and had to ferret around among all manner of contagions in order to retrieve it. The next incumbent, Britta, arrived with a trunkful of ball gowns and questions about the relative merits of Annabel's, Quag's and Tramp. Never having been to any of them, I wasn't a lot of help to her, and I rather feared she wouldn't be much use to me, either, but she was and we were fond of her. She got by on about half an hour's sleep a night before being stricken with appendicitis. So it was back to the hospital for Tim, while Muff looked after Suzy and I capered around a television studio with Bob Monkhouse. And so the succession of au pairs continued, with Inge, Charlotte, Pia, Wreni, Anke, Almut, Kathryn and Ruth. Ruth was a lovely girl and Suzy's favourite. We're still in touch and have visited her and her husband in Switzerland. She now has two strapping boys of her own.

Thanks to the au pairs, and knowing Mother was around to keep an eye on things, I was able to carry on working. Most of the girls were delightful and stayed with us from six months to a year, but Suzy was as pleased as we were when we finally had the house to ourselves.

Tim and I began our married life living in Tim's flat in Holland Villas Road. A year later he spotted a dear little two-up two-down in Addison Avenue – he seems to have a sixth sense about property. We bought it from Paul and Vena Wilkinson, an Australian dentist and his wife, and we are the best of friends to this day. We loved the house; however, with Suzy growing and a succession of au pairs to accommodate, the time came to find somewhere larger, with a garden and a school near by.

We happened to be having dinner in Kensington one evening with two friends, Tony and Sheelagh Williams, who were part of our squash-playing group. Tony ran the Old Carthusian squash club; he and Tim had been at Charterhouse together and had been friends for years. Tony and Sheelagh lived in Wimbledon, and they suggested we start looking for a house there.

'It must take you for ever to get home,' we said. Wimbledon seemed like the end of the world to us.

'OK,' said Tony. 'Whoever gets home first phones.'

We arrived at Addison Avenue, and Tim and I thought we'd have to wait about half an hour for their call, but a couple of minutes later the phone rang. Tony had proved his point, but he must have had to drive like Stirling Moss to do it. That rather long and boring story is just to explain how we came to live in Wimbledon in 1963, and have done so ever since.

Lincoln Avenue was a four-bedroomed neo-Georgian house with a long strip of ground at the back, in which Tim was able to indulge his enthusiasm for gardening. I'm told it can be rewarding, but as far as I'm concerned, an hour's gardening is an hour's wasted shopping time. Soon after we moved in, Tim was rooting around among the weeds, as was his wont, when he dug up a pistol and 300 rounds of ammunition. We told the police, who came and removed them, looking at us with suspicion – all of which is of no great consequence, except that it serves to strengthen the case against gardening.

We found ourselves among delightful neighbours, some of them Americans who were renting their accommodation. We became friends with Patty and Roger Mehle who had two boys of about Suzy's age. Suzy was collected and returned from her nursery school every day by the headmistress, 'Auntie', in the school bus. She took to school like a duck to water and couldn't wait to hop on the bus every morning. We stayed in the house for six years before moving to where we are now.

My work in radio and TV took me away from home during rehearsals – sometimes only in the morning – and for one long recording day and evening in the week. Work was intermittent, so I was at home more than most working mums with a nine to five job. Suzy is the only one who would know if she felt deprived, but I hope she feels her childhood wasn't too bad. We always enjoyed a good relationship, and still get on like a house on fire.

These days it must be a very hard decision for mums who don't have a back-up to leave their babies in the hands of others, only seeing them at breakfast and bedtime. I've no doubt it can work, but I am thankful I didn't have to leave Suzy in a crèche surrounded by strangers.

In the autumn of 1960 I took part in a pilot episode of a radio show with Sid James called *It's a Deal*. The BBC bosses liked it and we ended up doing a further twenty-one episodes. Sid played an unscrupulous property developer, and he was partnered by Dennis Price as the company's equally crooked, but exquisitely cultured, front man. I delivered a repertoire of debs, drabs and dotty old dears – sometimes Sid's secretary and sometimes his girlfriend. In radio you only meet on recording day, and then it's eyes down to rehearse, so you don't always get to know your fellow artists intimately, but I remember Sid saying he preferred to be *seen* by the audience, that way his wonderfully expressive crinkly face could come into play.

During the run of *It's a Deal*, Sid heard that Tony Hancock didn't want him to be in his next series. He and Tony had always got on well, and the news came as a complete shock. It was a separation that Sid found very upsetting. He was, of course, still very much in demand as a film and television actor, so he didn't suffer as a result of being dropped; indeed, Galton and Simpson wrote him a series of his own, *Citizen James*, but he still found Hancock's action incomprehensible. Sid felt there was a lot more mileage in the relationship between the two on-screen characters, and that it was a golden opportunity thrown away.

Tony's next series was called simply *Hancock*, and although many people thought his decision to do without his regular Railway Cuttings sidekicks was ill-advised, even arrogant, the series contained some of the best and funniest of all the Hancock shows: 'The Blood Donor', 'The Bowmans' and 'The Radio Ham'. When we think of a favourite Hancock situation or snatch of dialogue, more often than not it comes from this final series, which he did for the BBC in 1961, so Tony might not have been so wrong to insist on a change of direction after all. Where he most certainly did make a mistake was in ditching Galton and Simpson the following year.

I played the nurse in the classic episode 'The Blood Donor'. The rehearsals were a bit tense because Tony was suffering from the after-effects of a car accident. Cecily had been driving him home after a recording of the previous episode when she braked suddenly to avoid some roadworks, throwing Tony head first into the windscreen. For a while it was doubtful whether he would be well enough to do the show, but he insisted on going ahead with it. The bruises on his face were cleverly obscured by make-up and, since he had very little time to learn his lines, an autocue machine was hired to enable him to read his performance.

These machines were still in their infancy in 1961. They were free-standing or attached to the side of the camera, rather than fixed in front of the lens as they are nowadays. The words were printed on a large roll of yellow paper which scrolled down on rollers at a speed controlled by an operator. It required no little skill and a certain amount of practice to get both reader and operator in synch. Tony was a brilliant sight reader, so the arrangement worked well enough, but it meant that his eyeline was oddly directed to the side of the camera rather than towards the actor to whom he was speaking. It made one feel somewhat isolated. Initially the plan was for Tony to read only the longer speeches off the autocue and learn the rest, but he genuinely thought the blow to his head had affected his memory, so on the night he decided to read nearly the whole thing. It looked a little odd, as I say, but it didn't detract too much from his performance, which is rightly regarded as one of the classics of British television. Having discovered autocue, he began to rely on it more and more, but his best performances were the ones he committed to memory.

The final episode in the series was 'The Succession', the one where he decides to find a suitable wife and vets three possible mates who might provide him with an heir. I played Veronica Stillwell, a progressive beatnik who frightened the life out of him by spouting about philosophy and metaphysics. I wore a wig that made me look like a monkey and heavy glasses, through which I was able to glance at the autocue when I had to expound intellectually.

We made a record of 'The Blood Donor' a few months later, and Tony gave an even better performance. After that, I didn't see him again until his one-night stand at the Festival Hall in 1966. I was asked to be there to throw in an offstage line. A new script had been specially written and rehearsed for the show, but he abandoned it not far into the performance and fell back on tried and trusted routines, including some fairly antique material dating back to his pre-East Cheam days, impersonating the long-since deceased George Arliss and the Hunchback of Notre Dame, which was also a bit old hat. It was all rather embarrassing, and although an edited-down version of the show was eventually broadcast on BBC 2, and was not at all badly received, Tony knew it wasn't right, and was so disappointed with himself that he went into hiding immediately afterwards.

I think he really hated stand-up comedy, yet he forced himself to do it, possibly to demonstrate his independence from Galton and Simpson. His acting was naturalistic and contemporary, while as a stand-up comic his style belonged to the Windmill Theatre era. It was as if he couldn't bring himself to try anything new, and yet that was what he wanted to do more than anything else. He had developed this bee in his bonnet about the Hancock character and the world of Railway Cuttings being too limited and parochial. 'Where did Laurel and Hardy live?' he once asked. 'Where did Chaplin live? Nowhere.' So in searching for something different, he turned his back on what he did best, and what had earned him the love and loyalty of so many millions. It was a tragedy that he never truly valued his unique gifts.

The setting for Tony's final series on British television, *Hancock's*, was inspired by the nightclub sketch from the original series for Associated Rediffusion. I was somewhat miscast as a bunny girl, Esmeralda Stavely-Smythe, and together with Joe Ritchie as the wine waiter, Toulouse, we were all-purpose foils to Tony. There were guests such as Dick Haymes and Vicki Carr, of whom Tony was a great fan; and after one show he persuaded her to sing 'Funny, But There's That Rainy Day'. I think the song reflected his outlook on life.

The show began with Tony walking the length of the catwalk stage to face the studio audience. At one recording he said nothing for what seemed like hours, and was certainly several minutes. We thought he'd forgotten his opening line. He simply stood there, going through every one of his many facial expressions. Not a word was said, and Joe and I tried to look as though this was normal procedure. The audience eventually started to laugh, but one had the feeling they were only doing it out of sympathy or embarrassment.

I couldn't help thinking of the earlier nightclub sketch, in the days when Tony seemed a lot happier. *Hancock's* came to an end after six episodes, and within a year Tony was gone, too. It happened during the making of a new series in Australia; he took an overdose of tranquillizers while under the influence of alcohol. It was a terribly sad loss, and heartbreaking to think of the even greater heights this unique comedian might have achieved had he lived.

*

The light-entertainment output of radio and television in the Sixties was a rather successful combination of old and new. Alongside the character comedies, the satire and the sharp parodies of Benny Hill, Stanley Baxter and Dick Emery, ran the very popular variety shows. Variety is out of fashion nowadays and programmes tend to confine themselves to one specific form of entertainment: drama, soaps, comedy, music, dance and endless quiz and participation shows. But I miss the good old variety shows, with their spectacular routines, tumblers, conjurors and full orchestras. It's been a real pleasure to see the return of the Palladium Variety Show on TV, with the brilliant entertainer Bruce Forsyth in charge. During the Fifties and Sixties I took part in a number of shows, like *Holiday Music Hall* with Cyril Fletcher, *Starlight Hour* with Kenneth Horne, *London Lights*, *Star Parade* and several dozen editions of a long-running radio series called *Variety Playhouse*, which was recorded at the Playhouse Theatre in Northumberland Avenue and presented by Vic Oliver.

Variety Playhouse was an hour long and stretched the meaning of the word 'variety' to its limits; there were comedy monologues, interspersed with grand opera arias, piano and violin solos, sketches and even the occasional hymn. Ronnie Barker, Leslie Crowther and myself were the regular comedy trio, and I was sometimes cast as Vic's secretary for the purposes of light banter at the top of the show:

JUNE: Vic, there's a letter here from an old lady in Cockfosters. She wants a lock of your hair.

VIC: Is she kidding?

JUNE: No. Stuffing a mattress.

The sketches with Ronnie and Leslie required us to employ our repertoire of voices, which all three of us had a lot of fun with. The other items in the show were performed by various leading lights of the theatre and classical-music worlds. Guests included Cicely Courtneidge and Jack Hulbert, Donald Wolfit and many principal singers from Covent Garden. Heather Harper and Peter Glossop filled the theatre with their glorious voices and the bass Forbes

Robinson made the rafters tremble. We were thrilled to watch these wonderful stars in action.

Ronnie, Leslie and I would meet up with the writers, George Evans and Derek Collyer, before the show to read through the sketches and make sure our accents didn't clash horribly. We usually gathered beforehand in the Sherlock Holmes pub, just a few doors up from the Playhouse. Ronnie arrived one Sunday looking distinctly fragile and quailed at the suggestion of a drink. He explained that the previous day he had been scheduled to do some filming for *The Bargee*, but the weather had been awful and shooting was eventually cancelled for the day. While waiting for a break in the weather, Ronnie and one or two other cast members decided to spend their time in the local pub, toasting the Queen Mother. Hanging in every Young's pub was, and possibly still is, a photograph of the Queen Mum pulling a pint, and Ronnie being a loyal supporter of the Crown (and Anchor), demonstrated his loyalty strenuously throughout the afternoon, and on into the evening. He was eventually poured into a taxi and sent home. When we heard the story, we insisted he have a hair of the dog and pressed a small port and brandy into his hand – just to settle the stomach. Wincing a little, he raised his glass to an imaginary Queen Mum and downed the medicine. A warm smile spread over his face as it took effect, and after another small dose Ronnie was back on peak form and gave his usual magnificent performance.

Ronnie, Leslie and I worked well together and became good friends, and in 1963 we were teamed up for a new show, *Crowther's Crowd*, also written by George Evans and Derek Collyer. Micky Most and His Minutemen provided the hot music, and we enjoyed a run of three series. Leslie, Ronnie and I started off as three students planning to change the world and holding our summit meetings in the El Aroma coffee bar. We recorded the shows at the Paris Studio, which meant the script conferences shifted from the Sherlock Holmes to the Captain's Cabin, where the atmosphere seemed to concentrate minds just as effectively.

Ronnie and Joy, Leslie and Jean and Tim and I had some good times together, and we also became firm friends with George and Jo

Evans. George co-wrote *The Navy Lark* with Lawrie Wyman, as well as material for Jon Pertwee and Beryl Reid, among others. George reminded me of the evening we all spent at the Stork Club, a popular dinner, dance and cabaret venue in Streatham, in about 1968. We happened to mention that we were about to lose our secretary as she was expecting a baby. George offered his wife Jo's services – she was already secretary to Jon Pertwee – and Jo agreed and has been with us once or twice a week for about thirty years. A very happy arrangement.

Leslie and Jean Crowther often rented a house near us at Middleton-on-Sea, so we saw a great deal of them in the summer. One year Ronnie and Joy came down to stay at the Beach Hotel at Littlehampton, and after a very good dinner indeed, the six of us repaired to the bar to play bar billiards – a most frustrating game, particularly if one's concentration is not as clearly focused after dinner as before. Grandad would have been ashamed of me. Not only did I forget the skills he'd so carefully taught me, but each miscue was accompanied by a ripe expletive, causing Ronnie and Joy to wince – not out of prudishness, but from a growing awareness that they would have to face the eyes of their fellow guests in the dining room at breakfast the following morning. Fortunately, they forgave me and we remain friends.

Tim and I enjoyed several happy visits to the Crowthers' when they moved to their beautiful house near Bath. Tim and Leslie shared a passion for antique porcelain, about which Jean is also very knowledgeable. Leslie was an extraordinarily kind man and an indefatigable charity worker. His terrible car accident in the late Eighties left him partially paralysed and unable to speak. He eventually made a remarkable recovery and, though still very frail, he never lost his sense of humour. The year before he died he insisted on being on my *This Is Your Life*.

There is a tradition at the Theatre Royal in Bath. If you see 'the butterfly' when you're working there, it means the show will be successful. Tim and I attended Leslie's funeral in October 1996, and we couldn't believe our eyes when we saw a butterfly in the church, gently hovering over Leslie's coffin. Others saw it, too, a butterfly in

October! It was a very strange and moving coincidence, and a very affecting moment.

Ronnie and I worked together a good deal in the early Sixties. He was on the brink of great things, and would soon be acknowledged as one of our finest and funniest character actors. He would be the first to admit that his success over the years was greatly aided by the brilliant scripts of Gerald Wiley, Jonathan Cobbald, Bob Ferris, Jack Goetz, Dave Huggett and Larry Keith, all of which were in fact pseudo- nyms for one and the same writer: Ronnie Barker. The man is quite unfairly gifted, and it was a shame he decided to retire while at the peak of his powers. His terrific programmes are never off our screens for very long, and he still continues to delight us, even though he hasn't made a show since 1987. Come to think of it, that's not a bad way to earn a living!

Ronnie and I both consider ourselves to be character actors, and we never relished the prospect of appearing in front of an audience as our- selves. If and when we did, we would always think of it as playing a part. It was only in later years that I found the confidence to be 'me', and I'm still not that good at it. I also find it a lot easier to write about others rather than myself. It's quite difficult to recall what you thought about this or that when you were young, and even more so when my nature is to look forward rather than back, but I'm having a go.

Frank Muir and Denis Norden made the transition from radio to television with consummate ease, and the three *Faces of Jim* series, in which Ronnie and I appeared alongside Jimmy Edwards, were among the best things they ever wrote, as well as being extremely popular with the viewers. There were nineteen programmes in all, each one a self-contained comedy play featuring Jim as a different kind of overbearing rogue. Ronnie and I were cast as a whole range of characters; I was often Jim's daughter and Ronnie my suitor. The tone of Frank and Denis's scripts wasn't unlike the film or play parody that used to feature in the early *Take It From Here* shows. Jim set the self-mocking tone when he introduced one of the first programmes thus:

Our story is taken from a publication entitled 'The Fifty Most Hackneyed Plots in Fiction'. That fact alone should ensure the story's television worthiness. It has the *lot*: the much-beloved village doctor, who is a widower; his devoted daughter; the handsome, mysterious stranger; the dramatic emergency operation, with no sickening medical detail spared . . .

Most of the shows sent up one kind of storytelling or another; there was a melodrama called 'The Face of Guilt', set in a lighthouse, and a pastiche of the film *A Matter of Life and Death*, set in the office of a minicab firm, with me on the short-wave radio, guiding Richard Briers safely back to base through the fog – and the wall of the building! Dick Emery guested in a sci-fi episode about a 'Thing from Outer-Somewhere', then there was 'A Matter Of Spread-Eagling', set in ancient Britain; this had Ronnie as the poet Lascivius, spouting cod-Shakespeare, and myself as Rowena, the leader of the Saxon rebels. The setting prompted some memorable exchanges.

LASCIVIUS: Let us not turn them to martyrs.
HADRIAN: What have tomatoes got to do with it?

Jim was Hadrian, encamped at Wallsend and waiting to return to Rome after the completion of the wall. 'I will be glad to say goodbye to that brown Windsor soup,' he says. 'Tis a consommé devoutly to be missed . . . but for the time being I shall loiter – within tent.' How Frank and Denis loved their puns, and no-one does them better.

My association with Jimmy and the *TIFH* team continued many years beyond the programme's demise. After the *Faces of Jim* series I worked on Frank and Denis's ITV series *How to Be an Alien* – alien as in 'foreigner'. The programme examined the Americanization and Europeanization of British culture. They drew on Denis's encyclopaedic knowledge of old films to come up with unusual clips, which Ronnie Barker and I then revoiced. *How to Be an Alien* was ahead of its time, which is usually a polite way of saying that the viewing public hated it. It would probably go down far better now, but I expect the tapes have long since been wiped.

The *TIFH* connection continued during the Sixties and Seventies. I appeared on *Call My Bluff* several times, and Frank and I were featured in *The Tale of Two Microbes*, a twenty-minute educational film for Unilever. The script of this neglected masterpiece was by Frank and Jeff Inman, who directed us. It was primarily made for domestic science and hygiene classes in schools. We were Basil and Desdemona Salmonella, and our journey took us at breathtaking speed from the shop to the kitchen to the canteen or restaurant, leaving millions of baby Salmonellas behind us to contaminate whatever they touched. It was hoped that, through humour, the dangers lurking in the handling and preparation of food would be pressed home. Frank and I looked fairly strange in our silver microbe suits and wigs, with Frank adding the special touch of his trademark bow-tie. I don't know if we succeeded in putting the message across, but we had a great time trying. The more I think about it, the more grateful I am that I received that phone call from Frank and Denis one afternoon in 1952.

The Muir and Norden production line also churned out a seemingly endless quantity of episodes of the very popular school comedy *Whack-O!*, starring Jimmy Edwards as the crooked headmaster. I made occasional appearances as Matron in both the television and radio versions. One of the delights of these shows was working with Arthur Howard, who played the permanently terrified Mr Pettigrew. Arthur was a lovely man, but rather daunted by the success of his high-achieving family: his brother was the film star Leslie Howard, his wife's aunt was Fay Compton and her uncle was Sir Compton Mackenzie the novelist. Arthur need not have worried; he was a very fine character actor and a superb foil to Jimmy in *Whack-O!* His son, Alan Howard, has carried on the illustrious acting traditions of the family.

Whack-O! was transmitted live from the Television Theatre at Shepherd's Bush, often under fairly hair-raising conditions. The cast was large and the sets numerous. We played out a scene on one side of the studio, while on the other side the next scene was prepared – behind a black cloth so the audience wasn't unduly distracted. As usual the changes were barely accomplished in time. Props frequently failed to do what they were supposed to and actors were often obliged to react to silent telephones and non-existent knocks at the door, while keeping an eye open for falling scenery and equipment. Jimmy was quite unperturbed by all this, covering up mishaps by roaring loudly and wrenching recalcitrant drawers and windows into submission. The fact that he won the DFC for flying a bullet-ridden Dakota back from Arnhem probably put these kinds of problems into perspective; it must all have seemed like an enjoyable lark to him.

Jimmy was a charismatic person; when he walked into a room all eyes turned towards him. He wasn't particularly funny in private, indeed he described himself as a grumpy man, but he had tremendous energy and a wide range of interests which he pursued with great enthusiasm. As well as playing polo and farming, he loved brass bands, and the thing that gave him the most pleasure was when he conducted the Royal Artillery band at the Albert Hall. He had plans to do a musical about Falstaff, but it never came to anything, which was a shame, as I think he would have been very good. He was chairman of the Variety Artists Federation and was persuaded to stand as a Conservative candidate for North Paddington in the 1964 general election; he enjoyed the campaign but hated losing. He couldn't bear not to be the centre of attention, and admitted to being unhappy when he first arrived in America because nobody knew him there. He went on the *Johnny Carson Show*, and the next day a cab driver eyed him in the mirror and said, 'Hey, weren't you on the *Carson Show* last night?' Jim then relaxed and felt at home.

Jimmy spent a lot of time with his great friends Biddy and Alan Fletcher, who lived in Sussex, and as Tim and I had acquired a cottage near by, he introduced us, and we too became firm friends, often lingering over Biddy's delicious Sunday lunches, which we still enjoy today. We reminisce about Jim sometimes and his ability to consume vast amounts of alcohol with no obvious effect and his habit of plain speaking.

One Sunday there was a visitor – a friend of a friend probably as Biddy's hospitality is unbounded and there was usually a waif or stray in evidence. Jimmy conversed politely with this chap and asked him what he did.

'I'm a student,' he said.

'How old are you, then?' said Jim.

'I'm thirty-two.'

'What? You mean you're thirty-two and you've never done a day's work in your life.' Jim refilled his glass and mumbled into it, 'And I'm paying for it.' He said what he thought, did Jim.

During twenty years I did over 200 broadcasts with Jim. He also had a profound effect on our home life by virtue of a small dog called Rabbit.

Now then, are you sitting comfortably? Then I'll begin the story of a dog called Rabbit. It's quite a shaggy one – both dog and story – so you may require a comfortable pillow and perhaps some alcoholic fortification. If you're not a dog lover I strongly urge you to skip the next few pages.

To begin at the beginning; not long after we moved to Wimbledon, we acquired a Labrador. He was called Sid and was dearly loved by all of us. He made a bid for TV stardom in a BBC series called *John Bull*, and I was employed as his handler. Unfortunately Sid took one look at the cameras and ran for it. By the time I found him cowering in the scene dock some time later, another dog had been cast and Sid's chance of the big time was gone for ever. Both dog and handler were sent home in disgrace. As a family we stood together in this darkest hour of our shame, and Sid's 'blot on the escutcheon' was never mentioned again. He lived on happily with us for another six years before going to his kennel in the sky aged nineteen.

Jimmy Edwards was very sympathetic to our bereavement. He had a little dog of his own, Rubu – the product of an illicit union between a pure-bred Tibetan terrier and an uncouth Jack Russell known as Deadly Dudley – so when Jim had to go away he asked us to babysit Rubu. The name Rubu apparently means 'moustache' in Swahili – at least that's what Jim said but we have our suspicions it means something else. Jim had been to Kenya where he was known as 'Massa Rubu', Man with Moustache (or not). He also went to Australia quite often, and Rubu came to stay with us while he was away.

Biddy Fletcher, the owner of Rubu's mother, felt that it wasn't fair on the dog to be shunted back and forth between us, and suggested to Jim that Rubu come to live with us permanently. Jim wasn't terribly keen, but his absences were about to become even more frequent as he'd met the love of his life in Oz and eventually bought a house in Perth, where he settled down with his new Aussie partner, so it was agreed that Rubu should make his home in Wimbledon.

Jim had come close to marrying some years earlier, when he became engaged to a member of his polo-playing set – a very upper-crust young lady indeed. They were out riding one day when her hunter threw her into a pond.

'Help!' cried Jim's bride-to-be, sinking fast. 'What shall I do?'

'Throw out the ring,' said Jim. The wedding didn't take place.

There was a wild rumour that he was about to marry Joan Turner, but that was just Jim and Joan pulling a journalist's leg after a few noggins. He did, in fact, marry an air hostess, a lovely girl whom we met on several occasions, but it didn't work out.

However, at long last Jim happily settled in Australia and Rubu took up residence in Wimbledon with Tim, Suzy, me, my mother and a rabbit – who expired not long after Rubu's arrival. I know you're thinking I've been at the gin, but it will all make perfect sense in the end if you pay careful attention to the details. Tim took it upon himself to exercise Rubu morning and night on Wimbledon Common. In the course of his regular walks he fell into conversation, as one does, with other dog-owning locals, among them businessmen, actors, sportsmen and even an MP. He also spent many hours calling out 'Rubu'. People thought he was calling 'Ruby', and he wondered if a female figure might one night emerge from the darkness saying, 'Yes, dear, what can I do for you?' A name change was needed and, for reasons best known to himself, Tim decided to rechristen the dog in memory of our late rabbit. So Rubu became Rabbit. Unfortunately, that led to further difficulties as, for a while, there was a man who exercised his whippet on the common, and when Tim called out 'Rabbit' the whippet went berserk and had to be restrained. Tim took to whistling after that.

Rabbit came with us just about everywhere. He was equally at home in pubs, shops and restaurants, and when I was in pantomime he became a dressing-room dog. During the run of *Babes in the Wood* at Plymouth, Geoff Hughes, who was playing one of the robbers, along with Roy Hudd, spotted Rabbit sitting in my dressing room and said that he was exactly the kind of dog the robbers would have – I don't think this was necessarily meant as a compliment! I said, 'Well why don't you take him on?' Geoff clipped on Rabbit's lead and took him onstage for his next entrance, the scene in which the babes are kidnapped. The scheme carried an element of risk, since the *Babes in the Wood* set included quite a few trees, but Rabbit didn't disgrace himself and enjoyed his extra walk.

He lived on until just before Christmas 1998. We loved him dearly, and at the end of his life we had dogsitters for him if we were out of the house for more than two hours, and our good friends George and Jo moved in if we went away. He now lies in peace alongside his mother in the garden of the Fletchers' house, where he was born. He was a great little dog, and we really miss him. And that is more or less the story of the dog called Rabbit. But not quite.

Six months after he passed away, Tim and I were at the All England Tennis Club during Wimbledon fortnight. While we were standing around in a somewhat formal group of dignitaries, we were introduced to a prominent MP, who turned out to be one of the dog-owners with whom Tim had occasionally passed the time of day while walking Rabbit. I should point out that this took place in the aftermath of a spate of parliamentary sleaze scandals. When Tim was reintroduced to the Honourable Member, he said, 'Oh yes, we often used to meet on Wimbledon Common.' There was a general adjustment of ties and a sudden fascination with the contents of teacups.

In 1987 Rabbit's photo appeared on the cover of *Dogs Tales*, a canine anthology for which I wrote a foreword. The researcher found some amusing doggy stories and I love this one.

Mrs Patrick Campbell, the English actress famous for her high-handed manner, took her pekinese dog everywhere with her. She even attempted to smuggle him through customs by hiding him under her cloak. She nearly got away with it, and remarked afterwards, 'Everything was going splendidly until my bosom barked.'

1962 saw the appearance of one of the glories of television comedy,

Steptoe and Son. After the break with Hancock, Galton and Simpson were asked by Tom Sloan, the BBC's Assistant Head of Light Entertainment, what they would like to do next. At that stage in their careers, if they had said they wanted to dance the paso-doble naked on the six o'clock news the BBC would probably have given it serious consideration. However, they picked the one idea that Tom Sloan wouldn't sanction under any circumstances: a series for Frankie Howerd. 'Forget it. He's finished,' said Sloan. Ray and Alan were rather taken aback, but, being thorough professionals, they came up with a number of alternative proposals. Sloan bought them all, and the result was the birth of *Comedy Playhouse*, a series of ten individual Galton and Simpson scripted shows. I was in 'The Telephone Call', which was an Ealing Comedy sort of story. Peter Jones played a character who was concerned about the threat of nuclear war and tried to telephone Kruschev in Moscow, without success, but the publicity made him a national celebrity. I was his deeply unimpressed wife.

All the *Comedy Playhouse* programmes were of a predictably high standard, but one was outstanding: it was called 'The Offer' and it was about two rag-and-bone men named Steptoe. 'The Offer' became *Steptoe and Son*, and over the course of the show's long life I appeared as the girlfriend of both father and son. In the third series I was a gold-digging tart who got the old man into her clutches after he had a win on the premium bonds, but who gets frightened off when Harold clamps him into a straitjacket, claiming he's mad. In the radio version of the series I turned up as another of Albert's new fiancées, but with the added complication that she'd been Harold's girlfriend over twenty years earlier. Inevitably the relationships came to nothing and father and son were left, once again, with only each other. Galton and Simpson's scripts were always a joy, and Harry H. Corbett and Wilfrid Brambell were great to work with, though it did come as a bit of a shock when Wilfrid took his teeth out for authentic effect.

After four series of *Steptoe*, Ray and Alan felt in need of a change, and the BBC at last gave them the go-ahead to write a series for Frankie Howerd. The result was twelve superb half-hour shows that confirmed Frank as one of the foremost comedians of his generation. The format was simple. It began with a long opening monologue in which Frankie, seated on a stool, related his recent misadventures and grumbled about 'Thing' upstairs, then there was a long sketch linked to another long sketch, followed by a closing monologue. I appeared in the first of the series as a character called Beryl Cuttlebunt – Frankie's girlfriends often rejoiced in this surname. She was a neurotic, intellectual woman who he'd met through a dating agency. 'Don't touch me!' she shrieks when he shakes her hand. 'I can't bear men touching me!' Then shortly afterwards . . .

BERYL: Kiss me . . . violently and passionately.
FRANK: Madam . . . please . . .. control yourself. It's worse than Peyton Place.
BERYL: Kiss me, kiss me . . . bite me.
FRANK: Bite you? I'm a vegetarian. Let go of me.

When we were rehearsing the sketch I ran my fingers through Frank's hair, which seemed to me to be an appropriate gesture, but it alarmed Frank and he suggested I caress his shoulders instead. I'm not the most observant person and I hadn't noticed he wore a rug! But he felt confident enough to work with me again, and we did so dozens of times on radio, as well as on television. He and Dennis Heymer, his manager and partner, became our close friends.

Frank was always keen to try new things and made several forays into the world of satire and pop, and in 1968, he made an hour-long special, *Frankie Howerd Meets the Bee Gees*, again scripted by Galton and Simpson. After the recording we were invited to the Bee Gees' extremely luxurious flat where, in the middle of the living area, there was a fountain surrounded by a pool. They also had a Pyrenean mountain dog, which wasn't ideal since they were four floors up; however, they were lovely lads, so I'm sure they took it for walks.

One day in 1971, there was a call from April, my agent, offering me a chance to make a record with Frank. 'Absolutely, yes,' I said, having no idea what was expected of me.

I arrived at the studio to be greeted by Frank, Ray Galton and Alan Simpson who said, 'Do you know the song "Je T'Aime"?'

'No,' I said.

'Ah. Well, we'll play it to you.'

I heard the music a couple of times and said, 'I suppose I'm the heavy breathing.'

'That's it,' they said. Frank and I made the record; he did the dialogue and I made the noises. It must have been a success as it was banned by the BBC and could only occasionally be heard on Radio Luxembourg, but it was mild by today's standards.

I first set eyes on Frank at one of Noël Coward's parties in the Fifties, when he was having rather a lean time of it. He'd had some rotten luck with unscrupulous management and some woefully ill-conceived projects. The BBC once assigned him two writers, a Canadian and an American, only one of whom had ever seen him work before, and the results were predictably unfortunate. He acquired a reputation at the BBC for being difficult – hence Tom Sloan's resistance to him – but this was primarily a result of his trying to improve scripts that were badly in need of work. It's true that he did have a tendency to fiddle around with lines and jokes until he was happy with them – to 'Howerd it up', as he used to say. Frank wasn't difficult, just conscientious and a bit of a worrier, but his constant tinkering with scripts made his producers and writers despair.

It was through radio that Frank first came to prominence, but it wasn't a medium in which he ever felt really comfortable. He hated to be tied to a script. He needed direct eye-contact with the audience for the best reaction to his hilariously rude asides about his fellow performers. He got into a terrible state before a radio recording, and you would see him pacing up and down with the script in his hand, desperately trying to learn his lines so that he wouldn't have to read from the page and could look at the studio audience directly. When I listened to some of those shows again recently, I was struck by how funny he was; he sounds so natural and spontaneous, and there's no sign of the awful tension he suffered at the time.

It surprises some people that all his little asides were not only rehearsed but actually written into the final draft of the script. Writers always had difficulty with this aspect of his work, because if they put in all the 'oohs' and 'ahhs' he told them to stick to the jokes and leave the embellishments to him, but when they left them out he wanted to know where they were.

He didn't enjoy performing at all; he often said he hated it, and if he'd won the pools he probably would have happily retired and never set foot onstage again, but his earlier financial problems left their scars and drove him to work rather more than he needed to.

Later in life, he was well managed by his agent Tessa Le Bars, and well looked after by Dennis, with whom he lived in Edwardes Square in Kensington and a house in Somerset. Tim and I stayed with them there on several occasions, taking Rabbit, whom Frank adored. One evening Rabbit was let out to lift his leg and didn't return. We were very concerned because a number of dogs had been worrying sheep in the area, and the local farmers had their guns at the ready. Frank was very upset at the thought that Rabbit might have met with a trigger-happy farmer. After several hours of us calling, whistling and searching, Rabbit reappeared looking a bit ruffled and licking his lips.

Frank loved dogs, and he also loved 'the dogs'. We spent many an enjoyable evening together at Wimbledon dog track, and White City, before the BBC moved in. He would urge his fiver-each-way favourite down the finishing straight, then subject it to a torrent of withering abuse when it let him down. Dennis studied form and more often than not picked the winner.

Frank approached the business of socializing in his own individual way. He would phone up and say, 'Frank here, what are you doing on Thursday?

'Oh, well,' I'd say, wondering what sort of outing he might have in mind, 'nothing much.'

'Good. We'll be round for dinner at eight.'

Frank had simple tastes and found my no-frills cooking palatable, but he had quite the strangest relationship with alcohol that I've ever come across. He would start the evening by downing a triple vodka almost before anyone else had time to get a glass in their hands, then he'd have one or two more in double-quick succession, and then he'd stop and not another drop would pass his lips for the rest of the evening. For the last five years of his one-man show it was in his contract that in the interval he should be given a double brandy and soda with lots of ice. He could be an amusing companion, but on the whole he was a very serious man and a great philosopher. Conversations with Frank tended to be one-sided affairs. He talked, you listened.

After his renaissance in the Sixties he bought a house in Malta and called it The Forum, after the musical, *A Funny Thing Happened on the Way to the Forum*, which had helped to restore his fortunes. It was ironic as he didn't enjoy the show; he wasn't a singer and his character was hardly ever offstage. It was very hard work, and after two years he left, but he was invited to return for the last night of the run some time later, and he received a standing ovation. He invited Tim and me to stay at The Forum one summer, but Tim was busy, so I went on my own for a week or so. The house had to be quiet in the morning, as Frank was a late riser, and I remember silently swimming up and down the pool, taking great care not to splash Frank's bedroom window which faced the pool. Another house rule, which was much easier to obey, was that the large flat roof was out of bounds because that was where he sunbathed in the nude.

One day Frank hired a boat to take us round to the Blue Lagoon, one of the beautiful bays on the island. When we stopped, the swimming platform was lowered and I dived over the side into the sea and swam about for a few minutes to cool off. When I looked up the boat had drifted off, almost out of my range, but by employing my fastest breaststroke, and puffing a bit, I managed to get to safety. My next problem was how to get back on board. Johnny Weissmuller could probably have hoisted himself onto the platform, but for me it involved a lengthy and deeply undignified scramble, as they'd forgotten to attach the steps going into sea. I was finally heaved on board, and Frank leaned over the rail and watched in amusement. 'You went in like Esther Williams and came out all crotch and armpits,' he remarked.

When the time came for me to leave I thanked Frank for his

hospitality and remarked that, for the first time in my life, I appeared to have acquired the beginnings of a suntan.

'Yes,' he said, 'you've lost that embalmed look.'

I still can't believe I'll never again hear his instantly recognizable voice on the phone saying, 'Frank here. How about an evening at the dogs?' or, 'Do you and Tim fancy a trip up the Nile?' But we can at least be reminded of him through audio and videotapes. His signature tune was, 'You Can't Have Everything'. If we can no longer enjoy his company, Tim and I can treasure our memories of the times we spent with our kind, warm-hearted and generous friend, and we'll never forget him.

'Is he as funny off as he is on?' I am often asked. The answer is usually no, with some exceptions. Arthur Askey, Ted Ray and Eric Morecambe were men from whom the jokes just seemed to flow. They had computer-like brains and were able to recall and invent gags on the spot; in a sense they were never 'off'. All comedians are vulnerable and individual, and working with them over the years, my job has been to get on their personal wavelength. And the answer to, 'Who is your favourite?' is always, 'The one I'm working with at the time.'

Benny Hill was a withdrawn man, utterly dedicated to his work, and absorbed by it to the exclusion of just about everything else. You never really felt you got to know him. He lived alone in almost monastic simplicity, and had unpretentious, ordinary tastes. I remember seeing him in the street once. 'Hi, Benny,' I said. He looked up in surprise and smiled at me, and as he did so he revealed an extraordinary set of false teeth. Apparently they were his shopping disguise, but they weren't very effective because he was instantly recognizable. He wore them quite often on his shows; perhaps he was breaking them in?

Benny Hill always conjures up images of speeded-up chases and scantily clad girls cavorting about while Benny leers at them through his Fred Scuttle specs. But his first great television successes were with a more sophisticated kind of humour: sharp impressions and topical sketches. In his 1957 series he parodied a popular panel game of the time by impersonating the show's chairman and all four panellists, including Moira Lister and Kenneth Horne. It required each character to be recorded separately and cut together later, a simple enough process now, but not in 1957. No television show had attempted anything as technically ambitious before, and it provoked a terrific critical and public response. It assured Benny's future in television.

His early shows were written by Dave Freeman, and I was in a number of them with Henry McGee, Bob Todd and Patricia Hayes. We did various sketches and parodies, including current popular songs, and I took part in a send-up of a Cadbury's Flake ad. The Flake provided material for many sketches over the next twenty-five years, but I think I was the first to don the wispy, floral frock and prance around a field in slow motion. We filmed it on a farm near Weybridge, in the freezing cold, needless to say. I bit into the Flake, then turned to the camera, smiling and displaying a set of chocolate-covered teeth. It was, of course, a toothpaste commercial.

The sketch-show format suited Benny's talents perfectly. He was a brilliant mimic and created some wonderfully original characters and routines, which he recycled many times. He also introduced more mime, which guaranteed his success in any part of the world.

Stanley Baxter was another superb mimic and, like Benny, he was clear about what he wanted from everyone involved in the show, on the technical side and in front of the cameras. Stanley also had the best pair of legs in the business, and he used them to great advantage in his many impersonations of glamorous female stars.

The prime targets in his shows were television programmes and old films. His parodies – written by Ken Hoare – were so close to the originals that they were expensive to produce. Eventually they became prohibitively so, and after 1986 no television company felt they could afford to make another *Stanley Baxter Show*, popular though they were. I was teamed up with him for his 1964 series, *Baxter on . . .* It consisted of six half-hour shows, each with a different theme, but all with a high parody content. One of the best programmes included a composite British war film. Stanley played all the stock characters coming together in one scene; all the familiar types, from the cheery private – 'Permission to make jocular remarks, sir' – to the shifty Richard Attenborough character – 'I need a drink. I'm a coward and a drunkard'. I played the brave nurse in love with two stiff-upper-lipped officers – 'I can't decide. One of you will have to get killed in action'.

In another show we did a version of the famous eating scene from the film *Tom Jones*, with Stanley and me eating fish and chips and drinking Seven-up. I also sang a point number each week, which I didn't enjoy because I didn't think I was very good. Lack of confidence again – no character to hide behind.

I was bashing out a parody of the song 'Cinderella Rockefella' on *The Huddlines* recently when I had a sudden flash of déjà vu. I realized I'd done the same thing with Benny Hill thirty years earlier, but with different lyrics, of course. They say there are few new ideas in comedy themes and that most are recycled from time to time. There is, for example, the 'explorer sketch'. I first came across it in a send-up of Armand and Michaela Denis, and subsequently it became Hans and Lotte Hass. My first 'Armand and Michaela' was with Tony Hancock in 1956, then I did other versions with Michael Bentine, Terry Scott and two with Stanley Baxter. Nowadays the sketch is done by the comic on his own, dressed up as David Attenborough, which is a rotten swizz as it does me out of a job. Also popular in the Sixties were send-ups of *The Avengers*. I did a couple of those with Stanley Baxter and another with Norman Vaughan. For that one I entered as a leather-clad Fussy Galore, waving a machine gun and spraying bullets all round the place. The gun had quite a kick to it, and though I'd received instructions from the official armourer, I was a bit nervous when I noticed he had a pronounced limp; I couldn't help wondering if he'd shot himself in the foot.

Harry Worth, Jimmy Logan and Dickie Henderson were easy-going, hard-working professionals on whose shows I put in occasional appearances. Dickie Henderson's show was rather like an American sitcom, in that it was based on Dickie's life as a popular entertainer. It was one of the longest-running shows on British television. Dickie was a lovely man, greatly respected by his colleagues and blessed with a dry sense of humour. Like Leslie Crowther he was an energetic supporter of various charities. They were once on a committee charged with the task of trying to get wealthy businessmen to attend a fund-raising dinner at £250 a head. Leslie was trying to come up with a catchy slogan for the event. 'What about "All you can eat for two hundred and fifty quid"?' suggested Dickie.

I also worked with Bernard Braden, who pioneered the mixture of topical humour and serious stories about real events which later became *That's Life*. In fact, Esther Rantzen was a researcher for *On the Braden Beat*. He had been a successful film actor in his younger days, and was once invited by Vivien Leigh and Laurence Olivier to stay at their grand Oxfordshire home, Notley Abbey. Bernard got lost, but his directions said he should head for Thame and, driving through another immaculate village, he saw a policeman, wound down his window and said, 'Thame?'

'Five and twenty to one, sir,' answered the bobby.

Esther Rantzen and I probably first ran into each other during the making of the Braden shows, but neither of us can remember doing so. We didn't work together properly until many years later, in 1993, when Esther invited me to join *That's Life*. My job was to share with viewers some of the more amusing items that appeared in the papers. A few days before the show, Esther and I would sit in her office, or kneel on the floor, surrounded by news cuttings and letters, choosing what we hoped were the best bits. Esther was a great confidence-booster; she was a fan and always encouraging. Presenting a show is not the easiest job in the world, and Esther does it to perfection; she is also good company.

Working with such a diversity of comics and actors has been end-lessly fascinating and rewarding. I have often been asked if there is some special skill to it. The answer is yes: don't upset the comic. It sounds like a flippant response, but it isn't. I've always had a pro-found admiration for people who accept the daunting challenge of carrying the show, and perhaps those feelings somehow filter through to the comic, so that he knows I'm there in support rather than competition. In a competitive profession, it's reassuring to look across the stage or the studio floor and know that the person opposite you isn't trying to undermine you or steal your thunder, but simply back you up.

Some comics were easier to support than others. It was quite tricky working with Tommy Cooper. Being in a sketch with him could be an unnerving experience as you had absolutely no idea what he was going to say or do. You just had to throw him a line and hope that whatever came back offered you some slender chance of keeping the thread. As far as the audience was concerned it couldn't have mattered less, because they were invariably helpless with laughter at whatever he did, either scripted or extempore. Learning lines and practising moves held little appeal for Tommy. He'd arrive at rehearsals in the morning and, without even saying hello, he'd launch into one of his tricks.

'What d'you think of this?' he'd say. 'Might work.' More often than not he'd fail to remember how it was supposed to go and abandon it. 'Oh well, back to the drawing board.' He was a big, shambling man, who seemed almost as harassed offstage as he did on, but he tended to play by his own rules. He was alleged to have kept an entire production unit waiting once because he found a café he liked. And once, after a Royal Command Performance, he asked Her Majesty the Queen, 'Excuse me, ma'am, are you keen on football?'

'Not very.'

'Well, can I have your cup-final tickets, then?' said Tommy.

Many of the shows I worked on were produced and directed by Kenneth Carter. I must have done dozens of programmes with Ken over the years. He was a most easy-going chap, who was able to handle anybody, from the brooding Tony Hancock to the insecure Frankie Howerd. He could, and did, tackle anything from live musicals to straight plays and soaps. For much of the Fifties, Sixties and Seventies he was one of the leading light-entertainment producers in the country. He gave me a call one day in 1968 and asked me to come over to his house at Hurlingham for a drink and a chat about a new project he was setting up. There was a plan to revive a themed sketch show that had already had a few black-and-white airings some years before. The new version was to appear in BBC 2's *Show of the Week* slot and, depending on how things went, a series would follow. It was called *Scott On . . .* and its star – the person I had been summoned to Hurlingham to meet – was, of course, Terry Scott.

I was very nervous about meeting Terry as he had already made quite a name for himself, but we got on very well and he told me later that *he* was nervous about meeting *me*. When I left Ken's house, Terry apparently said, 'She'll do,' and so began a partnership that was to last twenty years.

Chapter Eight

MY HUSBANDS AND I

Back to TV last night came faces too long neglected by the small screen, June Whitfield, Pearl Hackney and Peter Butterworth, once all stalwarts of broadcast comedy. Terry Scott booked them for his *Show of the Week*, *Scott On Marriage*, and with these old stagers built one of the funniest slick and professional programmes in BBC 2's splendid series.

WHEN WAS THAT WRITTEN? 1968.
Terry had regularly starred in television shows from the mid-Fifties onwards. First he was teamed up with Bill Maynard for a sketch show called *Great Scott – It's Maynard!*, then he worked with Norman Vaughan in *Scott Free*, a sitcom about two entertainments officers at a run-down seaside town. *Scott On . . .* was Terry's biggest success to date. The shows were again written by Dave Freeman, with Barry Took and Marty Feldman. There was a different subject for every episode; *Scott On History*, *Scott On the Sex War*, *Scott On Girls* etc., and there was always a sketch with Terry and me as a suburban husband and wife. Sometimes the setting might be quite outlandish: for example, a stone-age sketch where I was moaning about not having anything to wear to the annual human sacrifice, and

Terry lost his temper because I was slow at getting ready. Whatever the situation, we were essentially the same sparring couple. The opening titles of that first programme, *Scott On Marriage*, showed us on a wedding cake as bride and groom, all smiles, then gradually turning away from each other as the pages of the calendar fluttered past. Thus the domestic theme of our long association was established.

At the start of the second series of *Scott On . . .* , the *Daily Express* welcomed 'the return of screen veteran June Whitfield'. If I was a stalwart old stager in '68 and a veteran in '69, what does that make me now? A candidate for the next series of *Walking With Dinosaurs?* *Scott On . . .* ran until 1974, by which time Terry and I had appeared in twenty-seven shows together. Other regulars in the cast included Peter Butterworth and Frank Thornton, who has a magnificent baritone voice, which was put to good use in the musical parodies that ended every show.

Terry was by no means the only screen husband or boyfriend I had at that time. In fact, there were dozens of them: Dick Emery, Kenneth Connor, Peter Jones, Terence Alexander, Terry-Thomas, Herbert Lom, Alfred Marks, Harry H. Corbett . . . the list goes on. Barry Took once said I had supported more actors than the Department of Health and Social Security.

Harry H. Corbett was more a fiancé than a husband, and that relationship formed the premise of *The Best Things in Life*, which was on the box between 1969 and 1970. The show was a will-they won't-they sitcom about a permanently engaged couple who never get round to taking things a stage further – shades of Ron and Eth again. I found it unnerving because it was the first time in my career – and remember I'd already been classified as a veteran – that I had ever appeared as myself. That is to say, I had no wig, specs, accent, or even much character to hide behind. It was a new experience and a rather frightening one. Harry was a committed method actor who always took trouble to research his characters and think himself into his part. He also liked to analyse the performance afterwards. I remember an evening when he gave Tim a severe ear-bashing about Lee Strasberg and the Actors' Studio. When Noël Coward was asked about his preparation for a role he was quoted as saying, 'Learn the lines and don't bump into the furniture,' which is rather my approach, but Harry and I got on well despite our different ways of working, and we even did a bit of Swinging Sixties socializing. He once took Tim and me to a posh club in a basement where the music was so loud that verbal communication was impossible; we sat for three hours beaming at each other and occasionally lip-reading while our eardrums withered under the onslaught. For me, amplified music is a curse. Bring back the Savoy Orpheans, I say!

Harry and I did our best in the show, but I don't think the results were very successful. Every week would find Mabel trying to snare Alfred into marriage by some ruse or other – often by buying a new frock or trying to make him jealous – then Alfred fecklessly wriggling out of it. It became somewhat repetitive. How many ways are there of saying, 'If this doesn't get him, nothing will'? We did two series before the men upstairs wisely decided to call it a day.

I have heard recently of the death of another one-time screen partner, Peter Jones. He was a dear man, a witty and amusing actor, well liked by his peers and all who knew him, and a great loss to his profession and his friends. He was possibly best known for his role as the factory manager in *The Rag Trade*, and his numerous radio shows, including over thirty years in *Just a Minute*. Peter and I first worked together in the Fifties, when I joined him and Peter Ustinov – remember them playing those two irrepressible sharks Morrie and Dudley in *In All Directions* – in an episode of their radio series *We're in Business*. We met up again in an Arthur Askey film called *Friends and Neighbours*, then there was Galton and Simpson's 'The Telephone Call' and odd sketches in an Eric Merriman series called *Mild and Bitter*. In 1966 we were asked to play husband and wife in another *Comedy Playhouse* pilot about a factory manager living next door to a highly paid fitter from the shop floor. It was called 'Beggar My Neighbour'.

The show struck a chord with the viewers immediately, possibly because it tapped into the way things were seen to be changing in the Sixties, with beleaguered toffs and upwardly mobile workers. Peter and I were the Garveys, with no money and delusions of grandeur, while Pat Coombs and Reg Varney were the Butts, with lots of dough and no taste. We looked down on them, but were very jealous of their lifestyle. In the pilot show we couldn't afford a holiday and didn't want them to know, so we drew the curtains, stayed in for two weeks and tried to get a tan from a sunlamp rigged above the kitchen table.

There were some hostile critical responses; Nancy Banks-Smith – esteemed *Guardian* reviewer, but at that time working for the *Sun* – said it was 'tosh'. The pilot was picked up and a series followed quickly afterwards. A long and healthy future for the show seemed assured. Unfortunately, Peter Jones left after the first series. His agent wanted more money from the BBC, but they said they couldn't pay him any more because of the 'credit squeeze' – you could fill a book with the reasons given by the BBC for keeping fees down. Peter left the show to go into a play and was replaced in the second run by Desmond Walter-Ellis. I had worked with Desmond in revue and he was an accomplished light-comedy actor, very effective at what were known as silly-arse parts. Good though Desmond was, the character was built around Peter's personality and I think the show missed him. Nevertheless, it remained popular and ran for another two series.

Playing my sister in the show, and forming one half of the common mob next door – who always seemed to get the lion's share of the laughs, incidentally – was Pat Coombs. Patti and I go back a long way. I think we first worked together on a forces radio show called *Bring on the Girls* some time in the Fifties. We were introduced as Girl Number One, Girl Number Two etc., and I had to interrupt proceedings with the line, 'Here is an important announcement for our fighting men in Piccadilly: stop fighting!' Last year, Pat and I appeared together in a radio series written by Mike Coleman and appropriately titled *Like They've Never Been Gone*, and I'm afraid that's probably how it seems to some listeners.

Reg Varney is a very inventive actor and comic; in the early days, Benny Hill was his feed. Give Reg a prop to play with and he'll perform for five minutes. I remember a scene in which he chased a solitary pickled onion round a jar, and another where he managed to get a disgraceful number of laughs by trying to butter pieces of melba toast, which of course kept breaking. He's also an excellent pianist and has entertained us with songs old and new on many occasions. I'm indebted to Reg for teaching me how to pull a table-cloth off a laden table without disturbing the crockery – a most spectacular and highly satisfying trick, requiring quick, decisive movement and steady nerve. When I appeared on his *This Is Your Life* I tried to persuade them to let us repeat the stunt on air, but the spoilsports wouldn't agree.

In *Beggar My Neighbour* Reg's character shared his personal interest in gadgets of all kinds, and there was an episode in which he designed a double teaspoon for use with a double egg cup. After the show went out, he received quite a few letters from gadget collectors, asking where the double spoons could be purchased. They couldn't; Reg had had it specially made, and in order for the device to register on camera it had to be dessert-spoon size, so you'd need a couple of ostrich eggs to make it worthwhile. Reg gave it to me as a memento of *Beggar My Neighbour*.

Marital relations between me and my screen husbands have never been entirely smooth. There have been countless scripted mis-understandings, rows and fallings out, though no divorces as far as I can remember, but I can't think of anyone with whom things were more acrimonious on the page than they were with Dick Emery. For some reason, whenever I was teamed up with Dick, usually as his wife, we were always at each other's throats. We once spent an entire show trying to poison each other, only to be thwarted by last-minute coincidences. In another he was a burglar and I was his nagging wife, who insisted that he take me out on a job, with fatal results. It reminds me of the old Sandy Powell gag: 'We've been together for forty years and never a thought of divorce. Murder, yes.'

In the host of programmes that Dick made for the BBC, I shared wifely duties with Joan Sims, Pat Coombs, Josephine Tewson and various other well-known comedy actresses, which wasn't in-appropriate as Dick had rather a lot of wives in real life. In spite of his liking for the opposite sex, he was a withdrawn fellow, shy even, and he hated being recognized. When we were filming he used to hide from curious onlookers, or 'Brentfords' as he called them. He was very reluctant to play himself – I know the feeling – which was, he said, why he developed those wonderful characters. He could be moody, but I don't remember it affecting his work, and he certainly had a great sense of humour. He was always trying to make me laugh during a recording. He would look as if he was about to have the giggles, and the moment he saw my face was slipping he would look very severe and shocked, which was even funnier. I was once told that a good way to stop yourself laughing is to tighten your buttocks. Working with Dick caused a great deal of buttock-tightening.

Dick was a fitness fanatic. He did so much running and vigorous training that I can't believe it was good for him. I'm the complete opposite. I watch exercise tapes and think, I really should do that, but I don't. If we were filming, Dick took his exercise bench and weights with him. Once I admired this equipment, saying, 'That's what I should do. I wouldn't mind losing a few pounds.' A few days after the filming finished, a padded exercise bench and a set of fearsome-looking dumb-bells arrived at our house. Dick had taken me at my word. I tried it out according to the instructions – you were supposed to lift the weights with your feet as well as your arms – but after some initial enthusiasm I was exhausted, and concluded that pumping iron wasn't really for me. The equipment was consigned to the attic, and we eventually passed it on to a friend's son, who was planning to set up as a personal trainer. He now runs his own gym, so Dick's kindness and generosity had a positive outcome, which makes me feel less guilty.

Dick's contribution to television comedy was prolific. He created many memorable characters that somehow managed to be both outrageous and true at the same time. The best remembered is the predatory blonde, Mandy – 'Ooh, you are awful, but I like you' – or the trembling brunette – 'Are you married?' Of today's generation, perhaps Harry Enfield comes closest to him. Dick made eighteen series and well over 150 programmes in all, many of them brilliant. I'm sure if the shows were to be repeated they would find a whole new audience, as well pleasing older fans.

*

Kenneth Connor was another sometime spouse over the years. Ken was extremely funny offstage and a very gentle, kind man. He was a regular in the *Carry On* films, and in *Carry On Abroad* I was his frigid wife, insisting on separate hotel rooms for our cheap package holiday, a situation that prompted this piece of dialogue with Sid James in the dining room:

SID: Drink?

ME: Not for me, thank you. I tried it once and didn't like it.

SID: Oh. Like a smoke then?

ME: No thank you. I tried it once and didn't like it.

SID: That's very strange.

ME: Not at all. My daughter's just the same.

SID: Your *only* child, I presume.

Carry On Abroad was my favourite *Carry On* role. My character opted to stay in the hotel while the rest of the team went to the local village 'Els Bells! I was wooed by the barman, Ray Brooks, my frigidity was melted and when Ken returned from the outing I was lying on the bed with outstretched arms. He was supposed to leap on the bed, sending it, and us, crashing through the floor. We were assured by the crew that there would be no problem, but Ken and I were, to say the least, apprehensive. He had to be very precise with his leap onto the bed, making sure he didn't leave his foot hanging over the edge. Of course he did it exactly right and we landed on the floor below as planned, with a bump but no bones broken. We offered up a silent prayer when Gerry called, 'Print it'; we couldn't have faced a second take.

When I was asked to take part in the film, I had visions of a trip to some sunny clime and made a note to stock up on sunblock cream. I needn't have bothered; the 'beach' was in a corner of the Pinewood carpark, with half a ton of builder's sand and a few stripy deckchairs to add authenticity. And it was cold and windy.

Abroad was written by Talbot Rothwell who scripted no fewer than twenty of the *Carry On*s, after which sheer exhaustion compelled him to retire. In *Carry On Girls*, one of the last that 'Tolly' wrote,

Ken played a dithering mayor of a seaside town and I was an over-bearing feminist councillor who, in one scene, bursts in on him while he's taking a mayoral bath – full of bubbles, of course.

'You're a weak-kneed ass,' I boomed at the end of the scene, then, as a parting shot, 'and from what I can see, as poorly equipped to deal with your domestic responsibilities as your civic ones.' When we rehearsed it there was some discussion about how to make the line less blunt. The script conference was punctuated by Ken desperately shouting for more bubbles – a *Carry On* moment if ever there was one.

Sandwiched between these two films with Ken I did *Bless This House*, a feature-length spin-off from the successful sitcom starring Sid James, but it was a *Carry On* in all but name, since it was produced by Peter Rogers and directed by Gerald Thomas with a *Carry On* cast. Terry Scott and I were engaged to play – guess what? – a suburban couple next door. We were now less than two years away from having our own show.

Also appearing in the film as Sid James's son was a young actor who was about to star in a string of comedies in his own right, Robin Askwith. When the *Confessions of . . .* series of films appeared in 1974 they threatened the *Carry On*s' share of the market, and with their X-rated humour they forced the *Carry On*s to become more sexually explicit. Not such a good idea. For years the *Carry On* scripts had been based on nudge-nudge suggestiveness; they got laughs more from what they *didn't* show than what they *did*. But the producer and writers decided to try and keep in step with the relaxing of taboos about sex. They immediately ran into a problem, which was that as soon as you actually *see* what is being suggested it ceases to be funny, and it's often not a pretty sight. It may have been more in keeping with the climate of the times, but it wasn't very effective as comedy, and after *Carry On Emmanuelle* the films disappeared from cinema screens.

Fourteen years later there was a brave attempt to revive the old formula with *Carry On Columbus*. I played the Queen of Spain, with Leslie Phillips joining my string of husbands as the king. Leslie and I had played illicit lovers in *Carry On Nurse* in 1959, and so it rounded things off rather nicely that we were married in the very last one.

With most of my film husbands my role was often a disapproving one. The Sixties and Seventies were the heyday of the sex comedy, so I spent much of my time being outraged by their suspected in-fidelities – in *Not Now, Comrade* I pushed poor Leslie Phillips into a very cold garden pond. Only once can I remember being allowed to be on the errant side, and that was in *Carry On Abroad*.

The film *The Magnificent Seven Deadly Sins* was an odd concoction, made up of seven separate stories, each written by different writers and directed by the actor Graham Stark. I was in the episode entitled 'Envy', and most of my scenes were with Harry Secombe. Graham relished his new-found role as director, and on the first day of shoot-ing he gave Harry detailed instructions as to how to say a line. In a break I asked Harry if he minded being told his job.

'Oh no, not at all,' said Harry. 'If he does it again I'll tread on his foot.'

We resumed work and, once again, Graham started issuing notes. Harry gave a convincing impression of trying to do what the director wanted and, in the process, contrived to tread on his foot. Harry was quite a substantial figure in those days, and poor Graham yelped. Harry was profusely apologetic and duly concerned for the condition of Graham's toes. I suddenly developed a nasty cough to stop me laughing. The desired result was achieved and, as predicted, Harry was allowed to do his job unhindered.

Graham reminded me recently of the scene where I was supposed to be in a bath full of bubbles, to hide my swimsuit. The bubbles wouldn't bubble and Graham was furious. He kept plunging his hand into the water and swishing in the vain hope of creating bubbles; he got some very funny looks from the crew.

By the end of the Sixties I'd managed to work my way through quite a few stage and screen husbands, but in 1970 the rate increased dramatically when Birds Eye asked me to do a series of commercials, in each of which I was to be the wife, girlfriend or mother of a different historical or fictional character: Mrs George Washington with Frank Thornton, Anne Hathaway with Terry-Thomas as Shakespeare, Mrs Charlie Chan with Herbert Lom, and Mrs Long John Silver with Harry H. Corbett. In the first one I was teamed up with Julian Orchard – we were a vicar and his wife – and we very soon learned that the secret of advertising food convincingly is not to swallow any of it, otherwise, by the end of the day, you will find the product coming out of your ears. I loved doing these commercials. They were lavishly produced and looked terrific. This was partly due to the involvement of two future Hollywood luminaries, renowned for their visual sense, Alan Parker and Ridley Scott. There were twenty Birds Eye commercials, each extolling the products' home-made qualities and promising to 'make a dishonest woman of you'. The character that seems to have stuck in people's minds is Pinocchio's mother, where my nose suddenly grew when I claimed the pie was home-made. In reality my nose receded, since it was tech-nically easier to start with a long nose, then hack bits off, and reverse the film. I remember having my head held firmly in one place by a sort of clamp for about an hour and a half while they painstakingly photographed each stage of the process. The trouble they took certainly paid off and it was a brilliant effect. The agency that made the commercials, CDP, have said that the Birds Eye campaign helped to put them on the map.

Making the commercials introduced me to a far wider public. This was brought home to me when I was driving through the main gate to BBC Television Centre on my way to record a show – you could park in the middle in those days. I passed a queue of kids waiting to be let into to *Top of the Pops*. One of them pointed at me and shouted, 'Oh look! There goes an advert.' Fame indeed.

There used to be some snobbery in the profession about doing commercials. In the early days, some actors took the view that it would demean their art to appear in an advertisement, but when they realized how lucrative commercials could be, most of them were queuing up to jump on the bandwagon in order to subsidize their not-so-well-paid theatre work. Some adverts are very well made and demean the art of acting not half as much as the programmes they interrupt. However, there are some strangely conceived examples. I was once offered a lucrative job advertising incontinence pants. I didn't fancy it, even though they pointed out that the American campaign was fronted by June Allyson, who had made a fortune from it. I thought it might be tempting fate, so I declined the offer.

I'm glad I no longer have to attend commercial castings because I gather they are cattle markets, and some of the people handing out the jobs don't even bother to say, 'Sorry, you're not quite right, but thank you for coming.' Lack of time is no excuse for bad manners, and there are a number of self-important employers who can destroy a young hopeful's confidence by their offhand attitudes.

Making commercials certainly hasn't harmed my career. When I was on *The Des O'Connor Show*, he asked me whether doing commercials had affected me in any way. 'And how!' I answered. 'We bought a cottage!'

By 1974 *Scott On . . .* had been running for six years and the producer Peter Whitmore suggested that Terry and I should do a sitcom together. Terry came up with an idea about a husband and wife whose children have flown the nest, leaving them suddenly alone with each other for the first time in twenty years and wondering what to do with the rest of their lives. It was a very simple idea that had occurred to Terry, so he claimed, in the way all his best ideas came: while he was sitting on the loo. We had several meetings at the BBC about the setting and the characters and how the situation might develop – at one point the idea was for my character to take a degree and become the breadwinner, but that never materialized. John Chapman and Eric Merriman teamed up to write the pilot script, and the title *Happy Ever After* was chosen.

The writers embellished the situation by introducing Aunt Lucy; a gem of a performance by Beryl Cooke. We thought she was coming for a short visit but she arrived with a good deal of luggage and a mynah bird in a cage. Of course we hadn't the heart to turn her out. For all the reputation the show later acquired for being middle of the road, it was this situation that led us into trouble with Mary Whitehouse and the Viewers and Listeners Association. The scenes with Aunt Lucy tended to take place in the early evening, after Terry had come home from work, and so, in a ritual repeated in households all over the country, he would naturally pour us all a drink. We never had time to drink it, or much inclination to do so, as it was usually cold tea or something equally nasty, however it offended the sensibilities of Mrs Whitehouse's organization, who complained that there was 'far too much drinking in the show'. The BBC took no notice and we carried on as normal, with Aunt Lucy having 'just a small one'.

By the time we came to do *Happy Ever After* I had forced myself not to worry too much about appearing without a heavy disguise. I had found a way of playing 'me' that wasn't really me, but rather a version of myself that fitted the show. For the most part my role was that of an unwilling accomplice in Terry's ill-thought-out schemes and enterprises. I was more like his mother than his wife; at first discouraging him, then witnessing his inevitable failure, and finally, depending on whether or not he deserved it, getting him out of trouble or letting him stew. As I say, it was only a version of me. The real June isn't so tolerant. And if I nagged Tim the way June nagged Terry I'd be in real trouble.

The routine for the show hardly varied throughout the many years of its life: on Monday we would do the read-through and set the moves; on Tuesday we'd have the day off to learn our lines; we'd have Wednesday, Thursday and Friday to rehearse; Saturday was a day off, and then we'd record on Sunday. Terry liked to spend as much time as possible rehearsing without the script. You can't look the other person in the eye if you're reading. By having Tuesday off to learn our lines, we could rehearse without books from Wednesday onwards. I won't say that's the best way to do it, but it was the way Terry wanted it, and it happened to suit me, too.

Noël Coward always wanted people to arrive at rehearsals knowing their lines, and I've always tried to follow that rule. Reading aloud was my favourite subject at school – the only one I was any good at – and my read-through is about the same as my performance. That's not necessarily something to be proud of, but that's it. Some actors like to grow into a part more slowly, working with the script for as long as possible and only arriving at a complete characterization on the day of performance. Indeed, this is the preferred method of some very fine performers, but it used to drive Terry mad.

'Why can't they learn their lines?' he'd grumble to me in private. 'I've learned mine.'

I tried to explain to him that people like to work in different ways, but he saw it as incompetence, and he could be rather intolerant if people didn't match his very high standards – in other words 'do it his way'.

I've no doubt it's a good thing to develop a character gradually, piecing together the different elements and mining the text for subtleties, but the truth is that in a half-hour sitcom the hidden depths are often simply not there. Also there isn't a great deal of time, so it's best to get on with it.

Happy Ever After and *Terry and June* were recorded in front of a studio audience, and Terry was very good at warming them up. He had plenty of material, acquired from his years in variety, including his little-boy act which could be hilarious; his confused account of the ballet *Swan Lake* was one of the funniest things I've ever seen. Terry would do about five minutes, then introduce me, as often as not, saying, 'Come on, June, tell us a joke,' knowing full well I hadn't got one. I've never been any good at that sort of thing. Unless I have a script I'm lost, so, in desperation I'd do my Margaret Rutherford impression. It seemed to answer well enough, and later on I added Margaret Thatcher, and Ruth Madoc and Su Pollard from *Hi-De-Hi!* thus managing to cobble together a warm-up routine that served me through the *Terry and June* years. I can still get away with Margaret Thatcher, but I think the time has arrived when I will have to preface my Margaret Rutherford in the way Tony Hancock introduced his George Arliss impression: 'Now then, here's one for the teenagers!'

Terry and I shared a complete inability to remember names and faces. People we'd worked with quite recently were puzzled when a friendly greeting was met with a slightly mystified smile. The BBC canteen became a terrifying place to both of us as it's always full of people one has worked with but can't quite put a name to. I used to be honest about it and say, 'I'm awfully sorry, but I've forgotten your name.' Tim has trained me out of this, telling me, 'Just wait. The name will crop up.' It's probably the reason actors say 'Dear' and 'Darling' so often, although that can be awkward if a third party comes along needing to be introduced – 'Dear, this is Darling,' won't quite do.

Terry was just as bad as me, if not worse. Even in scripted dialogue, which, as I've said, he was punctilious about learning, names had a way of flying out of his head at the crucial moment. There was one show in which he had to look at a Christmas card on the mantelpiece and say, 'Here's one from Gladys.' He couldn't think of the name and said, 'Here's one from Grace.' It wouldn't have mattered except that Gladys was mentioned repeatedly in the script. We somehow managed to substitute Grace for Gladys wherever necessary until the end of the recording, deliberately avoiding each other's eyes when the name occurred in case the giggles took over. Afterwards Terry was understandably pleased with himself and wondered if his memory for names might be improving. Not long after, we were lunching in the BBC canteen when Terry spotted an actress he knew. Normally he would have searched his memory in vain for the name, but for some reason it suddenly came to him. Delighted, he pointed at her across the canteen and shouted, 'Totti Truman Taylor!' She looked up, eyes also lighting up in recognition, and shouted, 'Bill Maynard!' That tickled Terry's sense of humour and tears of laughter ran down his cheeks.

The atmosphere on *Happy Ever After* was always fairly relaxed and the crews seemed to enjoy working on it. We also felt supported by the men in charge, although the days when departmental heads regularly turned up for recordings were already numbered. There was a time when Tom Sloan, Eric Maschwitz, James Gilbert, Frank Muir or whoever was the head of light entertainment would put in an appearance after the show, buy a round of drinks and generally make you feel valued. Then for some years the commercial element reigned supreme and you seldom saw, or even knew, the top brass. I'm glad to say that department heads like Jon Plowman,

Paul Jackson and others have now revived the hands-on approach. They do attend recordings, encourage their artists and make them feel they matter. Of course, as individuals we probably don't matter much – there will always be somebody else to play your part if you don't – but everyone responds to a little encouragement, particularly actors, since they are the ones who are directly in the public eye.

Happy Ever After and its successor *Terry and June* divided the viewing public into two camps, one of them fairly hostile. The highbrows hated it, but fortunately for us they were in the minority and there were 15 million others who were happy to tune in for an amiable and undemanding half-hour. The more popular it became and the longer it ran, the more it irritated the intellectuals. By the 1980s the vilification had reached a point where people seemed to be building careers in the media solely by knocking the show. We decided to regard it as a compliment, and we graciously accepted it as such, along with the more well-intentioned ones.

In 1977 Terry and I were honoured by the Variety Club of Great Britain with the joint BBC Television Personality Award. But without doubt the most gratifying reward for our work over the years came from the public. People were so friendly and appreciative of our efforts that it was very humbling. The nice thing about being in comedy is that people smile when they recognize you, and that's marvellous. It's a good feeling to know that you've cheered someone up. Being recognized or stopped in the street can be looked on as a hazard or a bonus, but if you're not prepared to recognize your public you can hardly expect them to recognize you.

It's best to grin and bear it, even when some well-meaning soul asks, 'Weren't you June Whitfield?'

Terry and I were now established as a team, and we were often asked to do things together: chat shows, commercials and public appearances. We judged the Bride of the Year show for Kodak, did a radio series, again called *Great Scott*, and, in 1975, we were asked to do a play, *A Bedful of Foreigners* written by Dave Freeman.

Bedful was a Feydeau-like farce about shenanigans in a French hotel room, and it was to occupy much of our time in the latter half of the Seventies. We performed it over four years and on three continents. We took it to South Africa in 1975, which was a wonderful trip as I was able to have Suzy with me for some of the time. Terry took his wife and four daughters and Lynda Baron, who was in the cast, took her children, too. So it was quite a caravan that moved around the country.

Playing my husband was Dennis Ramsden, known as Slim, a superb farce actor and an experienced director. Slim had played my husband just a few weeks before we set off for the Cape, when we filmed John Cleese's comedy, *Romance With a Double Bass*. We were chatting during a break when we discovered we were about to start touring together. Slim tells me I was rather hesitant and said, 'Don't they have cockroaches out there?'

'Don't be ridiculous,' said Slim. 'All the hotels have at least five stars.'

'But do the cockroaches know that?'

A few weeks later we were in a hotel room in Durban playing Scrabble when we noticed that a bowl of water under the radiator was slowly disappearing into the wall. We sent for the maintenance man, who arrived and said, 'Ah yes, that'll be the rat.' He stuffed material into the hole in the wall and left. I was glad I wasn't sleeping there. But that was a minor blemish in an otherwise marvellous couple of months.

We were the first show to be performed in the Nico Milan Opera House in Cape Town after it became multiracial. We also played in Soweto to an unusually boisterous audience, one of whom delivered a loud running commentary on the action. When Terry hatched a plan to conceal me outside the window, the commentator called out, 'Ohhh, Terry, for heaven's sake be careful!' Then, when my irate husband arrived, 'Oh no, that's torn it!' It was quite off-putting and difficult not to laugh, but we managed to plough on – another buttock-clenching moment!

Terry was never thrown by that kind of thing; he relished the opportunity to slip out of character and address the audience. It's a trick that seldom fails because of its apparent spontaneity. There are a wide range of ploys for getting laughs by this means: turning to talk to late-comers, for example, and waiting patiently while they take their seats, much to their embarrassment and the amusement of the rest of the house. However, if you happen to be sharing a stage with someone who goes off at an inspired tangent, you are held in a state of suspended animation, with nothing to do except wait like a lemon until the ad-lib comes to an end, so I was never very keen on Terry doing this. He once grumbled in an interview that I wouldn't let him do what he wanted, but my recollection is that he went ahead and did it anyway. It's a great skill, but one I prefer to admire from the safety of a seat in the stalls rather than from a frozen position onstage. We never really fell out over it, but it did make for a certain, shall we say, 'creative tension'.

Once Terry got the bit between his teeth there was no stopping him. It's quite usual for a leading man to make a short curtain speech at the end of a show, but his went on for about a quarter of an hour. While the audience rocked with laughter, we stood behind him, beaming but inwardly resenting the loss of drinking time.

When we were playing Durban, I had a large sitting room next to my bedroom in the hotel, and the cast would often gather there for 'drinks with . . .' and Scrabble. One night, while I was vehemently defending the legitimacy of the word 'Zpdv', we gradually became aware, by the guttural noises emanating from an armchair, that Terry had fallen asleep. The volume increased to such a pitch that Lynda Baron felt it should be recorded for posterity. We set her tape-recorder running, and she and I added an appropriate 'Armand and Michaela' commentary between suppressed giggles: 'Vee had been in ze jungle six weeks ven finally ve found vot ve vere looking for, Terridactus Brontosnorus . . .' The next day we told him we'd been on a safari trip, and that we wanted him to hear a tape-recording of an extraordinary animal we'd come across. Terry didn't recognize himself, but when we told him he had the good grace to laugh.

We took *Bedful* to Hong Kong for a three-week run of dinner theatre at the Hilton hotel. It was another fun trip, with some wonderful sightseeing. We had a jaunt on a junk, took the ferry over to Kowloon and had a picnic in the spectacular Ocean Park which had just opened and where we had a breathtaking cable-car ride. As our cable car set off from one of the boarding points several hundred feet up, I took it into my head to join the car in front just as it left the platform. I don't know why; it was the most idiotic thing and if I'd missed my footing I would have plummeted into the South China Sea. You do some silly things sometimes, but this one took the biscuit, and I can still see the astonished expressions of my fellow travellers as I joined their car.

Over the years we gave around 400 performances of *A Bedful of Foreigners*. In addition to the overseas trips, we toured at home and did a summer season in Bournemouth. By the time we finished we could have done it in our sleep, and I dare say we did on occasion.

Meanwhile *Happy Ever After* continued on television, and Terry and I became so closely associated that many people thought we really were husband and wife. If Tim and I were having a quiet dinner somewhere, people would sometimes wink knowingly at me, as if to say, 'We won't tell a soul.' Once someone asked me, 'Where's your husband, then?'

'Right here,' I said.

'Not that one, the real one,' was the answer.

Terry and Maggie suffered in much the same way. When we were in Hong Kong, the phone rang in their hotel suite one morning and a voice asked to speak to Terry Scott.

'I'm awfully sorry,' said Maggie, 'but he's still asleep.'

'Oh, is that June Whitfield?' said the voice.

'No,' said Maggie indignantly. 'This is *Mrs Scott*.'

Terry often fed the press the line that he had two wives, 'one for show and one for go', and sometimes he told interviewers that it would make life a great deal simpler if I married him and Maggie married Tim. It was a lucky thing the four of us were such good friends.

In the very hot summer of 1976, we played *A Bedful of Foreigners* at the Victoria Palace. Farces are quite energy-sapping to perform, with all that jumping in and out of cupboards and windows, and I remember us wilting from the strain of rehearsing *Happy Ever After* all day, then having to go into the Turkish-bath heat of central London every evening to do the play. Sometimes Terry and I would look at each other at half-past ten at night, not quite sure if we'd finished work for the day or if we still had another performance to give.

The television producer Jimmy Gilbert came to see us one night at the Victoria Palace and I gave him a lift home after the show. In the car I asked if he minded me learning my lines for *Happy Ever After* on the way home – I usually record my cues onto a cassette so I can rehearse when travelling. He was a bit surprised that I should be doing that after such a heavy day, but I pointed out that I had to test myself somehow, and it was better to do it while sitting in traffic than to stay up half the night trying to cram the words in at home. Oh, the glamour of it all.

A week or so before *A Bedful of Foreigners* opened in London, my agent rang and said that the *Sunday Pictorial* wanted to run a spread about the play and needed a set of shots before their Friday evening deadline. We had already been through all the pre-publicity photo sessions, and I felt they ought to be able to manage with the pictures that had already been taken, but April was insistent that it was crucial for the good of the show. Reluctantly, I agreed to meet the journalist Tony Lee for lunch and then go on to the theatre afterwards for a photo session. It all seemed to drag on rather, and after some highly inappropriate set-ups, involving me walking down the stairs like Gloria Swanson, I said they must surely have enough. As it happened Tony lived quite near us, so I gave him a lift, and when we got home I asked him in for a cup of tea. Tim let us in.

'There's someone to see you,' he said.

'I've just offered Tony a cup of tea,' I replied.

'No, I think you ought to come.' He took my rather large bag from my arm and frogmarched me towards the drawing room.

Oh no, I thought. I've double-booked something.

Tim opened the door and I was met by a battery of lights, cameras and microphones, which suddenly sprang to life to catch my expression of surprise. What *were* they doing there, with Suzy, my mother and Tim beaming from ear to ear? I had faced cameras and microphones on an almost daily basis for twenty-five years, but never in my home and never without warning. I was thoroughly confused. Then I saw Eamonn Andrews with the big red book.

'June Whitfield, this is your life.'

My jaw dropped. I think I said something really original like, 'That's ridiculous!' I couldn't believe it.

As I was changing before the drive to the Thames TV studios in Euston, I couldn't stop puzzling over how on earth they had managed to organize it all. I had appeared on the show several times as a guest, so I knew how much trouble they took to keep it secret from the subject – when I'd done Jimmy Edwards' *This Is Your Life*, the script was mysteriously titled 'Project One' on the top page – but I still couldn't believe that my family had arranged it without my knowledge.

The photo call at the theatre was a set-up by April, my agent, to get me out of the house for the morning, and she had done it with the full co-operation of the *Sunday Pictorial*.

Tim reminded me of when we'd been on holiday in Suffolk some weeks before, and to my great annoyance he had said we had to go home a day earlier than planned because he'd been called to an important business meeting in London – the meeting was at Thames Television to discuss making the programme.

Suzy had been taken out to buy a special frock for the occasion, and my mother had been questioned closely about my early life and career. Unable to locate my scrapbooks, poor Muff, whose memory for dates was worse even than mine, got them a bit muddled up, and the programme researcher said to her at one point, 'You're being most helpful, Mrs Whitfield, but according to your calculations June is now 123 years old!'

It was incredible how they'd managed to assemble such an array of family, friends and colleagues in the studio at the same time. On videotape came fulsome messages from Frankie Howerd in Canada, Frank Muir and Denis Norden at the Captain's Cabin pub, where we used to gather in the *TIFH* days, and also Jimmy Edwards and Eric Sykes from somewhere in the heart of Africa, where they were doing *Big Bad Mouse* and, by the look of them, enjoying serious 'drinks with . . .' Then, through the sliding doors came members of the Giles family, who we'd stayed with in Devon during the war, and my best friend Mog, who invited me to join her in a song we'd sung at one of the Brixton Empress displays; typically, I couldn't remember any of it.

Then came my brother John, his wife and my cousin Richard, childhood friends Mary and June, Pat Coombs, Reg Varney and Peter Jones, Leslie Crowther, Ronnie Barker, Bob Monkhouse, Peter Butterworth, Dora Bryan, Dick Bentley and Arthur Askey. Terry Scott caused much amusement by playing the recording of his snoring that Lynda Baron and I had made in South Africa. He was joined by the cast of *A Bedful of Foreigners*, and also Charlie Drake, who I had, in fact, only met once before in a sketch with Arthur. It was such a pity that dear old Dad wasn't there; he would have been so proud of me.

It's a very odd experience sitting there while people say nice things about you. It's embarrassing and uplifting; you go through a whole range of emotions, and at the same time you still can't quite believe they are talking about you.

The special surprise guest was my cousin Verena. When the phone rang in the early hours of the morning at her home in New Zealand, and an English voice asked, 'Are you June Whitfield's cousin?' she told me she'd thought I must have died; and when she was invited to fly over to be in the show she wondered if she was dreaming. It couldn't have come at a better time for her, as her father, Uncle Ron, wasn't at all well, and she was able to spend time with him and her mother in Yorkshire. So *This Is Your Life* served a useful purpose, as well as massaging my ego.

It was very flattering to have so many great comedians in attendance, but I was even more affected by the presence of my family. It struck me that, but for them, I wouldn't have been there at all. Without the support and encouragement of my parents, and without the tolerance and understanding of Tim and Suzy, I couldn't have had such a successful career. But I missed my dad.

Both Frankie Howerd and Terry Scott teased me for my lack of ambition, which isn't quite true. I have always loved my work and wanted to do well, but soon after Tim came into my life I knew where my priorities lay. My job has at all times been secondary to family. If you work at it, a marriage can last longer than a career, but if you put your career first, then the chances of that happening are very slim.

Far from putting a brake on my progress, my family is the means by which I have managed to survive for so long as an actress. I realize how lucky I am to have had the best of both worlds.

Chapter Nine

HOUSE, HOME AND HOLS

IN 1969 TIM SPOTTED A LARGE VICTORIAN HOUSE A BIT NEARER Wimbledon village, which had what estate agents like to call 'potential'. I fell in love with the staircase and the bay window on the first-floor landing, and although it needed doing up, we moved in and survived, living in reasonable chaos, for six months while builders attacked the kitchen. We lived in the front room, installing a cooker and siphoning water from a basin in the lobby next door. We tackled the house room by room, and the three of us, plus an au pair, labrador, tortoise and hamster settled happily into our new home.

We had not long become acquainted with our next-door neighbours, Mike and Lelia Popham, when we heard them in their garden calling for Sid. We couldn't understand why they were calling our dog, but it transpired that they too had a dog called Sid, who also happened to be a golden labrador. Not long after, we applied for, and got, some tickets to see the tennis at Wimbledon. Who should we find sitting right next to us on the day but Mike and Lelia? We were obviously destined to become firm friends.

The only member of the family who wasn't so pleased with her new living quarters was Hatty the hamster. Suzy went to feed her one morning and found her cage unoccupied and abandoned. A thorough search of the house revealed no trace of Hatty and we feared the worst. Eventually someone heard a faint rustling noise coming from behind the loo. Tim got down on his hands and knees and made conciliatory noises through a gap in the floorboards, but to no effect. Each of us in turn pleaded with Hatty to come out, wafting tempting bits of lettuce around the entrance to her bolt hole, again to no avail. The next morning Tim ripped up the floorboards, splitting a couple in the process, but Hatty only retreated further into the foundations. Several hours later she was driven by hunger to emerge, blinking and trembling, into the light. She was reunited with a very relieved Suzy and returned to her cage. A carpenter was called to replace the boards – quite an expensive hamster.

A sad fact of hamster life is that they live at about forty times the rate of humans; one day they can be happily rattling around on their wheels with all the high spirits of youth, then overnight they become doddery old rodents. It was distressing to see Hatty's rapid decline into decrepitude, but at least she didn't meet her end alone and entombed beneath the loo.

A far worse fate was to befall Henrietta the tortoise. One winter, Henrietta was given a hibernation box and, carefully following the instructions shown on *Blue Peter*, we filled it with straw and let her settle in. Once she was ensconced, we covered the box with polythene to prevent anything dropping on her and disturbing her winter slumber. In the spring, we gently raised the covering and found, to our dismay, a totally toasted tortoise. Suzy was distraught. Henrietta was given a burial ceremony, and a little later we were commiserating with, and comforting, Suzy when we saw, through the window, Sid the dog proudly approaching, having exhumed the tortoise, and about to come and present us with his prize. Tim rushed out and hastily reburied Henrietta while I consoled Suzy, who eventually calmed down and even managed a smile at the thought of Sid trying to behave like a gun dog.

There was an annexe to the house which had originally been a stable block, and we set about converting it for my mum. Mrs Suter was housekeeping for her but they were both getting on, and half the time Mother was looking after Mrs Suter, so it wasn't a very

Carry On Abroad with Kenneth Williams, Sally Geeson and Carol Hawkins – Ken's ready to go for a snorkel in the car park at Pinewood.

Birds Eye commercials: Pinnochio's mum, fibbing that the pies are
home-made and about to grow her nose, and Anne Hathaway
with Terry-Thomas as Shakespeare.

The Frankie Howerd Show, 1966 – a very striking Viking.

The Best Things In Life, 1969, with Harry H. Corbett.

LEFT: *The Fossett Saga*, 1969 – magician's assistant.

BELOW: *The Pallisers*, 1973, with Sarah Badel – I was Mrs Bontine mourning her husband, 'my poor dear lost one.' BBC

LEFT: *Carry On Abroad*, 1972, with Ken Connor, seconds before the bed, with us on it, plummeted through the floor.

Happy Ever After, 1974, with Terry. BBC

A Bedful of Foreigners, with Terry on Bournemouth pier, 1978,
keeping it under our hat – and eyelashes.

LEFT: *The Dick Emery Christmas Show*, 1980 – a policeman's lot can be a happy one.

BELOW: Royal Variety Show, 1980, with Arthur Askey, Terry Scott and Her Majesty the Queen Mum.

BELOW: *Mike Yarwood in Persons*, 1981 – he was Michael Foot as Hamlet; I was Mrs Thatcher as Juliet.

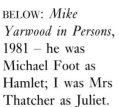

ABOVE: Jack and the Beanstalk, Chichester 1982 – spreading a little happiness with Frankie Howerd.

LEFT: Roy, Chris and me, 1986. Guess who has a birthday?

RIGHT: *Cluedo*, 1990, Mrs White, the cook – 'What's your poison?'

An Ideal Husband, Chichester, 1989, with Jo Lumley – 'the long and the short of it' when we stood up.

Three generations study holiday snaps.

Family snap 1990 – Suzy's birthday party.

satisfactory arrangement. When Mrs Suter went to live with her daughter, we became concerned about Muff being on her own, and when she let slip in a telephone conversation that she'd had a fall, but hadn't said anything because she didn't want us to worry, we realized that something had to be done.

Muff wasn't at all keen on the idea of coming to live in the annexe when it was first suggested. She didn't want to feel like a burden, and Wimbledon was, to her, a strange and distant place, full of hostile flora and fauna. Ideally, she would have liked a flat above Swann and Edgar overlooking Piccadilly Circus. Her flat in Cranley Mews had a large double garage underneath, which she had converted to a rehearsal-room, equipped with carpets, bookshelves and a very 1930s grey suede-fronted bar, complete with stools, from behind which she dispensed liquid refreshment. It was a popular meeting place for all her amateur-dramatic friends, and she was naturally reluctant to leave. But she finally realized it was too much for her and agreed to emigrate to Wimbledon in 1972.

She soon discovered that the natives were friendly. She joined the Hurlingham Players and the local Carlton Players – I am their President now – and continued to take part in Comedy Club productions at Vicarage Gate in Kensington. She went with them on several trips to the famous Minack Theatre, perched on the cliffs near Penzance, and she performed regularly in plays until she was in her eighties.

Tim loyally sat through dozens of amateur productions without complaint – perhaps not quite without complaint; he groans whenever the programme reads, 'Act 1: A drawing room in the home counties – early summer.' We once went to see a medieval play – not with Mother in it – in which the men wore enormous gold codpieces in various shapes and sizes, and all pretty phallic. We were with our friends Paul and Vena Wilkinson. Paul and Tim had great trouble controlling their giggles, and their suppressed laughter made the row of seats, which were all joined together, shake. Medieval plays are not for them; they really prefer football. But it is to Tim's credit that he has always been a steadfast supporter of all three generations of actresses in our family.

Tim has been a football fan since the days when he and his father followed Portsmouth. They were top of the First Division for two years running, and attracted large crowds to every match. He played soccer himself for Charterhouse and is a keen follower of the game. When we moved to Wimbledon the Dons were in the Southern League, and Tim became a season-ticket holder when they were in the Fourth Division. He and Paul Wilkinson regularly attended the matches at home, and sometimes away ones, too, when Vena and I would accompany them. They climbed to the Second Division, and there was an important match to be played in Huddersfield, the result of which could mean another leg up to the First Division. Paul, Vena, Tim and I – the Football Foursome – went up north to cheer them on. I recommended a hotel where Mother and I had spent some time during the war. Unfortunately, it turned out to be right on the railway station, and the metal-framed windows in the bedroom rattled and were sadly in need of repair.

'Are you sure you stayed here?' the others asked.

My Yorkshire cousin Margaret came for coffee, and Tim explained that we were in the hotel because I had stayed there and it was a nostalgic return.

'She did *not*,' said Margaret. 'She stayed at the Queen's, and that's long since been demolished.'

'Oh dear, sorry!'

On the day of the match, our friend Bernard Coleman, who was then a director of Crystal Palace, had kindly arranged for us to be in the directors' box. We were treated royally and invited to join the directors and their wives for lunch. Vena and I followed the men to the club room, but were gently told, 'The ladies have their own room; the gentlemen follow me.' It's still a man's world in Yorkshire! After a slap-up meal – exactly the same food as the men, we later discovered – we watched the match, and history was made with a 1–0 victory. The Dons were in the First Division.

There was great excitement from the Wimbledon fans, and about twenty minutes after the match I was asked by Peter Cork, a Wimbledon director, if I would like to meet the players.

'Of course, I'd be delighted,' I said.

I followed him along a corridor and was ushered into a crowded dressing room full of very tall men, although I did spot one woman, who turned out to be the physio. I was gently pushed to the front of the crowd, only to discover Dave Besant, the goalkeeper, standing on a bench, swaying slightly, absolutely starkers and looking like a Greek god. He had rightly been celebrating, and although the rest of the team were dressed or draped in towels, he hadn't quite got round to it. He had a bottle in each outstretched arm and – how shall I put this? – I was not exactly at handshaking height, so I gave him a pat on the ankle and offered my heartfelt congratulations to the others. Of course there was a reporter in the room, who couldn't resist the headline JUNE BURSTS INTO WIMBLEDON DRESSING ROOM! Dave and I cashed in on the publicity later; he posed in the bath with his head just visible, and I fed him grapes.

The Wimbledon story doesn't end there. In 1981 I was asked by Alf Lowne, a staunch Wimbledon supporter, if I would take on the role of president of the supporters club as, sadly, the current one had died. I explained that I knew little about the game and that work would prevent me from attending matches, but it didn't seem to matter, and I proudly became their president. As the 1988 season progressed I attended several games at Plough Lane, and each time we either drew or won, but never lost. As we reached the last sixteen, and then the last eight of the FA Cup, the chaps on the gate kept saying, 'You're coming next week, aren't you?' I became a sort of lucky mascot, and put in an appearance even if I had to leave before the game was over. It was a fantastic season, culminating in a great win over Liverpool at Wembley.

Wimbledon town went mad. I've never seen anything like it. The weather was good and the pubs were overflowing onto the streets. Traffic came to a halt and the atmosphere was electric. The following day, vast crowds greeted the triumphant team as they waved from their bus on their way to the town hall.

It was a wonderful experience and I'll never forget it. As time went by, Plough Lane was abandoned and Wimbledon now share Selhurst Park with Crystal Palace. When they moved I resigned as president of the supporters club, as I knew I would be unlikely to make the

South Circular trip. As we have a cottage in Sussex, Tim has returned to supporting his first club, Portsmouth, and I have settled for watching the occasional game on television.

Football, like many other sports, has become corporate entertainment, and I think a lot of the genuine supporters are priced out or unable to get the same seat each week, which is a shame, as half the fun is being with the same crowd. The downhearted Dons were relegated from the Premier League this season, but hopefully it won't be too long before they regain promotion.

I was never very sporty at school. I played netball and lacrosse, but could never get my feet warm. 'Run!' they said. 'I can't, I'm too cold.' Tennis wasn't much good because I always seemed to have the sun in my eyes. I was a dab hand at table tennis and not bad at darts, but on the whole it's just as well I stuck to acting.

The acting bug has travelled noticeably down the female line of my family, but the chaps have been touched by it to some extent. My father and uncle Ron enjoyed amateur performing when time allowed, and my brother John is an excellent after-dinner speaker. Like his father, John became a councillor, and he stood as the Conservative candidate for Pontefract and Castleford in the 1964 general election. He had little chance of winning, but he managed to reduce the Labour majority by 4½ per cent. It probably didn't help that I thoughtlessly turned up to support him wearing a red suit.

John's talents are considerable. He speaks Russian, French, German and Spanish and is now learning Italian. His other hobbies are bookbinding and golf, and he spends hours tramping the greens and fairways of his beloved Sunningdale Golf Club. He was club director for five years, has recently written a history of Sunningdale and has been made an honorary member.

His wife Rosemary, known as Bud, is also multi-talented. She paints, sculpts, sews, cooks and designs and makes wedding dresses. Her charming pastel of our dog Rabbit hangs in our hall, and she has had miniatures exhibited for three years running at the Royal Academy's Summer Exhibition. She is also the nicest person and a wonderful wife and mother. Don't you just hate people like that?

John and Bud recently celebrated their golden wedding anniversary, at Sunningdale Golf Club, naturally. They have two daughters, one of whom is now a grandmother, which makes me a great-great-aunt!

Many people from the world of arts and entertainment have been drawn to Wimbledon over the years. Joanna Lumley, Annette Crosbie, James Villiers and Richard Briers have all been Wombles at one time or another. The artist June Mendoza came to the area in the mid-Sixties, and the art critic and writer Brian Sewell has recently taken up residence. When June Mendoza arrived with her husband after many years in the Philippines, she was keen to find sitters. I was an early volunteer. Now she has a very grand studio, as befits a royal portrait painter, but then she worked in her bedroom. I perched at the bedhead end of the bed, leaning against it while she beavered away at her easel. June is so talented; I recognized myself as soon as she had outlined my head and shoulders and before she'd added any features. When I saw the completed work I was surprised to find that the bed was transformed on the canvas into an elegant sofa. Art and artifice combined. It is a brilliant portrait and hangs in Tim's study.

Our house has periodically served as a watering hole for friends playing at the Wimbledon Theatre, half a mile down the hill from us. Eric Morecambe and Ernie Wise came once to do what they called a 'bank raid' – they knew they would fill a theatre for two per-formances and walk away with a tidy sum at the end of the evening. They arrived for tea in between performances, and my mother and Suzy volunteered to make the tea and toast. They disappeared into the kitchen and, after a while, Suzy reappeared and said she was sorry for the hold-up but they'd had a slight problem with the grill.

'What have you done?' asked Eric. 'Toasted Granny?'

Eric belonged to that group of comedians who are funny offstage as well as on. Meeting Eric socially wasn't so different from watch-ing him on the box. When the doctors told him to stop work, it was the cruellest restriction that could possibly have been placed on him. He tried hard to do as he was told, but ultimately the temptation to work in front of an audience proved irresistible, with tragic results.

He is much missed but, thankfully, a part of him lives on through the recordings of those wonderful shows. His son Gary has written a book with Martin Sterling about his father called *Memories of Eric*.

I was flattered to be asked to appear on *The Morecambe and Wise Show*, and to be cast in one of Ernie's plays – 'what he wrote' – as the predatory wife of a colonial rubber-planter who tried to seduce Eric – me the wife, not Ernie the rubber-planter. All went well until the recording, when I saw Eric's baggy khaki shorts for the first time. They had wire in the turn-ups to stiffen them, and when he sat down next to me on the sofa, they shot up like two little crinolines. He then squeezed the wire hoops together to close the gaps and cover his modesty. In so doing he created two ridiculous khaki points. He hadn't done it in rehearsal, so it took me by surprise. Eric's expression and inspired business with the shorts was one of the funniest things I've ever seen.

Another visitor to our house in the mid-Seventies was that talented dancer/singer/actress, 'The Delightful Aimi Macdonald'. We met in *A Bedful of Foreigners* in Hong Kong, and during the run of the show we became friends and decided we would write together – just like that. Situation comedy was all the rage at the time, so we thought we would create one for ourselves. We sat down to work with great enthusiasm, paper, pencils and hot coffee at the ready. Whereupon inspiration completely deserted us. We came up with a few what-ifs – as in, What if we were a couple of nuns? Or, What if we were a pair of ex-cons? but no amount of caffeine, cigarettes, biscuits, wine, or anything else that was going could get us beyond that point. Suddenly, after several days of hopeful what-ifs we came up with a winning formula: What if we gave up the whole idea and stuck to performing? So we did. We remained friends and meet from time to time at charity shows and on panel games.

When Tim retired we bought the Corner Shop at Plaistow in Sussex. The upper floor was to be our country retreat, and the ground floor, which had been used as a grocery store, was refitted for Tim to sell his antiques there at weekends. It proved to be rather more time-consuming than we had bargained for, and we found ourselves spending most of the weekend minding the shop instead of relaxing, which, after all, was the main reason we'd bought the place, so after nearly four years we decided to sell up. Tim carried on dealing in porcelain via other outlets; first in the antiques market at Thames Ditton, subsequently in Knockhundred Row in Midhurst, and he currently plies his trade at Great Grooms in Billingshurst.

We still have a place in West Sussex, our favourite part of the country; it's relatively unspoiled and easily reached for short breaks. Sometimes we venture further afield, and we really miss the car-ferry service from Lydd airport. You used to be able to drive onto the plane and drive off at Le Touquet, and we spent many weekends there, enjoying gourmet meals at Flavio's, followed by bracing walks along the magnificent beach.

Once we visited Le Touquet with our neighbours the Pophams and the Robertses. Alan and Maddy Roberts had an apartment there and we all stayed with them, having some fun excursions and a lot of 'drinks with . . .' It was there that I recorded a golf score of 133 – not too bad, you might say, for a novice in a strong wind, but it was achieved over *nine* holes!

In a *Terry and June* episode about golf, there was a hole in Terry's golf bag and his clubs gradually dropped out. I was supposed to be a good player but Rosemary Frankau and I were given just half an hour's tuition prior to the filming. Peter Whitmore's clever camera angles made us look like professionals, and after the episode was shown I received two offers to take part in pro-am competitions, but I had to confess to the promoters that I didn't actually play. If only they could have seen me hacking my way round the Le Touquet course.

I saw a television programme recently in which people described their worst holiday experiences. It was compulsive viewing as well as amusing – which of us has not endured an unsuccessful holiday? Tim and I have been lucky on the whole, but we've had our ration of mishaps. There was the time we went to Alassio in Italy and found ourselves, with a couple of friends, in an apartment block, most of whose residents were night-shift workers who spent their time running up and down the stone stairs in clogs. Just when things had quietened down, an open-air cinema would start up outside, ruling out any chance of sleep and leaving us with nothing to do but hold an insect-swatting contest in our infested kitchen. Our friends had booked the place, so we were reluctant to suggest moving out. It wasn't possible to get to the front door without going through their room, so on the second night Tim climbed out of our window and went off in search of a hotel. When he mentioned the next morning that he'd found somewhere else, they were as relieved as us.

Then there was the time Tim and I set off with Annie and Derek Bond for a trip on the Rhine from Cologne to Frankfurt. We had become friendly after Derek and I appeared together in *Not Now, Darling* at the Savoy; Tim and Annie often came to watch the show, and we would all repair to Rules afterwards for supper; before long we were planning holidays together. For our Rhine jaunt, we met in Cologne, but unfortunately we'd chosen a hotel in a popular square. It was a weekend and beneath our window was a café that seemed to be the meeting place for all-night revellers, so once again not much sleep was had. We were due to board our vessel the next morning, but because there was fog in Frankfurt we were destined to travel by bus to Koblenz to catch the boat there. The bus's air-conditioning wasn't working, and we had to endure a very uncomfortable two-hour drive, but we assured each other all would be well when we got on the water. Once on board it was clear that our fellow passengers were mostly intending to use the trip to see how much beer they could consume before they reached Frankfurt – Singin' in the Rhine? We were summoned to the lounge, a large area with viewing windows, and were all introduced to each other in at least four different languages. There were few Brits, but we had to stand up and be counted when our country was called. The Rhine was suffering from pollution, and we floated serenely past the industrial areas on the outskirts of Frankfurt on a tide of grey-brown chemicals, with neither flora nor fauna to be seen. Every landmark we passed was described to us loudly and in four languages. On-board entertainment was provided by various Bavarian bands, and we were treated to a solo on a flugel-horn – shades of the sketch with Tony Hancock and Kenneth

Williams. Most of the passengers tottered unsteadily ashore at Frankfurt, but we had foolishly booked a return journey and so had to suffer a different set of drunks on the way back.

Of course we alighted at various ports of call and had a good many laughs, but we realized we would have been better off staying in a hotel on the Rhine and exploring the prettiest parts of the river from there. Luckily, Annie and Derek have remained close friends; we meet regularly and have enjoyed several rather more successful jaunts *à quatre*. Annie is a superb cook and hostess, and her dinner parties are memorable, especially the millennium bash.

I don't know what it is about me and boats. The relationship started to go wrong in Long Island Sound in 1949, and it hasn't really recovered since. When our friends Peter and Brenda Goddard invited us for a few days cruising on their splendid craft *La Bonita*, I should have warned them about my track record. We set off on the Hamble river, bound for Torquay, on a beautiful sunny morning. We swept past the Needles and out into the open sea, and with our course carefully programmed into the on-board computer, there was nothing for us to do but relax and enjoy the voyage, glass of champagne in hand. After a while I noticed that we had land on both sides – the computer had taken us round in a circle. We had circumnavigated the Isle of Wight and were almost back where we'd started. Peter decided to ignore the technology and consult a map, and we were soon headed in the right direction, passing the Needles once again. We had a glorious run to Torquay; the trip couldn't have been better. We stayed the night in a hotel, run by friends of Peter and Brenda, who had invited me to open a new section of the building before we returned to the Hamble the following day. That was when the gales blew up.

We bounced our way through rough seas to West Bay. The harbour has a bar, but we got in OK and weren't exactly welcomed by the fishermen, but were grudgingly allowed to moor as we only intended to stay for a short time in order to have a meal. When we returned our dinghy, which had been tied up by the steps, was nowhere to be seen as the tide had changed and the water had dropped twelve feet.

I spotted the dinghy on the far side of the harbour and Peter wanted to rescue it there and then, but was told firmly by Brenda that it wasn't a good idea to jump down the necessary twelve feet to get it. We returned to the hotel for a sleepless night, and at 6 a.m. we were roused by Peter and told we were leaving in five minutes as he had recovered the dinghy. The weather had improved and the tide was right to get over the bar.

Peter had been told by a friendly fisherman to 'keep between the Rock and the Race' while rounding Portland Bill. Away from the shelter of the harbour, we found ourselves in more rough seas in Lyme Bay. Peter tried to contact the coastguard on his ship-to-shore radio – 'La Bonita calling Portland Bill,' he said with increasing urgency. There was no reply, just a hissing sound. We were on our own, heading towards the dreaded Bill, being thrown about and hoping the boat would remain the right way up. We tackled the Bill between the Rock and the Race and, thanks to Peter's navigation and divine intervention, we got round it, narrowly missing the lobster pots that were dotted about.

Sighing with relief and nursing our bruises, we made for the nearest harbour, which was Weymouth. Just in time, Tim pointed out that we were approaching the naval base. We hastily diverted to the proper harbour and moored alongside the quay. One by one, boats came in to shelter from the storm and moored next to us. We ended up five boats deep and were mightily pleased to know that the night would be spent, if not on dry land, then at least tethered to it. The bonus was that no-one had been seasick.

The bad weather held for a further three days. I was due to return to work on the fourth and the decision was finally made to travel back to the Hamble by hire car. The driver informed us cheerily that it was his first job after his recent release from a rehabilitation centre, where he had been weaned off alcohol! We got back to where Peter had left his car in one piece, only to find the battery was flat – someone had left the phone plugged in. Our nautical adventure ended with us pushing the car, with Peter running alongside, steering with one hand, then jumping in at the last minute.

As I said, there is something about me and boats.

We have, of course, also enjoyed some wonderful holidays. We prefer short breaks and like to take the car. We've toured England, Scotland, Wales and Ireland, as well as exploring a great deal of Europe. When I was looking through some old scripts in search of material for this book, I found a note I'd scribbled on a page of a 1961 Benny Hill episode. I must have been trying to find a hotel in the South of France for a short break because there are various scribbled phone numbers and next to one I'd written 'Close to St-Tropez. Double room with baby. Sea view and dinner inc. £2 per day.' Maybe it was recommended by Benny.

In 1995, Judith Chalmers asked if Tim and I would like to visit Lake Garda for an edition of *Wish You Were Here*. We were very happy to accept and had a wonderful time in that most beautiful part of the world. As it was summer, there were a lot of holidaymakers about, but we had the luxury of travelling around in a minibus with the camera crew. We visited Limone, Maderno and Salò, towns and villages round the lake. We also went to the rather spooky house of the poet d'Annunzio who had somehow reassembled in his garden on the shore of the lake the boat he commanded in the First World War.

Not far away is Verona, home of the famous Roman arena, where opera is performed throughout the summer. We arrived there looking forward to an early dinner followed by *Aida*, but while we were in the restaurant the heavens opened. The opera should have started at seven thirty, and some people sat in the open air getting soaked for at least half an hour. We thought the show would be cancelled, but were finally told it would start at nine fifteen. It had stopped raining, but the roads were full of puddles, which, of course, I trod in in the dark. When we arrived at the arena it was like being in the middle of a football crowd, but we were guided in and purchased cushions and plastic macs, as the weather didn't look promising and the seats were wet. *Aida* was a magnificent spectacle, and the regulars around the arena had lit candles which added to the atmosphere. I took a sneaky photo of the leading lady when the music was quite loud, but my film then finished and, in the quiet moment that followed, I got a filthy look from the man in front of me as the film rewound. Verdi was never one to skimp a job, and so we finally made it back to base at 3 a.m.

When we returned from Italy, Tim had to be initiated into the mysteries of dubbing – that is, revoicing bits of the film that have either not recorded properly or need alteration for some other reason. Obviously the voice has to synchronize with the lip movements, and it's an interesting procedure. The film is played to you and, through earphones, you hear the original voice and try to match it. We had to recreate some of our conversations on the trips around the lake. Tim got the hang of it quite quickly and now isn't at all impressed when I say I have to go off and do some dubbing.

I've already mentioned my inability to withstand strong sunlight for any length of time without turning into a lobster. I am also highly susceptible to insect attack. If that didn't make me awkward enough when it comes to planning holidays, I recently added another no-go area. We were visiting Kandersteg in the Swiss Alps in early June, and as we went up the mountain in the cable car the wild flowers spread out below were quite stunning. We made the return trip on foot and I experienced, for the first time in my life, a bout of hay fever. I have suffered from it ever since. So while I may have acquired a reputation for being easy to work with in my professional life, I have become the most difficult holiday companion imaginable. How Tim manages to find a destination that accommodates my idiosyncrasies I do not know, but he does.

Our holidays have taken us all over Europe, from the Mediterranean to the fjords, but as foreign travel becomes easier and departure lounges become fuller, we find ourselves increasingly going off airports. When Noël Coward was once asked how his flight had gone, he replied, 'Aeronautically it was a great success; socially it left a lot to be desired.' To start with there's that eternal trek through the airport; it always seems to be the furthest gate and your hand luggage seems to get steadily heavier. You queue to get through security and passport control, and then to board the plane, and when you arrive home – usually plus heavy bottles – there's another endless walk before you even see a trolley. You wait at the carousel and endeavour to heave your luggage off before it disappears again. After all that you're completely exhausted. For pleasure, Tim and I would rather throw everything in the car and nip across the channel and drink a glass of champagne during the crossing.

As the years tick by I tend to agree with the great travel writer Dame Freya Stark, who, when she reached her nineties, decided that, with the rest of the world constantly on the move, it suddenly seemed much nicer to stay at home.

Chapter Ten

HERE AND THERE

ACTORS ARE REQUIRED TO PRESENT THEMSELVES AT ALL KINDS OF unsocial times and places: the 6 a.m. make-up call in some remote location; the night shoot; the evening journey to the theatre just as the rush hour is getting going, all of which pleasantly adds to life's variety, but also means spending a good deal of time in the car.

I have been driving since I was seventeen and have always enjoyed it. Until 1976 I usually drove myself to wherever I was working; I had a little Datsun which whizzed me about the place. But parking in central London has become more and more of a problem, and during the run of *A Bedful of Foreigners* at the Victoria Palace, I travelled with a local car-hire firm. The driver, one Barbara Welford, was the firm's proprietor, managing director and sole employee. She was a rather eccentric lady, but she delivered me in one piece and picked me up at the appointed hour, so before long it became a regular arrangement. She was getting on a bit when she first drove me, and by the time she retired, nearly twenty years later, her driving reduced strong men to quivering jellies.

Barbara was small, even by my standards, and I'm only five foot two and a half – probably one and a half now, as we all shrink, don't we? She certainly had. She was invisible from behind to other motorists, and to all the world her Ford Granada appeared to drive itself. She also had one leg shorter than the other – the result of a riding accident in her gilded youth – and it was a mystery how those little legs managed to reach the pedals. Her handicap entitled her to a disability badge, which meant there was nowhere she wouldn't venture to drive or park; double yellow lines and 'official vehicles only' signs deterred her not a jot. She could bring traffic to a stand-still while double-parked outside the favourite shops of her elderly clients. She wasn't a fast driver, but neither was she timid, and she was content to occupy the outside lane at a sedate 20 mph, respond-ing to the enraged hooting and flashing from behind by muttering, 'Ah yes, I know you're there,' while I shrank a little lower into my seat. When I did the serial *Family Money*, I stole this line of Barbara's. I had to ride round a corner on a bicycle and cut out in front of a bus. When the driver hooted and abused me, I answered, 'Ah yes, I know you're there.' How Barbara managed to get her commercial licence renewed was a mystery. Her clients gradually left her, and towards the end I was her only customer. I hadn't the heart to leave. Besides, in twenty years she never once delivered me late for an appointment or failed to be waiting outside to collect me – although her car did collect a few dents along the way.

She uttered some memorable malapropisms: she talked of 'bruis-ing through a magazine', in which she'd read a sensational story where 'allegorations had been made about a menagerie à trois'; and when we passed a service station she pointed disapprovingly at the sign and said, 'They're everywhere nowadays. You see, there's another Happy Easter.' Her work kept her going, and after she was forced to retire in 1994 she quickly faded away. However, in her last years she took on another driver, Jim Brady, to share the load. When Barbara died, Jim took over the business, and he has been driving us around ever since. I must admit, I feel safer with Jim. He is also always on time and never lets us down, and since Barbara's demise we've spent many hours travelling to the variety of obscure destin-ations that my job demands, and long may it continue – although he has warned me that when he wins the lottery I'll have to make other arrangements.

*

Ever since the invention of the celeb, many actors have been invited to show up in front of the cameras to do just about anything *except* practise their profession. Daytime television, quizzes and personal appearances, both charitable and promotional, are now part of the job. I have a slightly ambivalent attitude towards the latter, rather dreading having to 'say a few words' but not wanting to miss out on anything that might be fun or interesting. I have also always been conscious of the fact that memories are very short in this business, and it's not a bad idea to show your face in case people forget about you altogether. I'm not sure how reliable this theory is, but it's certainly one that has led me into some unusual situations.

I was once asked to take part in a trial at Brands Hatch for a celebrity race that would take place on a later date. The first thing I saw on my arrival there was an ambulance – bodes well, I thought. Then they gave me a form to sign, declaring that if I killed myself it would be entirely my own fault. I couldn't quite read the small print and asked what one of the questions was.

'Eyesight,' they said.

So I hastily ticked the box and made for the track. They shoved a crash helmet on my head, which is just what you want when you've come that morning from the hairdresser. After one circuit with an instructor in an ordinary car, it was time for the real thing. I was lowered into a motorized tin can and completely disappeared – cushions had to be piled under and behind me. I was strapped in, given a running shove and I was off round the track.

Driving lying flat on my back has never really appealed to me, but I tried to remember my instructor's words, 'Look for the "o" in Ferodo, then heel-and-toe – just drive as you normally would.' I didn't normally drive round and round at high speed in the midst of a group of actors, all eyeing each other in what could only be described as a competitive way. They shot past me on either side – not surprising, as I never got out of second gear. I came to a halt on the far side of the track, having hated every minute of it.

Strangely enough, I wasn't selected for the charity race. Most of my fellow actors loved the experience and couldn't wait to do it again. I found it utterly terrifying, as well as deafening. And I didn't enjoy lining up for the photographers, either, with my flattened hair-do.

Not long afterwards a complete stranger came up to me at a party and said, '*You* are a *terrible* driver!' Whether he was a disgruntled motor-racing enthusiast from Brands Hatch or someone I had inadvertently carved up in Wimbledon High Street I never knew, as he turned on his heel and walked away before I could find out.

My experience as a racing driver lasted for about the same length of time as my career as a sports commentator. I was hailed in a studio corridor by a high-up in the LWT sports department who asked if I knew anything about football.

'Not a lot,' I said. This was some years before my involvement with Wimbledon, but since Tim was a fanatic and I was rather curious to know what the director had in mind, I added that I'd absorbed some of the general principles, such as getting the ball in the net.

He eyed me carefully. 'And do you know what a *wall* is?'

'Of course I do. There's one round every ground with advertisements on it.'

He must have been desperate as, shortly afterwards, I found myself in the studio discussing a game with Jimmy Hill. I don't remember the teams, but I know it was during the 1970 World Cup. I have no idea what I said, but it certainly wasn't a turning point in my career.

Rather more my style was my annual day out at the Ideal Home Exhibition. Once or twice the *Daily Mail* sent me along with a photographer and, after a few shots, I was free to spend the rest of the day poking around, buying odd bits and pieces and helping myself to the freebies. I'm particularly susceptible to gadgets, and I have been known to buy some of the most useless labour-saving devices ever conceived by man. I have returned home with, amongst other things, an automatic sandwich cutter and the very latest hands-free tin opener. Tim despairs of my cupboard full of unused gadgets which might 'one day come in useful'. 'You haven't used that for years,' he says.

'Ah, but I might.'

I have at long last agreed to acknowledge sell-by dates, but it nearly broke my heart last year to throw out the half-pound box of paprika that my Hungarian friend Margit gave me in 1949.

The Ideal Home and I go back a very long way indeed. I was first taken as a child by my mother. Then, in the winter of 1950, I accepted an engagement to stand on a platform in a tailored two-piece and white gloves singing the praises of Atkinson's perfume. I had to say, 'Come along ladies, have you tried Atkinson's? Place a drop of scent on your wrist. It's so romantic when your fiancé kisses your hand.' I don't think I sold anything, but I attracted quite a few elderly ladies, clutching shopping bags and hoping for free samples.

Crowds have been drawn to Olympia over the years by the freebies – who could forget the miniature Hovis loaf? – though there are rather fewer on offer these days. Frank and Denis wrote a wonderful sketch on the subject for Ron and Eth in *Take It From Here*. This is a bit of it:

ETH: Ooh, Ron, if you eat any more of those free samples you'll be physically ill. Just what have you had so far?

RON: (*Savouring the memory of them*) A handful of jelly crystals, bit of Danish smoked herring, a tiny pot of apricot jam, a carton of cooking fat, some hot kidney soup, a swig of vanilla sauce, a slice of South African gorgonzola, twenty-eight frozen peas, a tiny little brown loaf and a tin of chocolate spread.

ETH: A tin of chocol— Ron! That was brown boot polish! Don't tell me you ate the whole tinful.

RON: Yes, Eth.

ETH: What are you going to do?

RON: (*pause*) I'll have to clean me boots with spit.

Advertising Atkinson's scent is the only out-of-work job I've ever taken. There was a time when things looked like being quiet for a while and I went to sign on at my local labour exchange. I was given a form to fill in, listing every job I'd had in the last five years. Five years! I need to look in my diary to tell me what I was doing five *days* ago! Luckily my agent phoned before too long and the form remained uncompleted.

There is a sort of halfway house between being unemployed and being in work as an actor; it's called 'being interviewed'. And of all the non-acting acting jobs, I relish this one least of all. There wasn't nearly as much of it when I first started in the theatre, but over the years it has become more common – a bit *too* common, some might say – for actors to be interviewed, and now it's just another part of the job.

In 1973 I was a castaway on *Desert Island Discs*. Roy Plomley took me to lunch at Veeraswamy's off Regent Street, and listened with courtly good manners as I burbled away about my life and work. It was such a relaxed and friendly sort of programme. My luxury was an endless supply of sunscreen, and my musical tastes were as un-original then as they are now. Later, after Sue Lawley took over the programme, I was invited back, and I chose more or less the same music, but I asked for a fax machine as my luxury the second time. I was denied it and had to settle for yet more sunscreen. Actually, I can't imagine anything worse than being stuck on a desert island, with or without a load of books and records.

Pieces of music become favourites as much for the happy memories they conjure up as for the quality of the music itself. I chose Noël Coward singing 'Alice Is at It Again' to remind me of the Café de Paris and the good times at White Cliffs and Gerald Road; I chose Judy Garland singing 'The Trolley Song' because of Hugh Martin and the *Love From Judy* days; Joyce Grenfell for 'Penny Plain'; Frank Sinatra and Ella Fitzgerald – they are the best, and also Tim's favourites – as reminders of our early days together; and finally Jack Hulbert singing 'The Flies Crawled Up the Window'. He was a favourite of my Uncle Billy, who used to play the record on his wind-up gramophone when I was very small. The sound of the song's lyrics echoing around the house is one of my earliest musical memories.

Million Dollar Bill was a Radio 2 programme in which one was supposedly given an unlimited budget to book any performers, dead or alive, to entertain you for an evening. I hired the casts of *South*

Pacific, *Guys and Dolls*, *Sweet Charity* and *Gigi*, and also the orchestra that played the theme from *Born Free* because it reminded me of when Suzy was small and someone asked her if she'd seen *Born Free* and, not wishing to be outdone, she said, 'No, but I've seen *Born 1*.' Music is a great way to recall happy periods in one's life, and I'm glad these programmes have allowed me to indulge my nostalgic inclinations.

I have always kept programmes of shows I've been in and mementoes of people I've worked with. They fill in the gaps in my memory, which is atrocious for details and dates. I'm also a great hoarder of photographs, and I have boxes and scrapbooks full of them. Some of the family photos date back to before I was born and are in a parlous state. When Terry and I did some work for Kodak I asked them if they had any means of restoring old photos. They kindly asked me to send them what I had, so they could see what they could do to revive them. A few weeks passed and I received several 'enhanced' photos and a polite letter saying that the negatives were so dense they had blown up their machine! The surviving photos were returned to their album, and some are reproduced in this book. Tim complains that I won't throw things away and he's right, although my hoarding instincts have proved invaluable while working on this project, but now it's published I suppose I will have to find another excuse for my squirrelling.

Probably the most common habitat for thesps who aren't actually thesping is the game show. As the television schedules encroached further into the daylight hours during the Seventies, there was a demand for more programmes, particularly those that could be produced more cheaply than the costly comedies and dramas. Part of the solution was game shows. I appeared at least once on *The Golden Shot*, several times on *Celebrity Squares*, *The Generation Game* and later *Blankety Blank*, as well as the more relaxed panel games such as *Looks Familiar*, *Jokers Wild*, *Call My Bluff* and *That's Showbusiness*. Roy Hudd and I made three series of *What's My Line?* for Meridian. It never quite made it onto the network, but it was fun to do, and Roy was on top form. Bernie Winters presented a popular show for

London Weekend Television called *Whose Baby?* The object was to find out the identity of someone's well-known parent by asking them questions. I appeared twice; once as a panellist and once when Suzy was the mystery offspring. Bernie was an adorable man, but his pooch Schnorbitz could have used a deodorant; he really did get up your nose! All these shows became well-known and achieved a reasonable level of popularity, but do you remember *Whodunnit?*, *The Zodiac Game*, *Funny You Should Ask*, *Mish-Mash*, *All Over the Shop* and *Crosswits*, all of which I appeared on at one time or another?

The closest I came to game-show immortality was when I was asked to be one of the captains for the pilot of *Give Us a Clue*, a version of charades, or 'the game' as it was known when it was all the rage in the Fifties. I did the pilot, but by the time the series was commissioned I was in *A Bedful of Foreigners* with Terry in Bournemouth, so sadly I had to refuse the offer. The programme ran for several years, and there's no doubt that part of the reason for its success was Una Stubbs, who turned out to be an absolute natural for the show and was far better than I would have been. They asked me on as a guest quite a few times, which made up for the initial disappointment.

The radio panel game *Does the Team Think?* started up in the Fifties. The show was co-devised by Jimmy Edwards and affection-ately known by those who regularly appeared as *Stinks*. It ran for about twenty years, in which time I was the mystery guest twice – the one who sat behind the screen, out of sight of the studio audience, and had to be identified by answering daft questions in a disguised voice. I popped up on other evergreen radio shows like *The Petticoat Line*, *Sounds Familiar* and *Twenty Questions*, and I was also a regular panellist for three series of *Fair Deal*. This was, as the *Radio Times* billing said, 'a game for four hands, devised and shuffled by Ian Messiter'. I wonder if there was ever a panel game that this amaz-ingly clever fellow *didn't* dream up. He must have filled several volumes with his endless outpouring of questions. David Nixon was chairman, and on the panel were Willy Rushton, Patrick Moore . . . and June Whitfield. You chose a suit, each one representing a different subject and, as always, you were expected to embellish your answers to the questions with an amusing remark or anecdote. You also had to remember the cards already played, as in bridge. I studied the rules and was able to give some of the answers, but I wasn't too good at the amusing remarks. Patrick was a real knight in shining armour, and whenever he sensed I was teetering on the edge of a verbal abyss he chivalrously came to my rescue.

On *The Impressionists*, you had to answer questions in the manner of various famous people. I really enjoyed that. I had steadily acquired a rep company of voices over the years; people like Katherine Hepburn, Ingrid Bergman, Zsa Zsa Gabor, plus copper-bottomed support from Margaret Rutherford and Mrs Thatcher. I was in my element, and even managed to ad lib a little in character in a way I couldn't have done as just 'me'. *Punchline* was a show that really sorted the men from the boys, or rather it emphasized the yawning chasm that exists between Bob Monkhouse and ordinary mortals when it comes to ad libbing. The man is extraordinary. He routinely came up with about six alternatives for every tag, while the rest of us struggled to make the one we were kindly given sound spontaneous.

I was busily occupied with these assorted shows, and with Terry, throughout the Seventies, and I also paid flying visits to *The Navy Lark* (meeting Leslie Phillips again), *Whoops Baghdad* (with Frankie Howerd), *The Rag Trade* (with Miriam Karlin, Peter Jones and Reg Varney) and *The Goodies* (in which I was a Russian adventuress, swathed in white furs and pulled along in a troika). In *It Ain't Half Hot, Mum* we were in the Malayan jungle, which was actually a wood near Esher. As part of the plot, Michael Knowles and I were lying along the branch of a tree. We were waiting for our cue when we noticed that the other actors and crew were gradually disappearing. They left us there for about five minutes, while we wondered how on earth we could reach the ground from twenty feet up without a ladder, then David Croft and the others returned, grinning, bearing cups of tea and feigning great surprise that we were still up in the tree.

*

I had always wanted to take part in a costume drama. The only period acting I had done on television was in historical send-up sketches, so I was more than pleased when I was offered the part of Mrs Bonteen in *The Pallisers*. All actresses love dressing up. I like being laced into a corset, partly for the relief of having it *un*laced again afterwards. A corset gives one a completely different deportment. Some of those heavy, elaborate nineteenth-century costumes can make you feel as though you're driving a small vehicle rather than wearing a frock.

When John Cleese co-adapted and starred in a Chekhov short story, *Romance With a Double Bass*, I was his employer, the Duchess Tatiana. We filmed at Wilton House near Salisbury, and walking along the wide, elegant corridors inspired us to get into the period. I began to believe it really was my house. John was brilliant as a musician who, on his way to give a concert at my palace, takes a swim in the river and has his clothes stolen. He had only his double bass to cover his nakedness throughout the rest of the piece. It was the kind of embarrassing situation that John Cleese excels at, and the result was wonderfully funny.

I have since appeared in other television period dramas, *Tom Jones*, Catherine Cookson's *The Secret* and the film *Jude*, and there's no doubt that the costume governs the way you walk, stand and sit. In *The Secret*, my character was described as over-made-up and wearing a wig, and since wigs often feature in period drama it was felt that mine would have to be more obviously wig-like than anyone else's. When we came to film it, the other characters' hair looked relatively normal while I was stuck with a bright-red bird's nest perched on my head. One critic mentioned that we had rather overstated the point.

When the time came for me to start playing mums, grans and even a dying role or two, I didn't worry too much about tempus fugiting. I was never a great beauty – I think I amused more than I aroused – but I never minded that too much, and consequently I didn't feel the pressures that many glamorous actresses feel when they reach a certain age. I actually think my looks improved when I passed the forty milestone. By that time you know what suits you and what doesn't; you get better at concealing your worst features. And there's one great advantage to being short-sighted: when you look in the mirror you don't see the wrinkles.

By 1978 *Happy Ever After* had been running for four years. The writers John Chapman and Eric Merriman had produced no fewer than forty-two episodes, and John felt they had said all there was to say about the two characters and decided to call it a day. However, the viewing figures were still regularly topping 10 million, and the BBC pressed them to change their minds. They couldn't be persuaded, so other writers were commissioned to carry on where they left off. Eric in particular was unwilling to waive his rights in the format and a disagreement developed. The BBC's solution was to change our surname from Fletcher to Medford, move us to Purley, replace the other regular characters and retitle the show *Terry and June*. Losing Aunt Lucy was a great shame, because Beryl Cooke was so good and had become an integral part of the set-up. The new programme acquired new characters: Terry's overbearing boss, Sir Dennis, was played superbly by Reginald Marsh; and Terry's rival in the firm was Tim Barrett, with Rosemary Frankau as his wife, Beattie. Otherwise everything was as before, with our characters remaining the same. Terry was headstrong, spoiled and reckless, and June was patient, practical and always picking up the pieces.

Terry and June ran for a further sixty-five episodes, making it the seventh longest running sitcom on British TV. The majority of the scripts came from John Kane, an actor and comedy writer who had been nurtured by Terry, who always liked to help and encourage young people. John gave a most moving address at Terry's memorial.

As the series went on, people still refused to believe that Terry and I weren't married, and we were often amused by the way in which events in real life mirrored those in the series. I remember Tim becoming crosser and crosser, trying to undo one of those tiny cartons of UHT milk in a motorway service station and getting squirted in the process, just as Terry would have done in the show. We were on our way to the theatre once with our glad rags on, and as we were a little early, Tim pulled up at a garage to give the car a wash. It was one of those jet-wash things that you aim yourself and he steadily worked his way round to my side. Suddenly I got the full flow of water smack in the chops – I'd left my window slightly open, and since he'd turned the ignition off I couldn't shut it. I shouted but the noise of the water jet drowned my voice. I waved frantically at Tim, and he waved back while the water continued to drench me. My first reaction was fury, then I realized it was a classic *Terry and June* situation and made a note to tell the writer.

Mishaps and bits of domestic slapstick were always part of *Terry and June*. Terry was fearless when it came to stunts, and I can only remember him having a stand-in once, and that was when he had to be catapulted from the roof of a car into the river. Normally he would leap into whatever needed to be leaped into and endure whatever indignities the writers conceived for him, regarding it simply as part of the job. I remember him jumping into the river Wye when it was in full flood, and nearly being carried away into the Bristol Channel before someone hauled him out with a boat hook.

Terry had a restless energy, not unlike the character he played, and he was also extremely hard-working. Once he got an idea in his head he pursued it with furious tenacity. He had very high standards as far as work was concerned, but he was often not very good at explaining what he wanted. He was usually right, but we had to listen to an awful lot of waffling before he made his point. He was a very volatile character who said what he thought – not always popular in a profession with an above-average number of sensitive egos.

He certainly didn't hide his emotions and members of the cast were left in no doubt if he disapproved of their performance, consequently he got quite a reputation for being difficult to work with. I always got on well with him and we liked working together, but he couldn't resist picking on someone in the show and having a go at them. He never tried it with me; I think he knew I'd answer back. He was like a naughty boy really.

He was devoted to his wife and four daughters and drew great strength from their support. That he achieved so much and was able to drive himself so hard was largely due to the security of his life at home in Godalming.

In 1979 we were asked to team up again onstage; this time the play was Ray Cooney and John Chapman's farce *Not Now Darling*. It had already been a great success with Donald Sinden and Bernard Cribbins some years earlier. Terry was to be alongside Leslie Phillips, with me as Leslie's long-suffering secretary. It is a very funny play, one of the pair's best, and since it had already proved itself we were going to the Savoy Theatre without a pre-London tour.

We went into rehearsals in October, but after a few days Terry began to suffer from bad headaches and was unable to work. Ray Cooney was directing us and, since he had played the part before, he stood in at rehearsals, hoping that Terry would return after a few days. But the headaches got worse and the doctors finally diagnosed a cerebral aneurism – a swelling of an artery often caused by high blood pressure. It seems that many of us have minor aneurisms without even noticing it, but when they occur in certain places they can be dangerous, and that's what had happened to Terry. His chances of survival weren't very good, but he underwent a four-hour brain operation to repair the damage.

Tim and I were celebrating our twenty-fourth wedding anniversary on the day that Terry had his operation. I went to see him at the Atkinson Morley hospital and he was a poorly sight, with his head shaved and a great railway line of stitches running across his scalp. His sense of humour was intact, though, and one of the first things he said to me was, 'They had to open up my head to let some of the steam out.' Although he was able to joke, it was obviously going to be a very long recovery. He was light-headed for the first few days, and did things like phone Maggie in the middle of the night to suggest a family picnic, then his spirits sank and he became convinced that he never wanted to go near a television studio or theatre ever again. There was no way of telling whether he would recover his appetite for performing, or even if he would be strong enough to do so; we could only wait and see.

Ray Cooney opened the play in Terry's place, before Andrew Sachs, who learned the part in a week, took over from him. Terry's illness was a great worry, and I did wonder if we would ever work together again. I had failed to take into account his determination and tremendous powers of recovery. By April 1980 we were filming for another series of *Terry and June*.

Chapter Eleven

OLD BUT ENERGETIC

TERRY SAID THAT HIS ILLNESS HAD MELLOWED HIM: 'A LOT OF
the aggression has gone out of me. I was blustering and stupid,
now I'm just stupid,' he joked to one of the papers. But his energy
was undiminished and he worked as hard as ever on the new series,
following it up with a summer show and a pantomime. At the end of
the year we did a sketch on the *Royal Variety Show*; him and me in a
sack, fumbling about and emerging in each other's clothes. I felt
rather embarrassed having to do it in front of the Queen Mum, and
I don't suppose she enjoyed it much, either. There was no doubt that
Terry was back to his old self, and it was a great relief that the
partnership, which had at one point looked like being cut off in its
prime, was now firmly re-established.

Terry and I were quite different in temperament. He was an
extrovert who liked to be in control, whereas I'm more inclined to go
with the flow and let others take on the responsibilities. I also like to
keep my private life private, particularly when it comes to giving
interviews to newspapers and magazines, whereas Terry had a fatal
inability to keep things to himself, and he spoke to the press about
every aspect of his private life, including his relationship with
Maggie and his daughters' love lives, to their understandable

annoyance and embarrassment. It was probably a combination of naivety, painkillers and one too many glasses of wine, but it was surprising how easily he allowed himself to be taken in by certain journalists, who promised their post-interview chats would be strictly off the record.

Terry was also somewhat accident-prone. One bank holiday he was giving me a lift home from rehearsals in his pink Jaguar when we had one of the strangest motoring mishaps possible. Suddenly, out of an alleyway charged a pair of dray horses, still harnessed to their cart, which terrifyingly scraped along the side of Terry's car – referred to as *our* car in the newspaper reports. Luckily the horses were unhurt and came to a slithering halt in front of a taxi. The driver was white-faced when he saw a horse's nose on a level with his windscreen, but all was well and the horses returned to base unharmed. It was a mystery why they acted as they did – *Terry and June* wasn't even on the air at the time!

Maggie said Terry had as many lives as the proverbial cat. There was a scar on his nose from the night he fell asleep at the wheel on the Edgware Road, and on another occasion he drove over the edge of a transporter bridge into thin air and landed in a safety net several feet below. Life with Terry can never have been dull. Maggie had a career of her own as a dancer, and later as a teacher at the Guildford School of Acting. She was also the co-author of Terry's popular song 'My Brother'.

Terry and June took up more of our time, often with two series a year and a Christmas special. Terry also committed himself to numerous theatre tours and pantos. Then, only three years after making a complete recovery from his operation, he was beset by further health problems. He began to feel pain in his hands and neck but kept quiet about it, hoping it would go away, but of course it didn't, and by the time we came to do a panto together at Bath in 1985, the condition had got so bad that he'd lost most of the feeling in his left hand and foot, and the numbness was spreading. He sometimes had to wear a surgical collar and was on painkillers for most of the time.

The part of the dame, especially the way Terry played it, was a very exhausting one. His pièce de résistance was a wildly energetic striptease, with which he closed the first half. I remember seeing him in his dressing room in obvious pain while his two dressers put him into the dozens of layers of costume necessary for his strip routine to work. He was clearly overworking, and quite early in the run his voice suddenly disappeared, and his understudy had to go on at short notice.

The understudy was a Cambridge graduate whom Terry had personally cast after seeing him in a Footlights revue just a few months earlier. His name was Christopher Luscombe. He went on to work at the Royal Shakespeare Company, and to devise and perform in *The Shakespeare Revue*, but then he was very new to the business. He was absolutely terrific, knew every line and deserved a medal for putting up with Terry's no doubt well-meant advice on how to play the part.

Terry loved teaching, and between shows he'd invite the dancers into his dressing room and advise them how to act. They lapped it up, but it didn't have quite the same effect when he tried giving a few nuggets of wisdom to experienced actors.

He recovered his voice and returned to the cast. We spent an evening with Jean and Leslie Crowther, who had moved down to Bath by then, during which Terry moaned on to Leslie about what he saw as the production's shortcomings. Eventually Leslie could contain his boredom no longer and said quietly, 'Well, it's no good telling me. I've got nothing to do with it.' That took the wind out of Terry's sails and the subject was dropped.

Terry was determined to fulfil his many commitments, including another series of *Terry and June*, in spite of his deteriorating health. The popularity of the show was as great as ever, but by now it was receiving a succession of broadsides, not just from the critics but from within the profession itself. Alternative comedy had arrived, and *Terry and June* became the focus for all that the newcomers disliked about so-called middle-class Middle England. The powers that be at the Beeb didn't know whether to take the show off and appease the younger critics, producers and comedians who were calling for our heads, or to keep it going for those millions of viewers who did not yet, and never would, appreciate alternative comedy. In 1987 the BBC decided to bow to critical pressure and announced the end of *Terry and June*. We thought that was that, but then the repeat showing of the final series attracted good viewing figures. This provoked a rethink, and the BBC asked the writer, John Kane, to come up with another six episodes. Since John had just been told his services were no longer required, and as he was an actor, he had sensibly accepted a job with the Royal Shakespeare Company, so was unavailable. He said he would be happy to write the scripts when his acting commitment ended, but the BBC wanted them immediately or not at all. So that, finally, was the end of it. A shame, but then 106 episodes wasn't a bad run.

Middle-class Middle England may not be fashionable but writers, actors and producers ignore it at their peril, because that's where the bulk of the audience is located. 'But we need to appeal to the younger viewers,' is the cry from the schedulers, so more and more programmes are aimed at the under-twenty-five-year-old age group. Although humour is now more PC it's much more vicious than in my early days. If explicit language isn't used within the first few minutes the show is deemed old-fashioned. The ladettes and extremists hold sway in entertainment at the moment, but a less in-your-face kind of comedy may return one of these days. The successful repeats of shows like *Dad's Army*, *The Good Life*, *The Rise and Fall of Reginald Perrin* and the current *As Time Goes By* indicate that gentler humour is still appreciated by many viewers. I'm not suggesting a return to the anyone-for-tennis school of light comedy, or that the young should not be catered for, but television needs to have a broad appeal. After all, the grey constituency increases every year.

Television bosses also seem to have got stuck on the idea that everyone wants to see their own lives on the screen, that programmes should involve the public, either playing games or revealing intimate details about themselves for the proverbial fifteen minutes of fame. There is a place for that, but audiences also like to be taken out of themselves. No-one will want to watch a repeated docusoap in ten years' time, but a well-made comedy series, like *Porridge*, can go on doing the rounds for decades.

Alternative comedy has itself passed out of fashion now and the younger elements of the movement have either faded away or become slightly older and mellower. Many have edged over into the middle of the road to claim the very same territory that *Terry and June* occupied before they got rid of us. I have worked with many of the younger generation of comedians and have found them utterly charming and thoroughly professional, not much different, in fact, from their predecessors, though I can't say I've always found their material to my taste, especially the obsession with bodily functions. In a way I have been working with alternative comedians all my life, people who want to try something new to make others laugh.

Terry and June acquired a reputation for cosiness, which it didn't really deserve. The scripts were certainly a lot sharper than has been claimed – maybe it was our fault. *Happy Ever After* and *Terry and June* kept us going for thirteen years, so they can't have been all that bad. UK Gold and Granada Plus have both repeated *Terry and June* so there's still an audience for that kind of humour, as well as the more antagonistic current style.

Not long ago someone sent me this cutting from the lonely-hearts section of a local paper:

Terry seeks sexy June. East London only.

The show is remembered, apparently, and not just in the home counties. I recently discovered that Reading Football Club supporters have adopted the *Terry and June* signature tune as their chant when they score!

The early Eighties saw a number of changes in our domestic lives. Muff was no longer able to take part in her amateur productions and really needed to be looked after. The stable block we had converted for her was too much to manage, even with help. Tim's stepmother, Irene, ran a nursing home in West Sussex and Muff went for a trial stay. She liked it and eventually moved in, but would still rather have overlooked Piccadilly Circus than the beautiful grounds and trees.

With her main interest in life gone, she sadly lost the will to live, and in 1982 she died, at the age of eighty-seven.

It's perhaps only when you lose a member of your family that you realize what a great influence they've been on your life. The hours my dear mum spent listening to my poetry readings, monologues and Shakespeare, and attending my dancing lessons, noting every step in that exercise book, always in bold print:

STAND FEET TOGETHER, LEFT FOOT TO SIDE, THEN FEET TOGETHER, JUMP FEET APART, ARMS FIFTH POSITION, JUMP FEET TOGETHER, ARMS DOWN.

She'd write down a whole dance routine so that she could help me remember the steps, and then take me through them. She accompanied me to endless competitions and dancing displays. She was always encouraging, and if it hadn't been for her I might never have embarked on the career that has served me so well. I owe her so much and loved her dearly.

Muff lived next door to us for many years and I still miss her. But she had a long life, a successful marriage, two children she was proud of and, though she may not have achieved the career she craved in her youth, her many years in amateur theatre were very fulfilling. She was thrilled to receive a medal from the National Operatic and Dramatic Association in 1973 for her contribution to amateur theatre over fifty years. There's no doubt I fulfilled her dreams. I know she was proud of me and enjoyed being part of my success.

Life regenerates itself, and in the year of Muff's death her granddaughter Suzy graduated from Birmingham University with a 2:1 in drama and took her first steps towards a career as a professional actress by appearing at the Edinburgh Festival. Muff would have been as proud to see her as I was, though perhaps a little bewildered as Suzy played Mosca, a part usually played by a man, in a fringe production of *Volpone* – shades of her mum and Peter Quince in *A Midsummer Night's Dream*. However, she was extremely good and clearly talented enough to have a future.

Coming from such a background, I suppose it was likely that Suzy would pursue a theatrical career. We neither encouraged nor discouraged her ambition to be an actress, and it perhaps wasn't so much an *ambition* but, like me, an *assumption* that she would end up onstage. She went to dancing classes, as I had done, but she was more gifted academically than her mum, and definitely more diligent. She took part in school plays and entertainments while at the same time achieving good O and A-level grades. I was determined not to be a theatrical mum, and Tim and I insisted that she should complete her education as a theatrical career cannot be guaranteed. My advice to would-be actors is, finish your education or take a computer course, you never know, it may come in handy when you're 'resting'. Actors' children are usually very employable as they are well aware of the less glamorous side of the business and what a precarious existence it is, however talented they may be.

Suzy's first professional engagement was, like mine, assistant stage managing in the West End. In 1943 I was in *Time and the Conways* at RADA, and later in rep at Wolverhampton. In 1983 Suzy understudied the leading role in the Chichester Festival Theatre production. At the dress rehearsal, she took over from Alexandra Bastedo who had suddenly fallen ill. Suzy had done her homework and knew the part well, and she played all the previews. We went to see her and she was a great success. Alexandra recovered in time for the opening night, and Suzy went back to the ranks of the small-part players, but her performance was much appreciated and her status in the company was given a great boost. As she said, 'Now at least they know my name.' Shortly after she went into the comedy *Daisy Pulls it Off* in the West End. She recently appeared at the Stephen Joseph Theatre in Scarborough, and at the time of writing is performing in Alan Ayckbourn's plays *House* and *Garden*, directed by the author at the Royal National Theatre.

Suzy has made her own way in her career, in spite of the hazard of having a well-known mum. Like most parents, what we want for her is good health and a happy and fulfilling life. I'll no doubt embarrass her by saying she is our pride and joy, and we love her to bits.

*

In 1982 I was offered *Jack and the Beanstalk* at Chichester. It was thirty-five years since I'd done my first pantomime with Wilfred Pickles in Leeds; in 1947 I was Cinderella, this time I was to be the Fairy. Instead of the six-month, twice-nightly sentence that was a Laidler panto, *Jack and the Beanstalk* was scheduled to run for a mere eight weeks, and instead of sub-zero digs I was able to stay in a nice warm flat in Chichester. I jumped at the chance to work with our dear friend and dog-racing companion Frankie Howerd. I was so looking forward to seeing him again, and when I arrived for the first morning's rehearsal to be greeted with the words 'Oh Gawd, it's her!' I knew we'd started off on the right foot.

At the Chichester Theatre the audience is on three sides of the stage, which makes scene changes slightly problematic, especially for a panto which needs a lot of sets. Finlay James designed a giant story book, with each page representing a different scene, and the huge pages were turned over by the performers as the plot unfolded. The Fairy and the Giant's henchman, Aubrey Woods, appeared from different places all around the theatre, surprising the audience. We emerged from the under-stage 'voms' – the vomitorium is the passage in an amphitheatre leading to or from the seats – and popped up on the balconies, threatening each other from either side. Traditionally, fairies always enter stage right and baddies stage left. At Chichester we had very good exercise, rushing up and down the stairs to reach our different vantage points – great for pantomime, but I prefer a proscenium arch and a curtain which rises to reveal the set and actors; I want to see their faces and their reactions rather than their backs.

I was the Vegetable Fairy but I didn't have a sad-looking leek for a wand, or a costume covered in rotting veg. I believe that, for the younger members of the audience, the fairy is the magic of the pantomime, and I have always tried to look as fairylike as possible – to start with anyway.

It was a pleasure working with Frank again. He really enjoyed himself and said it was one of the happiest pantos he'd ever been in. We sang a number which was a hit for Sting, 'Spread a Little Happiness', which was exactly what Frank did every time he went onstage. He really was marvellous with a live audience. I remember seeing him do his act on a Sunday night at Poole; he probably did about an hour, and I don't think I've ever seen an audience so enthralled by one performer. It was extraordinary for someone who, if you think about it, seldom actually told a joke. He got most of his laughs from his harassed, gossipy manner. In panto, of course, jokes are a vital element, but they are usually deliberately corny jokes, and this gave Frank plenty of scope to grumble about the material and berate both the audience and the rest of the cast in his inimitable way.

We went to stay with Frank in Somerset, shortly after he'd had an operation on his leg that made walking difficult. Like Terry, he was determined to recover. We would drive right onto the beach at Weston-Super-Mare and Frank would walk on his own, with Rabbit chasing after him. Tim and I followed in the car until Frank decided to call it a day, and then we drove home.

Frank sometimes rehearsed his act out loud on his lone walks along the beach – he would declaim in a field, surrounded by an audience of cows; or in a graveyard; or in his local church, where he could project his voice to the imaginary audience without disturbing anyone, and perfect his performance.

I was flattered and thrilled to be invited to play a small part in the television biography of Frank entitled *Please Yourselves*. He and I were seated in the Electric Cinema in Portobello Road watching the end of that wonderful weepy *Now Voyager* with Bette Davis and Paul Henreid. It led us into a conversation – well, I was listening, Frank was expounding – about comedy, and how different things made different people laugh. There are no rules; one man's meat is another man's poison. We came to the conclusion that most comics are neurotic and release their neuroses through their work.

Frank went through a very low time in the late Fifties and early Sixties. He said that no-one wanted him; he was unemployed, unfashionable and lost his nerve. He was very fond of his mother, and when she died he was devastated, and it made him realize that the important things in life are relationships and friendships. Suddenly people mattered more than his failing career. He said his attitude changed and, sure enough, a few days later he was asked to perform at the Establishment Club. The story goes that Frank followed the controversial American comic Lenny Bruce into the Establishment, and began his act with the words, 'If you're expecting this to be like last week, you can all **** off home now.' That led to an appearance on *That Was the Week That Was*, and his career took off again from there.

My next panto was *Dick Whittington* at Richmond the following year. It was to prove another turning point in my career. The experience ranks with getting the call to audition for *Take It From Here* and being invited to meet Terry Scott for the first time; the reason being that the show's star was a skinny feller called Roy Hudd.

I was the Fairy once more. The script was by John Morley, a master of pantomime scripts, and the strong cast ensured the show was a success. Honor Blackman was a very scary Queen Rat; we had the Red Shadow himself, John Hanson, Anthea Askey and her father's partner for so many years, Stinker Murdoch – partner in the original sense, that is.

Anthea donned a cat-skin most effectively, and she and I sang a song together. The Fairy and the Cat? Well, anything can happen in panto, and someone has to perform in front of the tabs while they change the scenery behind – sometimes not too quietly, either. I first met Anthea during her dad's series *Arthur's Treasured Volumes*, and I got to know her well through the panto. We shared a great many laughs backstage, and a few onstage, too. She manoeuvred her cat's tail magnificently during our little dance, but I nearly tripped over it a few times, which caused several unfairylike reactions.

Anthea died last year after a long battle against cancer. She always sounded so cheerful on the phone, despite being in great pain. She was lovingly cared for by her partner, Will Fyffe Junior, right to the end. Like her dad she was always the life and soul of the party and I miss her cheery face a great deal.

Roy Hudd is an expert on the art of pantomime. He is passionate about sticking to tradition and not filling the stage with TV celebrities who are unfamiliar with the medium. One thing I loved about that *Dick Whittington* panto was that after the who's-best walk-down we would do a rhyming couplet, referring to a particular group or a coachload in the audience. The comic is always given a list of firms or birthdays before the start of the show, and Roy and I would spend the interval making up a silly bit of doggerel for the finale. One night, towards the end of the run, we met as usual and I found Roy preoccupied. He said he was having problems with his radio show, *The News Huddlines*. Alison Steadman, who had been a regular member of the cast, along with Chris Emmett and Roy, had been offered a film she couldn't afford to turn down, so they were without a female. Janet Brown, who had also done the show, was unavailable, and Roy said they were getting desperate.

'We've tried *everyone*,' he said.

'Well, you haven't tried me,' I said.

'No, but it's a topical show, we need someone who can do impressions; Mrs Thatcher and that sort of thing.'

'Oh, I see.'

The climax of the panto was a duel to the death between Queen Rat and Dick. The fight was refereed, for reasons best known to the author, by Roy as Idle Jack and me as Fairy Bow Bells. At the next matinée, when the Fairy gave her instructions, they were delivered in my best Maggie Thatcher voice:

> Go to your corners – oh, isn't this exciting!
> And when you hear the bell, you come out fighting!

It raised quite a laugh, and during it Roy said, 'You've got the job.' And from then on, Mrs Thatcher organized the fight.

He was as good as his word and a few weeks later I was in the next edition of *The News Huddlines*. There I've stayed ever since. It has been one of the happiest associations of my career.

Mrs T became a regular, along with some other old favourites from my repertoire. The *Huddlines* brought back fond memories of *Take It From Here*, especially as, for years, we recorded it at our favourite Paris Studio. I hadn't used Eth's voice since *TIFH*, but when John Major came to power I played Norma Major as Eth, starting each sketch with, 'Ooh, John!'

It has been such a pleasure working with Roy and Chris Emmett over the years, and we all enjoy it so much that other work is turned down if it interferes with the twice-yearly *Huddlines*. So far, accommodating directors have arranged filming and rehearsal dates to avoid our recording days, though Roy did lose the chance to do a play at the National one year because it clashed with his favourite Thursday job. Roy is a fine actor, as casting directors have realized recently; he is also an authority on music hall. He has written books and regularly scripts pantomimes, as well as doing his one-man show, which is highly entertaining. His enthusiasm is inspiring. He is magnificent and holds the whole show together.

Roy and his wife Debbie have become good friends of ours. Roy has a fund of stories – with his permission I have borrowed one or two for this book – and we know we're in for a good laugh when we spend time together. He devotes a lot of time to charity, especially the Grand Order of Water Rats, and as I write he has just been elected King Rat for the second time – a great honour, as the past incumbents include Bud Flanagan, Will Hay, Little Tich and the great Dan Leno. He really deserves a knighthood. Debbie works hard for the Lady Ratlings, and has been their Queen. It would be wonderful to greet them as Sir Roy and Lady Debbie.

Chris Emmett is an excellent impressionist and a master of accents; he's also a great success as the pantomime dame. Peter Moss and The Huddliners provide the music and occasional noises off. The cast is completed by our announcer, Richard Clegg, who has been with the *Huddlines* for all of its twenty-five years. Our producers down the years have included some distinguished names, among them Simon Brett, John Lloyd, Jonathan James-Moore, Dirk Maggs, Alan Nixon, Richard Wilson, Phil Bowker, Paul Spencer, Mark Robson, Steve Dogherty and currently Carol Smith.

The show's script team is composed of commissioned writers and those who send material in on spec. If you count them all together it has probably run to three figures over the years, but some of the more notable contributors have been Tony Hare, Peter Hickey,

Michael Dines, Andy Hamilton, Mike Coleman, Malcolm Williamson, Martin Booth, Stuart Silver, Alan Whiting and the two brilliant writers who provide our musical parodies, Jeremy Browne and Richard Quick. These and countless others have ensured the show is sharp and topical. There is the occasional lavatorial joke that I'm not mad about but boys will be boys.

I was given the freedom of the City of London some years ago and was required to swear an oath of allegiance to the Crown. Thanks to the aforementioned funsters, I break my oath just about every time I record an edition of the *Huddlines*. Next time I'm driving my sheep over London Bridge I might well be stopped, but then, that's the price you sometimes have to pay for getting a laugh.

I'm not sure whether the writers would be pleased to know this or not, but sometimes I have been asked if we make it up as we go along, because it sounds so spontaneous. There is a little more to it than that. We meet at Broadcasting House at 10 a.m. in the rehearsal room, catch up on each other's activities for the past week, have a coffee and, at about ten thirty, our producer Carol suggests we read the script. Some of the characters we have done many times, so the political sketches or the 'royals' and the 'wrinklies' are already in our repertoire. Mine are more caricatures than impersonations, and if I'm really stuck I know I can get helpful suggestions from Chris, Roy or Carol. I can get by with a few accents, but not 'New-*cassel*', which, of course, the writers keep trying to make me do, in much the same spirit of malevolent mischief that Muir and Norden wrote a Red Indian character for Jimmy Edwards. When I went up to the north-east to film Catherine Cookson's *The Secret*, I heard the accent all around me, and after I returned, I went to Roy and said, 'Ah've bin ter New-*cassel* on a tray-un.' He and Chris Emmett just roared with laughter and said, 'Don't bother.'

Having read through and thrown out the odd sketch or 'quickie', we rehearse the songs, then the whole half-hour 'on mike', including sound effects. The show is then recorded at 1 p.m., or thereabouts, in front of an audience. If there are any retakes, we do those and are usually finished by 2 p.m. I love the immediacy of it. There isn't a lot of time to think about the characters; you just hope they come off the page and tell you who they are.

The News Huddlines became the longest-running radio comedy show when it overtook *The Navy Lark* in 1998. In October 2000 it had been on air for twenty-five years and is still going strong at the time of writing. The previous record holder was *Take It From Here*, so perhaps I should put an ad in *The Stage*: 'Long runs guaranteed, all accents attempted (except Newcastle).'

One morning in the summer of 1985 I opened a letter from Downing Street. Would I accept an MBE? I had no idea who had suggested it – I rather imagined a roomful of ladies in hats and floral frocks, deliberating over tea and fancies – but I was thrilled. The next day I received a phone call from Downing Street.

'Miss Whitfield, have you recently received a letter offering you the MBE?'

'Yes.'

'We're afraid there's been a mistake.'

Oh dear, I thought. They must have heard the royals being sent up on the *Huddlines* and had second thoughts. Oh well, it was nice while it lasted.

'Would you be prepared to accept an OBE instead?'

It was no doubt very ignorant of me, but I didn't know whether an OBE ranked above or below an MBE, so after my initial relief I wasn't sure whether to, as it were, stick or twist. I urgently whispered to Tim, who was standing by the phone. He told me to accept, which I did. They said they'd send a formal letter of acceptance accordingly, and there the conversation ended.

I looked at the letter again and saw the date on which I was to present myself at the Palace. It was 10 November; a recording day for *Terry and June*. Tim suggested I get in touch to see if the investiture date could be changed so, knowing it was my only hope, I phoned Downing Street. They were charming. 'No problem at all,' they said, and offered me 10 December. I agreed and flew to the post office with the written confirmation before they had time to change their minds again. A couple of days later I received another call asking if I could change to 12 December. I was convinced my dear mum had altered the date; 12 December was her birthday.

After the initial reaction of 'Why me?' and 'It's fantastic!' my next thought was, 'What do I wear?' I knew a hat was de rigueur, but I seldom wear one, so that was the first hurdle. I must have bought three outfits before deciding none was right for the occasion, and finally I settled on having one made; at least it was an excuse to stock up the wardrobe. On the great day, we set off with Barbara Welford – I couldn't do her out of a trip to the palace – and she loved every minute of it. Tim and Suzy were in loyal attendance. On arrival at Buckingham Palace a sniffer dog gave Barbara's Granada the once over, then we were escorted in different directions: Tim and Suzy to the ballroom and me to the adjoining long gallery to be briefed on the procedure, and to have a bar-pin attached so the gong could simply be hooked on it at the appropriate moment. An equerry told us the drill: 'When your name is called, move towards the dais, bow/curtsy, take four paces forward, receive the honour, shake hands, four paces back, bow/curtsy, then turn and move on, and take your place in the ballroom.' The slightly awkward moment, of course, is knowing when the brief chat with the Queen is over, but Her Majesty is an expert and a barely perceptible pressure of her hand sends you gently into your four backward paces. You are on your way, and thankful you managed to bow/curtsy without falling over.

There are, of course, a great many awards to be handed out, and to make the time pass, a military band plays 'songs from the shows', and I was amused to find myself sitting in the ballroom at Buckingham Palace listening to 'If I Were a Rich Man'. I looked for Tim and Suzy, but couldn't see them. They had found a vantage point on raised seats at the rear of the ballroom and had a splendid view of it all.

To top it off, we were invited to lunch by an old friend, Fergus Montgomery – now Sir Fergus Montgomery MP – who entertained us in a private dining room at the House of Commons. It was altogether an unforgettable day and I felt very honoured. At the end of it all I kicked my shoes off, slumped into an armchair and decided that the letters of the award stood for Old But Energetic.

Chapter Twelve

BACK ON THE BOARDS

S IMON CALLOW WROTE IN HIS BOOK ON ACTING THAT WHEN HE IS in a play he feels as though there is a voice in the back of his mind from the moment he wakes up saying, 'Show tonight.' I absolutely agree. Even though you may not have to set off for work until six o'clock in the evening, the play somehow looms over you throughout the day, placing a subtle restraint on your movements and making you look at your watch more often than usual. I was talking to Donald Sinden at a party once, and I happened to mention these and one or two other tiring disadvantages of working in the theatre – we were in a play together at the time. Sensing a certain lack of sympathy, I changed tack and said, 'But you like it, don't you, Donald.'

'What else would I do in the evenings?' he said.

There was a time when we actors had no choice but to work in the theatre, but since the advent of radio and television we have all become a little spoilt by only having to give a single performance, plus a few more for retakes. Leading actors are unwilling to commit themselves to long runs these days. Where a management once expected a year's commitment to a play as a matter of course, now they are lucky if a star agrees to three months, with the honourable exception of Sir Donald Sinden, of course. Noël Coward turned down the leading role in the original production of *The King and I* because he couldn't face giving what might be several hundred performances. The repetitive nature of the work over a long period of time can affect even the most robust constitutions.

However, the theatre is where it all began, and sometimes it's hard to resist the challenge of facing a live audience and being in control of the situation for once, rather than at the mercy of technology, as is often the case in television and films. Once Suzy had grown up I could see no reason why, providing the scheduled run wasn't too long, I shouldn't take on the occasional play and panto season.

There is no doubt that if you are in a good play with an appreciative audience, it's a very satisfying experience. Every performance is different; one time there'll be a big laugh, at other times nothing. You look for excuses like, 'Of course, they were all foreigners' or 'Something must have distracted them', but finally, you have to admit you probably didn't time the line very well. Live audiences certainly keep you on your toes. Once the show starts you are swept along by the audience and your fellow actors and it's exciting.

When I was asked to play Mrs Malaprop in Sheridan's *The Rivals* in 1986, I couldn't wait to utter all her convoluted words. The tricky bit was stopping myself thinking of the number of actresses who had previously taken on the role, and, as usual, I could think of a good half-dozen who would have done it better than I. But I nevertheless took it on, and had a great time, especially as Suzy was in the cast, too. It was lovely to be able to spend more time together – even though we hardly ever coincided onstage.

The Rivals was scheduled for a short three-week run – excellent! – then we were invited to add three more at Windsor. I thoroughly enjoyed the six weeks, but enough was enough, and when they decided to remount the tour some time later I declined. Suzy stayed and was promoted to one of the leading roles, in which she was excellent.

Oscar Wilde was arguably the greatest writer of comedies of

manners, and his play about political scandal, *An Ideal Husband*, has recently come to rival *The Importance of Being Earnest* as his most popular work – not surprisingly, perhaps, as its plot hinges on a case of 'insider dealing'. When the Chichester Festival Theatre mounted a production of *An Ideal Husband*, with Joanna Lumley, Lucy Fleming and Clive Francis, I was asked to join the cast. We think of Wilde as the most erudite of wits, but when the play was first produced it received some damning reviews, notably from the august critic Clement Scott, who pronounced that, 'Cleverness nowadays is nothing but elaborate contradiction, and the man or woman who can say that black is white or white is black in a fanciful fashion is considered a genius.' But the audience, which included the heir to the throne and many leading political figures of the day, cheered the play's anti-puritan attitude.

Our production was to have been directed by Ken Ives, a man with a distinguished television record, but unfortunately, as rehearsals progressed, Joanna and Lucy didn't quite see eye to eye with him. Ken withdrew and Tony Britton stepped in to replace him. As well as being a fine director, Tony is, of course, a superb actor, well-known for his work in the theatre, and television series like *Don't Wait Up*. It is a bonus when your director is also an actor, and Tony did a thoroughly good job, keeping a firm hand on the tiller through rehearsals, though thankfully not driving us quite as hard as the author drove the original cast – Wilde made them all rehearse on Christmas Day! Tony's main note to his cast was 'Find the tune of the text!' I understood what he meant. All spoken words have a tune; accents have a tune. If you can hear and reproduce it you're halfway there.

I played Lady Markby – a fashion victim of a certain age, a part played with notable success by Dame Irene Vanbrugh the year before I worked with her. Lady Markby is fun to play because she only appears in a few scenes, delivers some wonderful lines, then vanishes – rather like Mother in *Absolutely Fabulous*! Of all her idiotic theories, my favourite is this:

I have observed that the Season, as it goes on, produces a kind of softening of the brain. However, I think it is better than high intellectual pressure. That is the most unbecoming thing there is. It makes the noses of the young girls so particularly large. And there is nothing so difficult to marry as a large nose; men don't like them.

There was one guaranteed unplanned laugh at each performance. Joanna and I made an entrance together through double doors; Jo looking tall and gorgeous, with my round five-foot nothing standing next to her, dressed in purple velvet. We were framed in the doorway for a moment and could detect a titter from the audience at the incongruous sight. Mutt and Jeff had arrived.

Suzy was in the previous season at Chichester and was understudying in *The Sleeping Prince*, starring Omar Sharif. Tim and I happened to be seeing the show on the night he gave a party, and he very kindly invited us. It was in the garden of the house he was renting. There were fairy lights everywhere, trestle-tables groaning with food and gentle music wafting on the breeze. It was a beautiful evening and everyone was having a very jolly time. Gradually we became aware of a rather drunken female – not a member of the company, I hasten to add. Apparently she had been pestering Omar Sharif at the stage door for some time and had gatecrashed the party through the garden. He politely asked her to leave, to no avail, and eventually he frogmarched her out of the garden gate and bolted it, but not before she had struggled and managed to overturn a trestle-table that had just been laden with the puds. We all helped to clear up the mess and the party continued into the small hours, but I'm sure Omar was mortified, and furious that the lady in question had nearly ruined his party. Not at all what one would expect in Chichester.

Chichester was renowned for attracting star names, and it was a real coup for the theatre when they persuaded José Ferrer to appear in Christopher Fry's translation of Anouilh's *Ring Round the Moon*. A Hollywood veteran of over fifty films, including *Cyrano de Bergerac* for which he won an Oscar, he was a most interesting man and a charismatic actor; when he walked onto the stage, all eyes were focused on him.

In *Ring Round the Moon* I played the ambitious mother who is an embarrassment to her daughter and everyone else. Our director,

Elijah Moshinsky, wanted me to play the character as though she was jealous of her daughter's success. I thought Mother was just determined to get her girl into society, and in so doing jump on the bandwagon herself, which I felt gave more opportunity to bring out the humour in the role.

Leading the cast was Googie Withers. As well as being a brilliant actress, she is an expert needlewoman and is never idle during breaks between entrances. She is always 'tatting', and produces magnificent embroidery and petit point. It's very impressive and makes me feel rather guilty when I'm sitting around chatting or doing the crossword.

Christopher Fry successfully adapted a number of French plays during the Fifties. He lives not far from Chichester, in the same village as John Gale, who was the theatre's popular artistic director at the time and instigator of the Minerva Complex, which has proved so popular. He is no longer officially connected with the theatre, but is always well informed about what is appearing there. He and his wife, Lisel, live in West Sussex, and we have met Christopher at their house on several occasions. Christopher is in his nineties, still as bright as a button and giving lectures. I was thrilled when he said he approved of my portrayal of Mother.

Michael Denison added his unique touch to the play. His character was described as 'a crumbling butler', but in the final scene of the piece – an elaborate ball – he was anything but crumbly. Michael was an absolutely terrific dancer. Our nightly whirl round the stage was the highlight of my evening. He is, sadly, no longer with us, but he was a true servant of the British theatre, and his fifty-nine-year marriage to Dulcie Gray was one of the great theatrical partnerships of the last century. They met at drama school in the Thirties and were the toast of Broadway as recently as 1996, when they appeared together in Peter Hall's production of *An Ideal Husband*. It was at a party at the Denisons' house that Donald Sinden made the remark about needing to be in a play in order to lend some purpose to his evenings.

As it happened, Donald and I spent a great many evenings together. We appeared in a comedy thriller entitled *Over My Dead*

Body, which came to the West End in 1989 after a brief pre-London try-out. Donald, Frank Middlemass and I played a trio of has-been thriller writers who planned a real murder as a means of getting themselves back into the public eye. Needless to say, the crime was amusingly bungled. The public liked it and we enjoyed a respectable run at the Savoy.

I couldn't resist the chance to work with two actors I admire as much as Donald and Frank. I have an appalling memory for names, sometimes even faces, but visitors to Donald's dressing room after the show were always greeted like old friends. He made them so welcome. Occasionally I would join him and be vaguely introduced. 'I'd like you to meet my very good friends. You know June, of course.' When they'd gone he would say, 'Do you know who they were? Because I don't.' Donald was my friend for ever after that.

When we reached London, I was asked if I had any objection to having a male dresser assigned to me. 'None at all,' I said, and was introduced to someone who turned out to be a wonderfully efficient and eccentric character, Charles Routledge. He was neat as a pin and a snappy dresser, and had a reddish-brown rug on his head. He informed me that he always dressed Dame Diana Rigg but, as she didn't require his services, he was free.

I said, 'I'm sorry, Charles, this must be a bit of a come-down for you, then.'

'Ah well, you can't win 'em all,' he said, busying himself about the dressing room. We got on extremely well. He was in his seventies, but he ran up and down about fifty stairs to wardrobe like a two-year-old. I believe he continued to work on into his eighties. Diana gave him an eightieth birthday party, to which I was invited but was most upset because I was unable to attend as I was working. Charles was unique; professional, kind and helpful, with a wicked sense of humour. The definitive dresser. Every night, after the performance was over, I passed from the tender care of one eccentric to another, as, waiting for me outside in a large Granada, head barely visible above the dashboard, was the indefatigable Barbara Welford.

The opening night at the Savoy was enlivened by the appearance in the stalls of Fergie – Duchess of York – who attracted a great deal of attention from all parts of the house. At the cast party afterwards in the bar, we were discussing the audience reaction, and Fergie's presence, when the lady in charge of the bar succinctly summed up the situation, saying, 'You should never split yer focus on a first night.'

Galas or benefit nights where the celebs in the audience way outnumber those onstage have always been a feature of the London theatre scene. Usually the purpose is to raise money or celebrate something, and I have taken part in quite a number of them over the years. There was a star-studded tribute to Terence Rattigan on his seventieth birthday, in which Celia Johnson and Trevor Howard did a scene from *Separate Tables*, and an even more glamorous one was Noël Coward's seventieth birthday gala at Drury Lane, which featured contributions from just about everyone who had ever worked with him. I was roped in, along with Hy Hazell, Avril Angers and Stella Moray, to sing 'That Is the End of the News'. And in 1987 I was involved with another charity one-night stand, which featured a play written by the Master in 1926.

Semi Monde is probably the least-known of Coward's plays. It is certainly the least produced. There was a production of it at Glasgow, featuring a youthful Pierce Brosnan, but there was no London production until Tim Luscombe, brother of Chris, revived it for a single performance no less than sixty years after it was written.

The action of the play takes place at the Ritz Hotel in Paris, and is a typically Coward-like picture of shallow, spoilt people falling in and out of love with each other over a period of several years. It's a sort of spiced-up *Grand Hotel*. In fact, the enormous success of *Grand Hotel* a few years later was one reason why the play was quietly forgotten. Another reason was that it contained fifty-nine characters and enough male and female gay relationships to give the Lord Chamberlain a seizure.

Tim Luscombe assembled a star-studded cast for its London première, including Patricia Hodge, Sheila Gish, Judi Dench, Michael and Finty Williams, and anyone who was anyone, darling –

some playing walk-on parts. Sheila Gish had to drop out at the last minute and, in desperation, Tim asked me to come to the rescue. It wasn't exactly typecasting, but I enjoyed playing the somewhat loose rich woman who cheats on her husband by having an affair with a dubious Russian émigré, played by my old mate Lionel Blair; you can imagine the fun he had with that character, complete with Russian accent via most of Europe.

We rehearsed for a few days then gave a staged reading of the play at the Royalty Theatre. It was quite an achievement just getting the enormous cast together. No management could have afforded to produce it, which is a pity as scandal at the Ritz in Paris was hot news not so long ago. Coward is never out of fashion for long.

The recent hundredth anniversary of the Master's birth sparked off renewed interest in his work. There were many tributes to him, including one on Radio 2, in which I participated. I was asked to read a speech given by Noël to the troops during the war. It was a very good speech, but a strange choice for a woman to deliver – I had rather fancied singing 'Don't Put Your Daughter on the Stage, Mrs Worthington'.

I have kept in touch with Graham Payn since *Ace of Clubs* days, through Christmas cards and the odd phone call, and a few years ago we stayed with him in Switzerland, in the house he shared with Noël for the last fourteen years of his life. He has been busy helping to run the Coward estate, and he recently penned a charming memoir of their life together.

When Noël died in 1973 they dimmed the lights on Shaftesbury Avenue. It was the end of an era and a little of the sparkle went out of the theatre for ever.

Halls of Fame was a musical series presented by Roy Hudd for the BBC. Roy has occasionally tried to badger me out of my natural idleness to take on new challenges, and he persuaded me to do a couple of Marie Lloyd numbers in one of the episodes. Having done it once I had the confidence to repeat my performance for a charity show, *Night of a Hundred Stars* at the Shaftesbury Theatre. On the night I waited in vain for my entrance music, but the accompanist had gone missing and there was an ominous silence, so I walked onstage and explained to the audience that I was about to give a rendition of 'The Railway Song' and that we were running late due to unforeseen circumstances. Fortunately the pianist was hauled out of the pub and normal service was resumed.

I joined Roy in panto again in 1990. We did *Babes in the Wood* at Croydon then followed that with consecutive panto seasons at Plymouth and finally Cardiff – all traditional shows. The Dame, Jack Tripp, along with Terry Scott, was the best in the business. He was a wonderful dancer, with a wicked sense of humour. I learned a lot from watching Jack. That's one thing about this business, you never stop learning, it's *employing* what you've learned that's the tricky part.

In my Fairy role, my accomplice was a magic white rabbit, and I had to ask the children in the audience to help me find him. The rabbit popped up in various places around the theatre – in the orchestra pit, in one of the boxes, peeking round the scenery and so on, with different stagehands needed to manipulate the glove puppet for each appearance. The spotlight operator picked up the rabbit wherever he was. I was always looking the wrong way, of course, and the audience would shout, 'He's there,' or 'No, not there.' On one occasion, in Plymouth, the follow-spot shone on one of the boxes, revealing not only the rabbit but also a rather embarrassed mum who was breastfeeding her baby. The light went out quickly and the even more embarrassed glove-puppet holder hastily withdrew.

I thought, after the Cardiff panto, that it was probably time to hang up my wings, but when I was offered the Fairy Godmother in *Cinderella* at Wimbledon in 1994 I couldn't resist. The show starred Rolf Harris, whose talents are seemingly endless. He was supported by two excellent Ugly Sisters, Nigel Ellacott and Peter Robbins; a superb Buttons, Mark Curry; Robin Askwith – my son in *Carry On Girls* – and, as principal boy, Caroline Dennis. Also in the cast were GMTV's weathergirl, Sally Meen, and Ian Botham.

Rolf is a delightful man to work with; he always has a smile and a joke about the place. Rolf is also an ace photographer and he was never without his camera, snapping everybody in the show from the wings. He must use a colour filter, as all his photos have a mysterious pinky-mauvey look about them, which you wouldn't get with a box brownie. He gave me lots of photographs, and there is one of me with the little fairies, which I treasure.

When Rolf did an hour-long television variety show, he asked me to wander on at the end and attempt to play the wobble-board. He gave me a quick lesson before the show and said it was 'all in the wrist'. I think I managed to get it right once in every five beats, but he didn't hold it against me.

There's no doubt you need energy for panto, and, my goodness, Rolf's got plenty of that. I was in the wings ready to go on after his 'Jake the Peg' number, and although I watched every performance closely, I could never work out which was the extra leg. I knew which it was because he showed me once, but when he was performing I could never tell. He was so brilliant. We were never actually onstage at the same time during *Cinderella*, apart from the finale, when we met at the bottom of the steps, waiting to go up, usually muttering, 'Why are we *doing* this?' But on hearing our reception as we took our bows the question was always answered.

It was a very happy pantomime and had the advantage of being on my doorstep. Having survived twelve shows a week for six weeks without catching the company cold – always a hazard in pantomime – I decided that, in future, I would enjoy my pantos as a member of the audience, and that's the way it's going to stay. Oh, yes it is.

Chapter Thirteen

THE FABULOUS NINETIES

I HAD BEEN A FAN OF FRENCH AND SAUNDERS EVER SINCE I FIRST saw them, and I was thrilled when they asked me to appear in a sketch on their show. The girls played their TV 'extra' characters, and I was supposed to be going through my lines in the make-up room while they tried to remember my name. In the end I admitted that I was indeed Julie Andrews, and added a bit of ghastly singing to prove that I wasn't. In an earlier French and Saunders sketch, Jennifer played a spoiled, irresponsible brat, while Dawn was the sensible, hard-working one. Needless to say, the first was the mother, the second her daughter. The idea for a series continued to grow in Jennifer's mind over the years, and when it finally came to fruition she remembered me. The result had an effect on my career every bit as important as that day when Frank Muir and Denis Norden called me in 1952.

In 1991 I received the pilot script of *Absolutely Fabulous*, in which Jennifer wanted me to play the part of Mother. She subsequently told me that, before she wrote *Ab Fab*, she always wanted me to play her mother. It was a tiny part – only about thirty seconds of on-screen time – but Jennifer said she would develop the character if the pilot was picked up. That didn't seem very likely at the time, as the head of comedy's verdict was, 'I'm not sure that two women being drunk is funny.' My agent, too, was doubtful about me playing such an insignificant part. But I thought the script was hilarious; I laughed out loud when I read it, as did Tim, and he strongly encouraged me to accept.

The studio audience and the viewers responded to it immediately, which is a great tribute to Jennifer's insight and ability to gauge the public's taste. It was obvious from that first recording that the show was going to be a success, although just how big a success I don't think anyone realized.

The team was a mixture of old and new friends. I knew Joanna Lumley from *An Ideal Husband* at Chichester. Julia Sawalha and Jane Horrocks were two brilliant young actresses who I hadn't met before, but grew to like very much indeed. Our director was Bob Spiers, a sandy-haired Scot whose directing pedigree stretched back to *Fawlty Towers*. Bob later directed the Spice Girls movie, and I was roped in to do a cake-making demonstration at the beginning of one of their videos, *An Audience with the Spice Girls*. Posh and the others weren't around, but I was given a Spice Girls Polaroid camera, which at present sits unused in the cupboard next to the one I won in New York in 1949. The comedienne Ruby Wax also had an influence on *Ab Fab*, and sat in at rehearsals, supplying the odd one-liner.

As promised, Jennifer fleshed out the character of Mother in the subsequent scripts, and soon she emerged as more than a merely dis- approving presence and became slightly unhinged, helping herself to household items and old clothes, and donating them to her local WI. When Eddie's father died, her reaction was, 'Oh, it's me next,' to which Patsy replied, 'You can't die. What about me?' Saffy – Julia – was the only one who was upset. Mother, busy with her puzzle book, said her husband's death would make more room at home, and she'd have to try and alter a bridge date in order to attend the funeral. A cynical view from our author, but with an uncomfortable element of truth.

It's rather embarrassing to reveal that I mostly wore my own clothes for the part. My habit of hoarding things meant I was able to dig out all my old M&S stuff from ten years earlier – good quality, but just that bit out of date, which was perfect for the character. By the time we got to the third series the *Sun* newspaper decided that Mother needed a makeover, and I was sent to Lacroix with a photographer. They put me into some wonderful outfits and some fun photos resulted. There were some gorgeous leggings which I had my eye on, and I think I might have managed to wangle a pair if I'd played my cards right. But when I saw the price was £350 – reduced from £700 – I blurted out that it was a ridiculous amount for a pair of leggings and, of course, the *Sun* quoted me. If only I'd said what marvellous value they were they might be sitting in my drawer right now. Sometimes my Yorkshire blood will out at inappropriate moments.

Reaction to *Ab Fab* was extraordinary. It soon became the object of frenzied media attention, and the viewing figures were such that it moved from BBC 2 to BBC 1 for its second series. It duly won every award going, so many, in fact, that Jennifer was simply unable to accept them all in person. I went to pick up the Television and Radio Industries Club (TRIC) award on her behalf, and when I tried to pass it on to her she asked me if I'd mind keeping it. Although she didn't say so in as many words, her shelves were obviously groaning already. And so it sits in my drawing room, and very proud I am to have it. It was a great thrill to be involved in such a successful show. There's no doubt that it was a real shot in the arm to my career. Suddenly directors began to realize that I wasn't either dead or mouldering away in a deckchair in Sussex, and more jobs started to come in. The show also reignited Joanna's career, and she has gone on to star in her own series since then. We are both extremely grateful for the new lease of life *Ab Fab* gave us.

There was a plan afoot to make a film version of the show, but in the end Jennifer decided the script would work better as an hour-long special. Dora Bryan was brought in to play my sister, who had married a GI during the war. For reasons best known to Jennifer, I took on Dora's American accent, which confused everyone, not least ourselves. Then again, perhaps it wasn't so odd, as I remember that Muff, within seconds of meeting an American or any foreigner, would start copying their accent. Dora was on top form in the show, and even did the splits at one point, although I don't think the camera quite caught the stunt in all its glory. Dora and I have been friends since the war, when she had a little flat in Denman Street, where a group of us would sometimes gather for tea and gossip. She has had to endure some difficult times, but has always bounced back. She can still do the splits, and is working as hard as ever.

A highlight of my *Ab Fab* experience came in 1995 when the Comedy Channel in America gave the third series a spectacular New York launch. Joanna wasn't free, and neither was Julia, but Jennifer, Jane Horrocks, the producer Jon Plowman, now Head of Comedy at the BBC, and yours truly were flown out first class, installed in the lap of luxury, wined, dined and generally made to feel welcome. They spent 1.5 million dollars on publicity, and from the moment we arrived it was clear they meant business. Our accommodation was at the Four Seasons Hotel on 57th Street, where we were allotted a suite each. Jennifer had a splendid one, and she invited us all to join her to watch the Emmies and have dinner served 'at her place'. We were able to make rude remarks about everybody appearing on the show without anyone around to hear us.

The purpose of our visit was to attend an Eddy and Patsy lookalike competition, which was taking place at the Puck Building, a vast space in downtown New York. It was my first time being ferried around in a stretch limo, and I quite took to it. As we rolled up, we could see the crowds waiting to get in, but of course they couldn't see us through the limo's darkened windows. When we got inside, the place was seething with fellers in frocks, showing off their Eddy and Patsy outfits. I even spotted a solitary Mother, wearing the only cardigan in the room. We were introduced to various dignitaries, including Bob Kreek, the managing director of the Comedy Channel, and one of the few men flouting convention by wearing trousers. Then there was a screening of an *Ab Fab* episode for the journalists present, followed by questions. Jennifer, Jon, Jane and I sat on a raised platform waiting in eager anticipation, but all the questions were addressed to Jennifer, apart from one person, who asked Jane where she got her accent from. That over, we were taken through the vast warehouse, nodding and smiling at all the Patsies and Eddies;

the winner of the competition was over six feet tall – in drag, of course – with a Patsy hairdo. He couldn't have looked less like Joanna, but he'd made a great effort. We gave a few radio interviews in a roped-off section and made semaphore conversation with a few visiting VIPs, including Helen Mirren, who was working in New York. We were whisked away from the ear-splitting decibels to the relative quiet of the Barolo, a courtyard restaurant in SoHo, then back to the hotel at 1 a.m.

No sooner had my head hit the pillow than the phone started ringing and a voice told me it was ten to seven and why wasn't I in reception ready to travel to the airport. My wake-up call had been overlooked, but I was in the lobby by 7.05. At the British Airways check-in desk, the girl told us they were looking for people to upgrade and were we interested? Since we were already travelling first class, I couldn't see how it was possible to upgrade us.

'Do you care to fly Concorde?' she asked.

We did.

My first transatlantic trip in 1949 took five days, and one was expected to have a different dress for each evening of the voyage; this time it was hardly worth taking my coat off. Three hours and twenty minutes – just incredible! Concorde is a great deal noisier than the *Queen Mary*, and not nearly as comfortable, but it does go about 1,300 miles an hour faster. As we approached Mach 2, I was passed a note from Jennifer which read simply, 'Fast enough for you, Mother?' They plied us with quantities of food and drink, and I was invited into the surprisingly cramped cockpit. I met the captain and his crew, who kindly allowed me to stay there for the landing at Heathrow. It was quite an experience!

Jennifer has been commissioned to write a new series called *Mirrorball*: we have recorded the pilot, and the series will follow in 2001. More of that later. My admiration for her is unbounded. She has combined the roles of actress, writer, wife and mother with great success. She has managed to become one of the hottest properties in television, and at the same time bring up three of the best-behaved little girls I've ever come across.

*

Absolutely Fabulous introduced me to a new generation of viewers and directors. When they were casting the film *Jude*, I was asked to go along and discuss the possibility of playing the part of Jude's aunt Drusilla. I didn't know the story, but asked the producer and director what made them think of me. They said they wanted Aunt Drusilla to be a warm character, and Jude's only real friend. I immediately bought the book in case I got the job. In the novel *Jude the Obscure*, the character is described as a tall and gaunt woman, so I was somewhat surprised when I was cast, but very pleased to take on the part. I reckoned it wasn't my fault if Thomas Hardy spun in his grave.

It was strange to be playing a serious role for the first time at the age of seventy. I think it was also my first dying role. The producers kindly accommodated my *News Huddlines* commitments; however, one of the filming days happened to be the day before I was needed for a recording in London. As the afternoon wore on, there I was in costume in Durham and beginning to worry about missing the last train. I was assured I'd make it in plenty of time, but filming is unpredictable and the hours ticked by. One of the film's producers came to the rescue and kindly drove me at speed to Newcastle airport, managing to get me on the last plane south with minutes to spare.

The film company then contacted my agent to say they would need me for an extra day, as the director wanted to add my character into the wedding scene. It is one of the perks of playing mums, aunties and the like that you are often booked for an extra day just to stand around on the church steps. The unusual part of it was that the wedding scene was being filmed in New Zealand, so I was off on my travels again.

It is one of the laws of filming that if you fly off in search of good weather, no matter how sunny the clime, as soon as you get there conditions will immediately change to resemble a wet Wednesday in Merthyr Tydfil. It poured. The director had no option but to plough on, and thanks to clever lighting and camera work, when the finished product came out it looked as though the weather had been perfect. I made my brief but telling appearance at the wedding breakfast, then tried to cram as much as possible into the rest of the time available. I stayed with my cousin Verena, whom I hadn't seen for twenty years, and on a spare day in Dunedin I took a boat trip along Otago Harbour, a beautiful, ten-mile stretch of water leading out into the Pacific. The captain, who was also a guide, was extremely knowledgeable about the flora and fauna of the place; she was a real old sea dog and could spot a shag at a hundred yards! She gave us an illuminating commentary on everything we passed, which included shags, seals, dolphins, yellow-eyed penguins, small blue penguins and, towards the end of the inlet, at Taiaroa Head, albatrosses and their nests. It was surprising to see these giant creatures just a few miles from a busy city. Normally I prefer my encounters with the wilds of nature to come via the medium of television, which I find reduces the risk of being bitten or stung, but this was a fantastic trip and I wouldn't have missed it, or the informative commentary, for anything.

Christopher Ecclestone played Jude and his co-star was Kate Winslet. It was a pleasure to meet them and refreshing to find that screen goddesses can also be delightfully down to earth. I enjoyed their company a great deal.

I do admire the courage of young actresses these days. They are often required to strip off. I'm so glad I didn't have to go through that when I was young. Mercifully I have reached an age where it's unlikely to be a problem.

Or so I thought. When I was asked to play Edward Woodward's girlfriend in *Common as Muck*, I read the script and thought it was great – until the scene in which Edward and I were supposed to be undressing each other. I felt the viewers should be spared such a spectacle, and told the producers I would love to be in it, but didn't feel I could unless that particular scene was revised. I was told not to worry, the scene would be cut. However, come the day of the read-through, there it was still in the script. I asked Edward what he thought about it.

'Oh, I told them that one had to go ages ago,' he said, much to my relief.

The scene remained unrevised throughout the various drafts, and even on the day we came to film it, it was still in the shooting script. So Edward and I simply rewrote it. We cobbled together our own version, in which we remained dressed. The scene faded on a loving kiss, letting the viewers decide what happened next.

Since I was playing the love interest, the BBC paid for me to go to one of the smartest hairdressers in town, Michael van Clark, to tart me up a bit. He did a splendid job and I arrived for the first day of shooting with my hair looking as good as it possibly could. The first scene was on the end of the pier at Blackpool, where it was blowing a gale, and within a minute or two my hair was standing on end and I looked as though I'd been electrocuted. The make-up people were going frantic; they'd spent all that money, only to see their investment blown away by the wind. Edward and Roy Hudd, who was also in the scene, both wore hats – stuck on, I suspect – and Roy, like the true and loyal friend he is, responded to my predicament by laughing. I must remember to push him into the sea next time we're on the end of the pier together.

The two-episode story was touching as well as funny and it was a privilege to be a part of what became a great critical, as well as popular, success. My character was a terminally ill kleptomaniac – my second dying role. Were they trying to tell me something?

There were one or two other, what you might call straight parts at this time, in *Tom Jones* and *Family Money*, although a friend said the sight of me wobbling down the road on my bicycle in *Family Money* made her laugh out loud. I was all right on the flat, it was the camber in the middle of the road that exposed my rusty technique. Well, it had been a good thirty years since I'd last been on two wheels, in an equally unstable effort in the title sequence for *Beggar My Neighbour*. In *Tom Jones*, which was directed by Metin Hüseyin, who also directed *Common as Muck*, I was the landlady, Mrs Whitfield. I wonder what made him think of me? There were comedy elements to all these scripts, so it wasn't really a question of 'going straight', as some of the newspapers put it. Shortly afterwards I began working with someone who could not by any stretch of the imagination be called 'straight': the gorgeous Julian Clary.

We met in 1992, during the filming of *Carry On Columbus*, the last brave hurrah of this much-loved sequence of films. Sadly, many of the original regulars of the team were dead or unavailable, and some of the younger comedians who replaced the old guard had a different approach and weren't quite on the same wavelength as Dave Freeman's script – not surprisingly, perhaps, as some of them were not even born when the *Carry Ons* began. But Julian Clary managed to recapture the spirit of the earlier films and was extremely funny as the camp gaoler. He told me he was planning his series *Terry and Julian* – sounds familiar! He said there was a part for me in one of the episodes.

'Oh, yes,' I said. 'What's that?'

'The wife of the Governor of the Bank of England.'

'I see. And what does she do?'

'As a matter of fact, she tries to seduce me. Now there's a challenge.'

How could I resist?

It was an unruly sort of show, in which Julian addressed the studio audience and, occasionally, even pulled people onto the set to read small parts in the script. For my husband, the Governor, Julian cast Reginald Marsh, Terry's old boss in *Terry and June*. Reg and I duly took part and Julian was most welcoming, although as we sat backstage, waiting for our cue, Reg and I were rather taken aback by the warm-up man's excessive use of the 'F' word. How different from the days when the warm-up man started proceedings by telling the audience to 'Stand up, turn to the person on your right, shake hands and say, "How are you?" Then turn to the person on your left and say, "Mind your own business,"' followed, after the hysterical laughter had died down, by community singing of 'Daisy, Daisy'.

I worked with Julian again in *All Rise for Julian Clary*. The idea of the show was that Julian would tackle people's real-life problems, and then, assuming the role of judge, mete out punishment or reward accordingly. I took over from Frank Thornton, who had played Julian's Clerk of the Court in the first series, but was no longer available because he'd been head-hunted for *Last of the Summer Wine*.

Not many people can claim to have taken over from Sheila Gish *and* Frank Thornton in the space of a few years. Versatile or what? The format of the show was altered, and I insisted on being Julian's Auntie June; that way I could misunderstand his innuendo and smile fondly at him as though he was my favourite nephew who could do no wrong. I turned many a blind eye, and several shades of pink from time to time.

So now I was part of the alternative comedy scene. When I'm asked how I've managed to adapt, I reply that I'm acting the same way I always have. It's what goes on around me that has changed.

The changes in television comedy have been quite marked. Not just the evolving of different styles of humour, but the technological developments have been truly mind-boggling since the live and dangerous days at Lime Grove, where I did my first TV show in 1951. As more technicians are needed to make a programme, production costs have risen, and so there is more pressure on shows to recover the costs. As a result, there isn't as much leeway to allow a series to settle in and find its audience; if it doesn't show results pretty soon, off it comes. Scripts might be more challenging nowadays, and cover a wide range of subjects including sex, politics and religion, which were strictly taboo fifty years ago, but the basic technique for getting a laugh from a funny line is the same now as it was fifty or a hundred and fifty years ago, and will be the same in a hundred years' time.

When I took part in a special English episode of *Friends*, it was fascinating to observe the working methods of a big-budget American show. They were very methodical and left nothing to chance; even flying in their own camera crew, which meant they had to recompense ours. The story was set in England and they brought in Tom Conti, Hugh Laurie, Jennifer Saunders and myself to play a variety of rather unpleasant Brits. Jen was a high-flying executive who was never off the phone, Tom was a stingy father of the bride, Hugh was an unhelpful aircraft passenger and I was the toffee-nosed housekeeper. Rehearsals were conducted with great thoroughness, making sure every line, look and nuance was as it should be. During one rehearsal a group of about twenty people came into the studio. I assumed it was a tour being shown round, but I later discovered they were the *Friends* writers, who had also been flown in from America. Twenty writers for one sitcom! When I first worked for the BBC there were probably only about twenty full-time television comedy writers in the country!

The recording of an American show is a painstaking process. In fact, it takes at least twice as long as a British sitcom. The audience was in the studio from four o'clock in the afternoon until eleven o'clock at night, poor souls, but they enjoyed themselves. I spoke to two of them who had travelled down from Scotland to see their idols, and when I asked them how long they were staying they replied, 'As long as they're here.' The audience was kept entertained during the many hold-ups by warm-up men, who organized quizzes about the show and the characters. Prizes, in the form of *Friends* fridge magnets, T-shirts and baseball caps, were handed out to the jubilant winners.

The actors themselves were extremely professional, absolutely word-perfect and completely unfazed by any number of retakes they were required to do. They were also well aware that they had struck gold and worked very hard to maintain their success. Their professionalism has certainly paid off as they now collect $500,000 each per episode. A well-earned slice of the enormous cake. It was an eye-opening experience, and the way of working was quite different from ours. Not better, not worse, just different. In the final analysis, the working methods don't matter too much; the reason that *Hancock*, *Steptoe and Son*, *Ab Fab* and *Friends* are all great sitcoms is because of the scripts and the performances. In the end, that's what counts.

In 1995, not long after we finished the third series of *Ab Fab*, Jennifer, Joanna, Julia and I were called in one day to do some dubbing, and while recording in the small studio, I saw Michael Aspel making his way towards me. I almost waved him away as I was concentrating on the matter in hand, then he said the magic words and produced the red book.

'No, no,' I said. 'There must be a mistake. I've been done.'

They cut that bit out!

I really thought he was there to nobble one of the others, but I soon realized from their grins that they'd known all about it. I was taken to the studio and once again basked in the deeply flattering process. The funny thing was that a few weeks before a woman had turned to me in the audience of a charity show and said, 'Are you looking forward to your *This Is Your Life*?' I told her I'd been done twenty years ago, but she smiled knowingly, and I just thought she was touched. The producer of the programme recently admitted to me that a list of possible subjects had been taken from his office and circulated at the time, so presumably this woman must have had access to it. However, I was still completely unprepared.

I wasn't thrown by it quite as much as the first time, but I did wonder how on earth they would manage to scrape together enough people to walk through the sliding doors. In the event, they rounded up rather more than the first time. Some of the old crowd had faded away, but I had acquired several new theatrical families in the intervening years, the *Huddlines* and *Ab Fab* teams to name but two.

The surprise guest at the end, and it really was a surprise, because no-one thought he'd be well enough to manage the journey, was Leslie Crowther. I had done his *This Is Your Life* some time earlier, and he was determined to appear on mine, even though he'd been very ill.

The recording of the show was delayed by about forty-five minutes because the traffic in West London had come to a standstill following a shooting incident in Castlenau, near Hammersmith Bridge. The extra time that Leslie was kept waiting didn't do him a lot of good, and I know Jean was worried about him, but he did wonderfully well and I really appreciated the effort he'd made to be there.

Yet again, it was an overwhelming experience. For the second time in twenty years I was left gobsmacked with wonder at all the research and effort that must have gone into the show, and I greatly appreciated the trouble my friends and colleagues had taken to turn up.

As a result of *Ab Fab*, the last ten years have been busier than any time in my career since the Fifties. There's always something new to learn and new people to meet and work with. Tim enjoys the show-biz part of my life, even if he does grumble occasionally about having to attend another 'Hello Darlings' evening.

My career has taken me into a wide variety of areas, whether it's comedy, drama, children's TV or just popping up on a panel game. Of course, they don't always get what they bargain for with a senior citizen like me. I caused looks of utter horror on *Master Chef* when I said I didn't go along with the fashion for serving pink lamb: 'I like mine well-done and crispy-skinned. Good old falling-apart lamb, like Granny used to cook,' I said. 'Why do we have to copy the French?' Needless to say I wasn't invited back.

I also had the cheek to present a series of keep-fit programmes called *It Doesn't Have to Hurt*. Now I'm the last person to pontificate on this particular subject, never having paid a great deal of attention to fitness. I insisted that I shouldn't set myself up as a trainer, but rather pass on the advice of the experts. The programme suggested healthy alternatives to the lazy way most of us move around in the course of a day, things like walking upstairs rather than taking the lift. We encouraged people to go dancing, and I was seen doing my stuff at the disco with a strap on my wrist monitoring my heart rate. The programmes were fun to make and I found them quite in-structive. I did take the stairs for some time after, but I didn't manage to put into practice all the lessons.

A by-product of being on TV over a long period of time is that you're occasionally given honours you don't necessarily deserve, but which are quite impossible to refuse. I have, for example, a ward named after me at St Helier hospital, for which I did hardly anything except front a fund-raising campaign. A more frivolous boost to my ego came in the course of a chance interview I did with Gloria Hunniford at the Hampton Court Flower Show. My opinions on gardening carry about as much weight as my views on physical fitness, but we chatted on regardless. Gloria asked me if I had ever had a rose named after me. When I said no, she asked me if I would like one.

'Of course,' I said. 'I'm sure everyone would like a rose named after them.'

Fake fashion shoot for the *Sun*, 1991, with me in Lacroix – a brave try.

My *This Is Your Life*, 1995, with Rolf Harris, ace photographer.

Terry and June.

With statue – 'So she's got longer arms.' BBC

Jack and the Beanstalk with Terry, Bath, 1985.

Dick Whittington with Honor Blackman, Richmond, 1983.

Babes in the Wood with Roy, Cardiff, 1992.

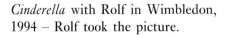

Cinderella with Rolf in Wimbledon, 1994 – Rolf took the picture.

ABOVE: Reopening of the Paris Theatre.

ABOVE: *The News Huddlines*, rehearsal with Roy and Chris. I joined in 1984 and we're still going strong.

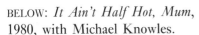

BELOW: *It Ain't Half Hot, Mum*, 1980, with Michael Knowles.

ABOVE: *What's My Line?*, 1994, with Roy, Kate Robbins, Emma Forbes and Peter Smith.

BELOW: *The Rivals* with Suzy, Bath and Windsor 1986 – 'Don't let your simplicity be imposed on.'

RIGHT: *Over My Dead Body* at the Savoy Theatre, with Donald Sinden and Frank Middlemass.

BELOW: Leslie Crowther's *Life*, 1994.

RIGHT: *Common As Muck*, 1996, with Edward Woodward.

ABOVE: My very own rose, 1995.

RIGHT: *All Rise for Judge Julian Clary*, 1997, with me as his Auntie June! BBC

LEFT: Cartoon of *Abfab* by Gary. © Daily Mail/Atlantic

TOP RIGHT: 'You'll soon get the hang of this.' BBC

BOTTOM RIGHT: 'Downed in one again.' BBC

LEFT: USA Comedy Central launch of the third series of *Abfab* – on Concorde; where else?

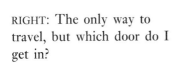

RIGHT: The only way to travel, but which door do I get in?

ABOVE: *This Is Your Life* the second time around, in 1995 with Jennifer, Joanna and Michael Aspel.

ABOVE: BBC Radio 4's *Miss Marple*, 1994 – 'I hope I'm not intruding.'

RIGHT: *Carry On Columbus*, 1992, as King and Queen of Spain, with Leslie Phillips. BFI

Three proud faces on 12 December 1985 – an amazing coincidence,
my mother's birthday.

'Well, here's the man to do it,' she said, and introduced me to Ken Grapes of the Rose Society. Peter Harkness of the British Rose Growers Association was also there, and he offered to grow a rose for me. So, thanks to Gloria, a few weeks later we went to the Harkness Nurseries in Hertfordshire to choose from a number of new hybrids. These plants, although not yet officially named, have a sort of working title by which they are identified. I picked out a hybrid tea-bush rose called Harchutzpah, which is pinkish with a yellow base. After you've chosen the rose, you have to wait for it to be brought on in the nursery for a couple of seasons before it's ready for the market. I launched mine at the Hampton Court Show, and in due course we took delivery of several June Whitfield roses. It's described in the brochure as follows: 'A peachy pink, overlaid with bold tones of scarlet and gold. Vigorous, leafy, superb for bedding, grows readily, even in testing conditions.' There now.

Another sought-after accolade was bestowed upon me during a recording of *The News Huddlines*. The cast was told the World Service was going to take the show, and we needed to record a ten-minute promotional sketch for them. The script we were given was very poor indeed, with a great many sound effects which kept going wrong. In one sketch Roy was playing Bill Clinton and I was Hillary, and before we were very far into it, a woman in the audience stood up and said, 'I'm an American and I don't like to hear that kind of thing being said about our First Lady!'

There was stunned silence, and then I said, 'I'm terribly sorry, but this is the *Huddlines* and we are inclined to say things about all kinds of people. You should hear what we say about Mrs Thatcher and she's very well respected here.'

The heckler wasn't much mollified, and as the argument continued I noticed Roy and Chris smirking.

'Anyway,' I said, 'there's so much going wrong with this sketch I don't think it'll ever be heard.'

We resumed the dialogue to an accompaniment of sheep baaing and car horns honking. Then the producer came down and announced that the sound-effects man had been taken ill and we were to have a replacement. When the new man appeared at his post behind the screen, I thought, 'What's Rolf Harris doing here?' It was, of course, Noel Edmonds wearing a false beard, but I didn't look too closely as I was trying to concentrate on the words of the deadly sketch. When the thing ground to a halt once again I said, 'Oh really, this is like a Gotcha.'

Roy and Chris looked suddenly suspicious, and Roy went behind the screen, as I later learned, to say to Noel, 'You'd better come out. I think she's sussed you.'

I hadn't twigged at all, but Noel emerged, whipped off his beard and announced the Gotcha to the amusement of all present, including me.

Afterwards, Roy asked me, 'Didn't you think it was odd that Chris and I stood there and didn't say anything to the heckler?'

I said, 'No, she spoke to me, so I thought it was up to me to answer.'

'But I would have rushed to your rescue if it was for real,' he said. 'I wouldn't have just stood there.'

So there's a comforting thought to bear in mind if we ever get heckled again.

When I attended the studio presentation of the Gotcha after watching the playback, I said to Noel, 'I really enjoyed that.'

He said, 'You're not supposed to enjoy it. It's meant to upset you.'

After sixteen years of the *Huddlines*, not likely!

Roy himself has experienced the occasional sticky moment in the studio. He's very quick to pick up gags and routines, but he met his Waterloo when he was given a parody song to sing about the Polish ex-premier, General Jaruzelski. The words went to the tune of 'When Johnny Comes Marching Home', so he had to sing 'When General Jaruzelski comes marching home again . . .' Roy was going frantic in rehearsal, effing and blinding and saying, 'It doesn't scan; it doesn't scan.'

Peter Moss, the musical director, said to him, 'It's simple, Roy. It's in fifteen/sixteen time. Anybody can do it.'

'Well I ******* can't,' said Roy.

Eventually the producer's voice came from the control box: 'I think we'd better get on or we'll never get this April Fool edition in the can.'

Roy was given another hot flush when he was recording the links for a *Behind the Huddlines* tape. He did an extremely good Neil Kinnock impression which he was using for the recording. Chris Emmett had spotted the Ginger Ninja himself in the building, and persuaded him to sneak up behind Roy and surprise him while he was doing his stuff at the microphone. When Roy finished the link he heard a familiar Welsh voice behind him say, 'Not bad, but I think I could've done that better.'

The *Huddlines* has been my main regular stable over the last sixteen years, but I have partnered Roy in a number of other series on Radio 2 and 4: *The Crowned Hudds*, a historical sketch show written by Michael Dines, and *The Newly Discovered Casebook of Sherlock Holmes*, written by Tony Hare, in which Roy was Holmes, Chris Emmett was Watson and I played the housekeeper Mrs Hudson. We also teamed up with Chris for a Channel 4 sketch show in which Roy and I were an outrageous pair of punks. Suzy was also in that show. We have made two series of Mike Coleman's *Like They've Never Been Gone* for Radio 4, playing a bickering old 1950s singing duo trying to make one more comeback, in which we had the bonus of Pat Coombs being very funny as my ex-dresser-cum-dogsbody. A third series is scheduled for 2001. One way or another Roy has been responsible for keeping me gainfully employed for a good part of the last sixteen years, and we're still talking.

Before the war there was an advertisement for the radio showing a child being asked by his mother why he preferred radio to films, 'Why, Mother,' he said angelically, 'because the pictures are better.' Children may not express themselves quite like that now, but the idea still holds true. I have always had a particular fondness for radio; it was where I first achieved a measure of success, and in the last ten or fifteen years I have done as much radio as ever. As well as the regular work with Roy, there have been series with the Pasadena Roof Orchestra, and the sharply written *Kalangadog Junction* and *The Law*

Game, and also plays and a classic serial, plus a revival of the musical *Gigi*, in which Joss Ackland and I did our best to escape from the shadows of Hermione Gingold and Maurice Chevalier, in the number 'I Remember It Well'. I also partnered Tony Britton in the same number for a charity show at Chichester.

In 1993 I had to follow in some more illustrious footsteps when Radio 4 commissioned an adaptation of *Murder at the Vicarage*. Enyd Williams cast me as Miss Marple. Joan Hickson was so perfect on TV and Margaret Rutherford memorably Marpled on film, and they were both hard acts to follow. There have been many comedy sketches in the course of my career in which I have sent up Miss Marple with my Margaret Rutherford impression, but I realized I had to find another way of playing her. I based my portrayal on her polite enquiry, 'I hope I'm not intruding,' which, of course, she always was. With the splendid adaptations of Michael Bakewell and the brilliant direction of Enyd, we have now done eight further Miss Marple mysteries. Miss Marple often narrates events, and most of the action involves the other characters. Enyd is one of the most experienced producers working for the BBC, and with her excellent instinct for casting she manages to get some superb performances out of our large casts and various visiting guest stars.

I've worked in just about every branch of the entertainment business except the circus, but over the last fifty-six years my main employer has been the BBC. I did my very first radio job in 1947, and am about to start another run of *The News Huddlines* at the time of writing. In 1997 Tony Hare compiled, and I introduced, a cassette, *June Whitfield at the Beeb*, which included excerpts from some of the programmes in which I have appeared. Believe it or not, I have contributed to over 1,300 BBC radio and television shows over the last fifty-three years, so Tony had his work cut out to whittle *June Whitfield at the Beeb* down to just two cassettes. He must have been sick of the sound of my voice! Thanks Tony, and thanks BBC.

Tapes and audio books are now essential equipment for long car journeys, and I have recorded a number of them, some for children, such as *Brambly Hedge*, *George's Marvellous Medicine* by Roald Dahl and several Dick King-Smith stories; also Terry Pratchett's *The*

Wyrd Sisters, nine Agatha Christie *Miss Marple* stories, four *Miss Read*s, a Rosamund Pilcher, and I've also contributed to poetry tapes. It's probably enough to get you past at least three junctions on the M25!

The words 'lifetime achievement' provoke mixed feelings because they carry a suggestion that the lifetime might be coming to an end. Having said that, it was wonderful to be given the British Comedy Awards' Lifetime Achievement in 1994, and another from Channel 4 in 1998, presented by Women in Film and TV. Last year I was presented with a Talkie for 'contribution to the spoken word', and I was also inducted into the Royal Television Society's Hall of Fame. My lifetime has certainly gone past three-score years and ten, but I hope to be allowed to achieve a little more before they roll the credits.

In 1998 I officially became June Whitfield CBE – Caught Before Expiry? I was absolutely flabbergasted. To quote Frankie Howerd, my flabber had never been so gasted. Until the Birthday Honours are officially announced, you have to keep the news under your hat, and at the same time you have to set about finding that hat. I felt it wouldn't do to wear the same one I wore for the OBE. Her Majesty would spot it immediately! I consulted my friends at Usher, and Tom Bowker solved the problem by using the same midnight blue material to create both the elegant outfit and the titfer. Incidentally, when you receive your CBE you are requested to hand in your OBE. Presumably my CBE was passed down from someone who had themselves been upgraded. I'd love to know who it was.

When I attended the investiture at Buckingham Palace, I found myself in a different ante-room from the previous occasion; this time I was mingling with the 'K's and the DBEs, while Tim, Suzy and brother John – my three permitted guests – were allowed to move a little closer to the action in the ballroom. I was gallantly gonged by Prince Charles, whom I'd met only a few weeks before at a Stage For Age event.

'Who would have thought we'd be meeting again so soon?' he said, which I thought showed pretty impressive powers of recollection.

It was another unforgettable day, and wonderful to have the family with me. Afterwards we were given lunch at Windows, a splendid restaurant on the top of the Hilton Hotel, where John's wife Bud and a couple of other friends joined us.

Exciting though it is to receive such an honour, it's hard to find an occasion on which to wear it. It's not really right for shopping at Sainsbury's or lunch in the pub. When the Queen came to open the BBC Experience exhibition at Broadcasting House, I was asked to be part of a reception group, and I thought that was the ideal opportunity to wear my gong. If you can't wear it to meet the Queen, then when can you? As anyone who has visited the exhibition will know, there are sound-effects desks for members of the public to try their hand at sound cues. The Queen arrived and I, along with Terry Wogan, Sue McGregor and various others, demonstrated an assortment of dog barks, car horns and thunderclaps, then waited for Her Majesty to walk between the desks and exchange a few words. First she spoke to Sue McGregor and then to Terry. Mine was the last desk and, as the Queen neared it, I dropped the deepest curtsy I could manage. By the time I got up Her Majesty had been gently ushered on to the next part of the exhibition, leaving me smiling respectfully at thin air. Terry says he dined out on the story many times. From now on the gong stays in its box. But I know it's there and am inordinately proud to be a Commander of the British Empire.

Chapter Fourteen

ROLL THE CREDITS

I SPENT TWENTY VERY HAPPY YEARS WORKING WITH TERRY SCOTT, six years with Arthur Askey, and with Roy Hudd the tally is sixteen and counting, but these valued associations seem almost like brief flings in comparison with the partnership I have enjoyed with my agent, April Young. April and I are now into our forty-sixth year together. We have never had a formal contract because we totally trust each other and have never felt it necessary.

April's background is partly theatrical; her mother was the actress Joan Young, who in later life became a favoured stooge of Jimmy Edwards and Eric Sykes; her father was the night news editor of the *Daily Express* for many years. April was married to Peter Glaze, the comedian who worked with the Crazy Gang and later with Leslie Crowther in *Crackerjack*. I wonder if April still has her *Crackerjack* pencil. She joined Kavanagh's, the agency established by *ITMA*'s creator Ted Kavanagh, in the early Fifties. At the time I was represented by Foster's, but the arrangement didn't turn out to be entirely successful as they were mainly a variety agency. My relationship with Foster's cooled after I went into the office to ask them if there was any work about; they said they'd put me up for this and that job, then added, 'And we did get you *Take It From Here.*' Oh no they didn't; Frank and Denis did. So in 1955 I made a move. Frank and Denis were both clients of Kavanagh's, as were Dick and Jimmy, and I welcomed the opportunity to join the *TIFH* clan under the one roof. April represented every one of the Glums at one point, including Alma Cogan. Kavanagh's went through a number of transformations over the next twenty years, then, in 1975, April set up on her own in an office in Neal's Yard. She was joined by Lesley Kay, and we have all become good friends. Together they prospered, while shifting their base further and further westwards as the years went by; I remember one office in Chelsea with particular affection as it was opposite Peter Jones. Now April Young Ltd is in Barnes. April is the kind of agent who inspires strong loyalties and I am not the only one who has been with her for many years; Denis Norden is another – I think he joined round about the time of Marconi's experiments.

When I completed my fiftieth year in showbusiness, Tim and Suzy gave me a surprise party. Actually, the party wasn't entirely a surprise; I knew something was afoot the day before when I was banished from the house in the morning and told not to show my face until evening. When I returned there was a big marquee attached to the house filled with flowers. The big surprise came the next day. I had no idea who would be turning up and was delighted to see so many old friends and colleagues with whom I'd worked over the years. Denis Norden, Leslie Crowther, Bob Monkhouse, Miriam Karlin, Ronnie Barker, Roy Hudd, and more recent old friends, such as Joanna Lumley and Jennifer Saunders, were among the sixty or so guests. Every time the doorbell went I opened another window on the past. It was quite an emotional experience.

There were, of course, a few notable absentees. One of the penalties of living a long life is the loss of old friends. There was a time in the Nineties when one sadness followed upon another with awful regularity. We lost many to whom I was close and who the public had looked on as family friends: Jimmy Edwards, Benny Hill, Dick Emery, Frankie Howerd, Terry Scott, Kenneth Connor, Frank Muir and our *TIFH* producer Charles Maxwell. Terry battled with cancer for seven years, but never complained, and it was a very sad time when he died. His funeral was at his home town of Godalming. I managed to keep a grip until the congregation started to sing the first hymn. Terry had always been a great embarrassment to his family in church because they said he sang too loudly. That moment was when it really got to me.

It's hard to get through an occasion which not only marks a private loss, but is also a media event. Frankie Howerd's funeral packed his local parish church in Somerset. Outside, there were photographers perched on ladders and peering over hedges. Both before and after, reporters kept coming up and asking for a few words. You don't want to snub people because they are only doing their jobs, but it's not really the moment. I dived into Cilla Black's car and her husband Bobby drove us home.

These were sad days, but with the passage of time my strongest memories are of the happy years I spent working or playing with these wonderfully interesting, funny men. If they're all up there in heaven, I'd love to know who gets top billing. It's a sobering thought that Denis Norden and I are the only surviving members of the cast of *TIFH*. We all have to go eventually, but I'll take a leaf out of Scarlett O'Hara's book and 'think about that tomorrow'.

Comic Heritage, a charity formed by David Graham, has done much to keep alive the memories of popular post-war entertainers. Blue plaques have gone up at places like Pinewood Studios, where the *Carry On*s were made, the BBC stage door canteen and outside the former homes of the artists themselves. The unveiling ceremonies are followed by a lunch, attended by paying guests. There is usually an auction of memorabilia, and the money raised goes to various charities. Cilla Black and I jointly pulled the cord on the plaque outside Frankie Howerd's house in Edwardes Square, and I have also unveiled one to my dear old mate Terry Scott at the BBC.

There are a number of charities to which members of the theatrical profession give their time and services. The Variety Club, the Water Rats, the Society of Stars, the Lord's Taverners and the Lady Taverners all raise money for various charities or individual cases. Judith Chalmers is the Lady Taverners President, and she works tirelessly for them and does a tremendous job. A few years ago they gave her a tribute lunch, and invited some of her friends and colleagues to say a few words about her. It was such a success, and raised so much money for the charity, that Judy decided there should be a yearly lunch given for a particular person, and she very kindly selected me as the next guest.

It was an amazing and heart-warming experience, surrounded by family and friends, and a day I'll never forget. Suzy was working, but sent such a sweet message that it brought a tear to Judy's eye, let alone mine, as she read it out. There were so many nice things said about me by my chums that by the time I had to say a few words I was all choked up. The star of the show was Liz Fraser, who made a hilarious speech and had the whole room rocking with laughter; she's a good friend and sent me up rotten. Last year the tribute lunch was for Dame Thora Hird, and was again a success and a great money-raiser. I'm looking forward to seeing who is next in the hot seat. I can promise them a day to remember.

Another favourite charity is SAGE – Stage For Age – started by Sir Ian Trethowan in 1989. It's a fund-raising arm of Help the Aged, not a charity for old actors, though I'm glad to say there are those as well. Robert Powell is a past president, as is Lionel Blair, and Diana Moran is currently in charge. They have all done great work, and we are kept in order and closely in touch with Help the Aged by our secretary Pat Baron, assisted by Sheila Rawsthorne and Judith's sister, Sandy Chalmers, who works for Help the Aged. They plan the various events which we members happily support, knowing that the money raised will help to improve the quality of life of elderly people who are frail, isolated or poor. So far we have raised over £100,000 and will continue to help all we can.

In 1995 we had to say goodbye to another stalwart of post-war comedy, the Paris Studio. The BBC's lease had run out and they decided not to renew it, so comedy shows were moved to the old Concert Hall in Broadcasting House, which had been renovated and rechristened the Radio Theatre. It was sad to vacate the Paris after so many years. Its intimacy made it an ideal venue for radio comedy. There were around 200 seats, separated by a central aisle, and no-one in the audience was more than about ten yards from the performers.

The stage area was raised, but only by a foot or so, and the seating was gently raked so that everyone had a good view.

The Paris started life as a cinema in 1939 and only became a studio when the BBC was looking for underground premises during the blitz. It was requisitioned by the Ministry of Information on the corporation's behalf at a rent of £40 a week. The first programme to be broadcast from the Paris was a Cochrane revue. A BBC internal memo reports that after the performance, 'a large number of those who accepted BBC hospitality on Saturday became quite unpleasant; they sat drinking and carousing until 3 a.m., keeping everyone else awake and leaving a filthy litter of broken glass, crown corks and cigarette ends.' Nothing like starting as you mean to go on.

Shortly after the decision was made to let the Paris go, I was at a lunch and happened to be seated next to John Birt, the then director general and architect of many controversial cost-effective schemes. On my other side was a very senior accountant, who was in complete sympathy with the reorganization that was taking place. I asked if there was no hope of keeping the Paris.

'Something has to go,' the accountant said. A number of studios were under threat, such as Maida Vale and Golders Green, and the Paris was to be the unlucky one. I explained how we all felt about losing the home of radio comedy. Mr Birt listened courteously and said, 'I'll take that on board.' It obviously dived off again as, pretty soon after that, on 26 February 1995, Roy and I were taking part in the two-hour *Farewell to the Paris* programme on Radio 2. The show was hosted by Bob Holness and featured a large cast of old Paris lags. Afterwards there was quite a wake, at which we did our best to reproduce the atmosphere created after that very first Cochrane revue.

Our party was in the office of the then head of radio comedy, Jonathan James-Moore. Roy's wife Debbie said to Jonathan, 'I'm sure Roy would love to have a souvenir.' The walls of the stairway leading down from street level had been lined with photos of the stars who had appeared there over the years. Within an hour of the show ending, every photo had disappeared. 'I'm sorry,' Jonathan told Roy, 'but everything's been nicked.' However, in front of the double doors leading into the auditorium was a large oblong piece of coconut matting, bearing the words 'The Paris', so Debbie asked Jonathan if they could have it. The mat was rolled up and transported in triumph to the Hudd residence in Clapham. Having got it home they realized the thing was as wide as the house, and I think Debbie rather regretted having suggested it, but it's a splendid memento all the same.

So that was how we said goodbye to the studio that had played host to *The Goons*, *TIFH*, *Hancock's Half-Hour*, *Round the Horne* and more recent shows like *The Hitchhiker's Guide to the Galaxy*, *Radioactive* and *The News Huddlines*. It's probably true that the technical facilities were inferior to those at the Radio Theatre – certainly, in the forty years I worked at the Paris they never managed to banish the smell of drains from the narration suite – but the auditorium had a special feel which I'm sure added to the quality of all the great shows made there.

When the move from the Paris was announced to the press, its technical shortcomings were stressed, and also the fact that, before a recording, the audience had to queue outside in Lower Regent Street in all weathers. It was promised that, with the move to Broadcasting House, all that would change, and indeed it did, now they get soaked in Portland Place until it's time for them to be let in.

The Radio Theatre doesn't lack atmosphere or history – it was where *ITMA* and *Band Waggon* were performed, together with a host of big-band shows, dating right back to the early Thirties. It's certainly a period architectural gem, but it isn't by any means intimate, and some shows don't benefit from being done in such a large space. To try and give the place a more cosy acoustic, they slung a giant net in the ceiling which hangs down and reduces the height of the theatre. Roy ran a competition among the audience to name this monstrosity, and someone came up with Auntie's Bloomers. The bloomers have been taken down now and shows have simply had to adapt to the surroundings.

The Paris was the last in a long line of studios the BBC have dispensed with over the years: the Camden Theatre, now the Camden Palace, where I recorded *Leave It to the Boys* with Bob Monkhouse; the Aeolian Hall in Bond Street, where I auditioned for *TIFH* and later worked with Bob again on *The Big Noise*, one of Frank and Denis's series about a disc jockey; then there were Piccadilly 1 and 2 where I did a *Juke Box Jury* and Jimmy Edwards' *This Is Your Life*, and which is now the headquarters of BAFTA. Of the theatres which were used as studios, the Hackney Empire and the Playhouse in Northumberland Avenue are happily still in theatrical use, as are the Riverside Studios in Hammersmith, where *Dixon of Dock Green* and the early *Hancock*s were recorded, but the Chelsea Palace, where *The Army Game* was made, and the Wood Green Empire have gone. The Golders Green Hippodrome survives as a music studio – we recorded *Gigi* there recently – as does the strangely elongated building in Delaware Road known as the Maida Vale Studios. It was once an ice rink, and the corridor there is so long between the studio and the canteen that, by the time you've pushed through all the swing doors to get to the read-through, there's nothing left of your coffee.

Broadcasting House has grown in size over the years, as has Television Centre in Wood Lane, vast labyrinths the pair of them, in which it's all too easy to get lost. After Jonathan James-Moore's farewell lunch, we Huddliners and several of our writers ended up in JJM's office, which was in a different part of the building. I was with a group who knew the way, but Tim was talking to Richard Quick and another writer, Glen Mitchell, and with a confident, 'Follow me', Richard led them off on a short cut. They followed blindly while Richard took them along several miles of corridors, into the lifts, along more corridors, up and down stairs, cheerfully saying, 'We're nearly there.' They went into the medical centre, the archives, the weather studio and finally blundered into an office marked 'Controller'. Richard was carrying a glass and Tim had my tapestry holdall slung over his shoulder, so they must have raised a few eyebrows. They missed the party and we finally met up in the foyer – another day to remember.

We've said goodbye to so many pillars of the BBC – real and metaphorical – and yet it's surprising how little has changed. It still takes about the same length of time to make a show as it did fifty years ago. Studio audiences haven't altered much, except that they are less impressed by the technology. Filming follows a time-honoured routine; you can still be called at six in the morning and not get in front of a camera until five in the afternoon, by which time both you and your costume, not to mention your crossword, are in rather a creased state. The main technical change in television has been the improvement in the look of the finished product, brought about by the introduction of the playback monitor. This device, which came in a little over twenty years ago, enables a director to review the recording immediately. If there's a microphone in view or an obvious mistake, the scene is reshot, whereas before, if nobody noticed the boom or someone walking past the camera when they shouldn't, the errors remained and were duly transmitted.

The relaxation in censorship has had an effect, but nothing on radio frightens the horses in quite the same way it does on late-night television, and in most respects radio is virtually unchanged. It still thrives, despite predictions that TV would kill it off. When we have recorded the *Huddlines* live in some of the big regional theatres in Glasgow, Leeds and Newcastle, the response has been thrilling, and we are made to feel so welcome. Roy, Chris and I are looking forward to our next outside broadcast.

1999 was a very busy and varied year for me. As well as writing this book I taped another *Miss Marple Mystery*, several talking books, commercials and Catherine Cookson's *The Secret* for ITV. I also took part in a film for TV, *The Last of the Blonde Bombshells*, Alan Plater's story about a 1940s all-girl band getting back together again, and graced by a star-studded cast, including Judi Dench, Ian Holm, Cleo Laine, Olympia Dukakis, Leslie Caron, Joan Sims, Billie Whitelaw, Thelma Ruby, Felicity Dean, Nicholas Pallister and a delightful eleven-year-old called Millie Findlay. It was a joy to meet Judi and discover what a delightful, caring and funny person she is, as well as mega-talented. It was also good to see Joan again, and in such good form. She has had a marvellous career, and was a stalwart of the *Carry On*s. I was in four, but Joan was in twenty-four and was one of the main reasons for their success. As I write, *Bombshells* is set to go out in September.

My character in *Bombshells* was discovered playing the trombone in a Salvation Army band. Pete Strange of the Humphrey Lyttelton band kindly came to instruct me in some basic trombone techniques, and he devised a map of slide positions for me to follow, from 1 to 6. Fortunately, the tune didn't require me to go to 6, as I don't think I could have stretched that far. In rehearsal, I was concentrating so hard on the slide position Pete had to remind me to keep the mouthpiece clamped to my lips, and to breathe occasionally. He taught me that wonderful evergreen number, '111 111 111 111 1 1 212 11331 24 23 221', which you might know better as 'It Don't Mean a Thing If It Ain't Got That Swing'.

This year and next there will be two more series of the *Huddlines*, hopefully another *Miss Marple*, and the *Ab Fab* cast are looking forward to meeting again to record *Mirrorball*. I play Dora Vermouth (pronounced ver-mooth), who has been in a long-running musical, *Sleepy Time Girl*, since the Fifties. She has played Little Sally, Sally and Sally's mother, and is now consigned to the role of 'Mysterious Lady in Bath Chair' and isn't very happy about it. Jennifer, Joanna, Julia and Jane gave their usual brilliant and funny performances in the pilot show. We were all nervous but the studio audience loved it and laughed a lot, so it's fingers crossed for next year when we make the series, to be directed by Jennifer's husband Adrian Edmonson.

Tim encourages me to keep working; he knows I'd be impossible to live with if I gave up. But it is probably true to say that I have retired from the theatre; it would have to be something quite exceptional to tempt me back into the eight-shows-a-week routine, and there aren't too many exceptional parts for actresses of my vintage. When I went to the Wimbledon Theatre recently to see a show, Mike the chief electrician said to me, 'There's one more panto in you,' but I'm pretty sure there isn't. In fact, I'm absolutely certain there isn't. I think.

So there it is; not a rags-to-riches story, or one bursting with revelations; there isn't even an unhappy childhood, only a life full of love,

affection and laughter, of gigs, gags and a couple of gongs. None of
it could have happened without a lot of help and encouragement
along the way, especially from my nearest and dearest, Tim and Suzy,
from my agents for their friendship and guidance over forty-five
years, and from the endless list of producers, writers and fellow performers who have shared the failures, and the successes, of my
lengthy career. My thanks to all of them, not forgetting the
audiences, viewers, listeners and now you the reader. Thank you for
staying with me.

> That's all folks.
> It's been good fun,
> Telling tales and jokes,
> Now my story's done –
>
> For the present, that is.
> Who knows what's in store?
> In twenty years' time,
> I may write some more.

JW (eternal optimist)

CAREER HISTORY

MOST OF MY CAREER IS LISTED BELOW. IF THERE ARE OMISSIONS, they are not intentional, merely lapses of memory for which I offer my apologies and blame my advancing years.

1942–44   RADA. Awarded scholarship at end of first term, December 1942. Arthur Talbot Smith Prize – good all-round work.
Shared Gertrude Lawrence Prize for Character.

1944   *Pink String and Sealing Wax*, Duke of York Theatre – assistant stage manager and understudy.
Dear Brutus, Q Theatre – Margaret (first professional role).
The Land of Promise, Q Theatre – Various small parts.

1945   *Little Women*, Q Theatre – Amy.
Dear Brutus and *Land of Promise*, tour.
Appointment with Fear (with Dame Irene Vanbrugh), tour – 'The Girl'.
Pink String and Sealing Wax, Intimate Theatre, Palmer's

Green – Jessie.
Fit for Heroes, tour and Whitehall Theatre – stage
manager.

1946   *Quiet Weekend*, film. Associated British Corp – 'A
        Dancer'.
        Pink String and Sealing Wax, Penge Empire – Eva.
        The First Mrs Fraser, repertory, Worthing.
        The Cure for Love (with Wilfred Pickles), tour – Janey.

1947   *Oak Leaves and Lavender* by Sean O'Casey, King's
        Theatre, Hammersmith and tour – 'a land girl' and 'a
        seller of lavender'.
        Focus on Nursing, BBC radio drama/documentary –
        small parts.
        Heaven and Charing Cross Road, repertory,
        Wolverhampton – Bella.
        Time and the Conways, repertory, Wolverhampton –
        Carol.
        London's Dance Bands, BBC radio drama/documentary
        – 'A Fan'.
        Cinderella (with Wilfred Pickles), Bradford Alhambra –
        Cinders.
        Wilfred Pickles' Christmas Party, BBC radio.

1948   *The Desert Song*, tour – chorus and understudy.
        Cinderella (with Wilfred Pickles), Leeds Theatre Royal
        – Cinders.
        Wilfred Pickles' Christmas Party, BBC radio.

1949   *The Twenty Questions Murder Mystery*, film – small part.

1950   *Ace of Clubs* by Noël Coward, tour and Cambridge
        Theatre, London – Sunny Claire.

1951   Cabaret, Studio Club, Knightsbridge.

The Passing Show (popular music 1900–10), BBC TV.

Penny Plain, revue with Joyce Grenfell, St Martin's Theatre.

South Pacific, Drury Lane – Ensign Sue Jaeger.

See You Later, revue, Watergate Theatre.

1952 *Women of Twilight*, UK tour and Plymouth Theater, New York – Rosie.

Miss Hargreaves, CBS TV play – 'A Maid'.

Love From Judy, tour and Saville Theatre – Sally McBride.

1953 'Seven Lonely Days', 'Dancing With Someone', 'Diamonds are a Girl's Best Friend' and 'Bye Bye Baby', records, Philips.

Take It From Here (with Jimmy Edwards, Dick Bentley, Alma Cogan and Wallas Eaton), series, BBC radio.

1954 *Take It From Here*, series, BBC radio.

Fast and Loose (with Bob Monkhouse), series, BBC TV.

1955 *Before Your Very Eyes* (with Arthur Askey), series, Associated Rediffusion TV.

No Peace for the Wicked, BBC radio.

These Radio Times, BBC radio.

Henry Hall's Guest Night, BBC radio.

From Here and There, revue, Royal Court Theatre.

Star Struck, sketches, BBC radio.

Man About Town (variety with Jack Buchanan), BBC radio.

Bring on the Girls, variety, BBC radio.

Take It From Here, series, BBC radio.

New Faces, BBC radio.

Your Kind of Music, ITV.

Late Show, revue, BBC TV.

Fast and Loose (with Bob Monkhouse), series, BBC TV.

Here We Go (with Bruce Forsyth and Billy Dainty), sketches, Associated Rediffusion TV.

1956   *Idiot Weekly, Price 2d.* (with Peter Sellers, Spike Milligan, Kenneth Connor etc.), series, Associated Rediffusion TV.

Before Your Very Eyes (with Arthur Askey), series, Associated Rediffusion TV.

Take It From Here, series, BBC radio.

The Tony Hancock Show, series, Associated Rediffusion TV.

Curiouser and Curiouser (with Peter Sellers), BBC radio.

The Straker Special, musical, Associated Rediffusion TV.

1957   *The Spice of Life* (with Ted Ray), series, BBC radio.

Take It From Here, series, BBC radio.

Yes, It's the Cathode-Ray Tube Show! (with Peter Sellers and Michael Bentine), series, Associated Rediffusion TV.

Hancock's Half-Hour, 'The Alpine Holiday', BBC TV.

The Peers Parade (with Donald Peers), BBC Radio.

Chelsea at Nine, Granada TV.

Before Your Very Eyes (with Arthur Askey), series, Associated Rediffusion TV.

Friday the 13th (with Ted Ray), BBC TV.

1958   *Early to Braden*, BBC TV.

My Pal Bob (with Bob Monkhouse), BBC TV.

Many Happy Returns, variety, ABC TV.

Dixon of Dock Green, BBC TV.

Before Your Very Eyes (with Arthur Askey), series, Associated Rediffusion TV.

On With the Show (with Alan White), series, Associated Rediffusion TV.

Take It From Here, series, BBC radio.

Welcome to London, BBC radio.
Whack-O! (with Jimmy Edwards), sitcom, BBC TV.
This Is Your Life (Jimmy Edwards), BBC TV
The Army Game, sitcom, Granada TV.
Carry On Nurse, film.
Murder Bag (with Raymond Francis), Associated Rediffusion TV.

1959 *The Army Game*, Granada TV.
Friends and Neighbours (with Arthur Askey), film.
Take It From Here, two series, BBC radio.
We're in Business (with Peter Jones and Peter Ustinov), sitcom, BBC radio.
Whack-O! (with Jimmy Edwards), BBC TV.
Saturday Spectacular (with Bernard Bresslaw), ITV.
It's Saturday Night (with Ted Ray), BBC TV.
London Lights, BBC radio.

1960 *Take It From Here*, final series, BBC radio.
Arthur's Treasured Volumes (with Arthur Askey), series, ATV.
The Vera Lynn Show, BBC TV.
Leave It to the Boys, (with Bob Monkhouse), series, BBC radio.
Take It From Here, record, Philips.

1961 *Leave It to the Boys* (with Bob Monkhouse), series, BBC radio.
Beyond Our Ken (with Kenneth Horne and Kenneth Williams), BBC radio.
What's the Odds (with Sid James), two series, BBC radio.
It's a Deal, BBC radio.
The Benny Hill Show, BBC TV.
London Lights, BBC radio.
Whack-O! (with Jimmy Edwards), series, BBC radio.
Variety Playhouse (with Vic Oliver), series, BBC radio.

The Arthur Askey Show, sitcom, ATV.
~~*Hancock*, 'The Blood Donor' and 'The Succession',~~
BBC TV.
The Man in Bed (with Bernard Braden), BBC TV.
Juke Box Jury (with David Jacobs), BBC TV.
The Seven Faces of Jim (with Jimmy Edwards), series,
BBC TV.
Hancock, 'The Blood Donor' and 'The Radio Ham',
record, Pye.
Does the Team Think?, BBC radio.

1962   'The Telephone Call' (with Peter Jones), Galton and
Simpson's *Comedy Playhouse*, BBC TV.
Variety Playhouse, two series, BBC radio.
Whack-O! (with Jimmy Edwards), series, BBC radio.
Benny Hill, series, BBC TV.
The Rag Trade, BBC TV.
Six More Faces of Jim (with Jimmy Edwards), series,
BBC TV.
Holiday Music Hall, BBC radio.
Christmas Night with the Stars, BBC TV.
London Lights, BBC radio.
Hotel Paradiso, play, BBC TV.
The Men From the Ministry, BBC radio.
The Rag Trade, BBC TV.

1963   *More Faces of Jim* (with Jimmy Edwards and Ronnie
Barker), series, BBC TV.
Whack-O! (with Jimmy Edwards), series, BBC radio.
Star Parade, BBC radio.
Crowther's Crowd (with Leslie Crowther and Ronnie
Barker), series, BBC radio.
How to Be an Alien (with Frank Muir and Denis
Norden), voices alongside Ronnie Barker, series,
Associated Rediffusion TV.

1964   *Steptoe and Son*, BBC TV.
     Norman Vaughan, ITV.
     Round Trip (with Jimmy Edwards), BBC radio.
     Variety Playhouse, two series, BBC radio.
     Baxter On . . ., series, BBC TV.
     Comedy Parade, BBC radio.
     The Big Noise (with Bob Monkhouse), series, BBC TV.
     Starlight Hour (with Ronnie Barker), BBC radio.

1965   *Call it What You Like* (with Eric Merriman), series,
      BBC TV.
     This Is Your Jim (with Jimmy Edwards), series, BBC
      radio.
     Light Up the Night, BBC radio.
     On the Braden Beat, ATV.
     Porterhouse Private Eye (with Peter Butterworth), play,
      ATV.
     The Des O'Connor Show, ITV.
     Crowther's Crowd (with Leslie Crowther and Ronnie
      Barker), two series, BBC radio.
     Not for Children, BBC radio.

1966   *Mild and Bitter* (with Eric Merriman and Peter Jones),
      series, BBC TV.
     Frankie Howerd, BBC TV.
     Frankie Howerd, series, BBC radio.
     The Spy with the Cold Nose, film.
     Rikki, Scottish TV.
     On the Braden Beat, ATV.
     The Sound of Laughter, ABC TV.
     The Dickie Henderson Show, BBC TV.
     Beggar My Neighbour, (with Peter Jones, Reg Varney
      and Pat Coombs), *Comedy Playhouse* followed by
      series, BBC TV.

1967   *Life with Cooper* (with Tommy Cooper), ABC TV.

Hancock's, series, ABC TV.

~~*Beggar My Neighbour*~~ (with Desmond Walter-Ellis, Reg
    Varney and Pat Coombs), two series, BBC TV.

In Lieu of Cash, play, BBC radio.

Take a Cool Look, ATV.

The Young Pioneers, drama, BBC radio.

Christmas Night With the Stars, BBC TV.

Million Dollar Bill, BBC radio.

1968   'What's a Mother For?' (with Joe Brown and Mona
    Washbourne), *Armchair Theatre*, ABC TV.

The Benny Hill Show, BBC TV.

Frankie Howerd Meets the Bee Gees, Thames TV.

Never a Cross Word (with Paul Daneman and Nyree
    Dawn Porter), sitcom, LWT.

Show of the Week (with Terry Scott), BBC TV.

Father, Dear Father (with Patrick Cargill), Thames TV.

The Benny Hill Show, BBC TV.

Harry Worth, BBC TV.

The Fossett Saga (with Jimmy Edwards), sitcom, BBC
    TV.

1969   *The Jimmy Logan Show*, BBC TV.

Scott On . . . (with Terry Scott), series, BBC TV.

According to Dora (with Dora Bryan), BBC TV.

The Best Things in Life (with Harry H. Corbett), sitcom,
    ITV.

Late Night Line Up, BBC radio.

Birds Eye commercial.

My Favourite Broad (with Richard Briers), play, BBC
    radio.

Barry Humphries' Scandals, BBC TV.

The Dave King Show, ATV.

Frost on Saturday, LWT.

1970   *Scott On . . .*, series, BBC TV.

Give a Dog a Name, BBC radio.
The Best Things in Life (with Harry H. Corbett), second
 series, ATV.
Christmas Night With the Stars, BBC TV.
Do Me a Favour (with Peter Jones and Terence
 Alexander), sitcom pilot, LWT.
Birds Eye commercial.

1971   *Steptoe and Son*, BBC radio.
        Scott On . . ., series, BBC TV.
        Two's Company, BBC radio.
        The Dickie Henderson Show, LWT.
        The Dick Emery Show, BBC TV.
        The Magnificent Seven Deadly Sins, film.
        Great Scott, pilot and series, BBC radio.
        Birds Eye commercial.
        The Goodies, BBC TV.
        'Up Je T'Aime' (with Frankie Howerd), record. Banned
         by Radio 1!
        The Val Doonican Show, BBC radio.

1972   *The Dick Emery Show*, BBC TV.
        Saturday Variety, ATV.
        The Navy Lark, BBC radio.
        Tarbuck's Luck, BBC TV.
        Commuter Tales, BBC radio.
        Carry On Abroad, film.
        Bless This House, film.
        Scott On . . ., series, BBC TV.
        The Frankie Howerd Show, BBC radio.
        Whoops Baghdad (with Frankie Howerd), BBC TV.
        Frankie Howerd's Christmas Gala, BBC radio.
        Wonderful Children's Songs, Contour Records.
        A Friend Indeed (with David Tomlinson), play, Anglia
         TV.

1973 *The Frankie Howerd Show*, series, BBC radio.
Frankie Howerd in Ulster, BBC TV.
The Dick Emery Show, BBC TV.
Birds Eye commercial.
Carry On Girls, film.
The Entertainers: Frankie Howerd, BBC radio.
An Evening With Francis Howerd, series, BBC TV.
The Navy Lark, BBC radio.
Desert Island Discs (with Roy Plomley), BBC radio.
Scott On . . ., series, BBC TV.
The Pallisers (with Susan Hampshire), serial, BBC TV.
A Friend Indeed (with David Tomlinson, Dawn Addams, Richard Vernon and Fiona Fullerton), TV play, Anglia.

1974 *Birds Eye* commercial.
Happy Ever After (with Terry Scott), *Comedy Playhouse* followed by series, BBC TV.
Menace, BBC radio.
The Frankie Howerd Show, series, BBC radio.
The Morecambe and Wise Show, BBC TV.
The Dick Emery Show, BBC TV.
Romance With a Double Bass (with John Cleese), film, BBC TV.
The Golden Shot (with Bob Monkhouse), ATV.
Kenneth Williams Playhouse, BBC radio.
The Val Doonican Show, ATV.
Morning Story, BBC radio.

1975 *A Bedful of Foreigners* (with Terry Scott), tour of South Africa.
Jon Pertwee's Sketchbook, BBC radio.
Happy Ever After (with Terry Scott), second series, BBC TV.
A Bedful of Foreigners (with Terry Scott), UK tour.

1976   *Not Now, Comrade* (with Leslie Phillips), film.
         A Bedful of Foreigners (with Terry Scott), Victoria
             Palace Theatre, London.
         Happy Ever After (with Terry Scott), third series, BBC
             TV.
         This Is Your Life (June Whitfield), Thames TV.
         Polydor Nursery Stories, record.
         Birds Eye commercial.

1977   *Vivat Rex*, play, BBC radio.
         Happy Ever After (with Terry Scott), fourth series and
             Christmas special, BBC TV.
         This Happy Breed by Noël Coward, BBC radio.
         A Bedful of Foreigners (with Terry Scott), Hong Kong
             tour.
         Jackanory (2 stories), BBC TV.
         Pickwick Papers, serial, BBC radio.
         The Dick Emery Christmas Show, BBC TV.
         Joint recipient (with Terry Scott) of the Variety Club
             TV Personality of the Year Award.

1978   *Weekly Ferret* (with Jon Pertwee), pilot, BBC radio.
         The Lie, play, BBC radio.
         Birds Eye commercial.
         Happy Ever After (with Terry Scott), fifth series, BBC
             TV.
         A Bedful of Foreigners, summer season at the Pier
             Theatre, Bournemouth.

1979   *Birds Eye* commercial.
         Terry and June (with Terry Scott), first series, BBC TV.
         What About the Workers? (with Peter Sellers), record.
         Jackanory, BBC TV.
         Not Now, Darling, Savoy Theatre.

1980   *Birds Eye* commercial.

Terry and June (with Terry Scott), second series and Christmas special, BBC TV.
It Ain't Half Hot, Mum, BBC TV.
The Dick Emery Christmas Show, BBC TV.
Royal Variety Show, the Palladium, BBC TV.

1981   *Birds Eye* commercial.
Terry and June (with Terry Scott), third series and Christmas special, BBC TV.
Mike Yarwood in Persons, BBC TV.

1982   *Terry and June* (with Terry Scott), fourth series and Christmas special, BBC TV.
Rupert the Bear (with Paul McCartney), cartoon.
Jack and the Beanstalk (with Frankie Howerd), Chichester Festival Theatre.

1983   *Terry and June* (with Terry Scott), fifth series, BBC TV.
Karen Kay Show, BBC TV.
Sharing Time (with Anton Rogers and Gwen Watford), play, BBC TV.
Tribute to Tony Hancock, BBC TV.
Dick Whittington (with Roy Hudd), Richmond Theatre.

1984   *The News Huddlines* (with Roy Hudd and Chris Emmett), two series, BBC radio.
It's Going to Be All Right, pilot, Yorkshire TV.
3-2-1 panto, TV.
Halls of Fame, BBC TV.
The Des O'Connor Show, BBC TV.

1985   *Some of These Days*, BBC radio.
Joyful Joyce, BBC radio.
The News Huddlines, two series, BBC radio.
Terry and June, sixth series, BBC TV.

Jack and the Beanstalk (with Terry Scott), Theatre Royal, Bath.

OBE.

1986   *The News Huddlines*, two series and a Cup Final special, BBC radio.

Some of These Days, BBC radio.

Night of a Hundred Stars, Shaftesbury Theatre.

The Rivals, tour – Mrs Malaprop.

Jack and the Beanstalk (with Terry Scott), Yvonne Arnaud Theatre, Guildford.

1987   *Terry and June*, seventh and final series, BBC TV.

The News Huddlines, two series, BBC radio.

An Ideal Husband (with Joanna Lumley and Clive Francis), Chichester Festival Theatre.

Yesterday's Huddlines (with Roy Hudd, Chris Emmett and Suzy Aitchison), Anglia TV.

Semi Monde by Noël Coward, The Royalty Theatre.

1988   *The Law Game*, play, BBC radio.

Second Chance, play, Radio Bristol.

Ring Round the Moon (with Googie Withers, Michael Denison and José Ferrer), Chichester Festival Theatre.

The News Huddlines, two series, BBC radio.

French and Saunders, BBC TV.

1989   *Over My Dead Body* (with Donald Sinden and Frank Middlemass), two-week tour and Savoy Theatre.

1990   *It Doesn't Have to Hurt*, keep-fit series, BBC TV.

Arena, special on Frankie Howerd, BBC TV.

The News Huddlines, two series, BBC radio.

Desert Island Discs (with Sue Lawley), BBC radio.

Hinge and Bracket, BBC radio.

Babes in the Wood (with Roy Hudd), Ashcroft Theatre, Croydon.

Wogan, BBC TV.

1991 *The News Huddlines*, two series, BBC radio.

Absolutely Fabulous (with Jennifer Saunders, Joanna Lumley, Julia Sawalha and Jane Horrocks), pilot episode, BBC TV.

Some of These Days, BBC radio.

Pasadena Roof Orchestra, series, BBC radio.

Babes in the Wood (with Roy Hudd), Theatre Royal, Plymouth.

The Craig Ferguson Show (with Peter Cook).

1992 *The News Huddlines*, two series, BBC radio.

June Whitfield's Variety Special, BBC radio.

Absolutely Fabulous, first series, BBC TV.

Carry On Columbus, film.

Noel's House Party, BBC TV.

Terry and Julian, Channel 4 TV.

Babes in the Wood (with Roy Hudd), New Theatre, Cardiff.

1993 *The News Huddlines*, two series, BBC TV.

That's Life, series, BBC TV.

Murder at the Vicarage, Radio 4 – Miss Marple.

1994 *The News Huddlines*, two series (including 300th edition), BBC TV.

Absolutely Fabulous, second series, BBC TV.

All Time Greats, BBC radio.

The Crowned Hudds, series, BBC radio.

That's Life, BBC TV.

Noel's House Party and *Noel's Garden Party*, BBC TV.

Cinderella (with Rolf Harris), Wimbledon Theatre.

The British Comedy Awards – 'Lifetime Achievement Award'.
Any Other Business, series, BBC radio.

1995   *Absolutely Fabulous*, third series, BBC TV.
The News Huddlines, two series, BBC radio.
Noel's House Party, BBC TV.
Farewell to the Paris, BBC radio.
This Is Your Life, June Whitfield, BBC TV.
Wish You Were Here, Carlton TV.
All Time Greats, BBC radio.
The Crowned Hudds, series, BBC radio.
Kalangadog Junction, series, BBC radio.
Peter Pan, BBC radio.
Jude (with Christopher Ecclestone and Kate Winslet), film.

1996   *The News Huddlines*, two series and *Christmas Huddlines*, BBC radio.
Common as Muck (with Edward Woodward), BBC TV.
Family Money (with Claire Bloom), serial, Channel 4.
Absolutely Fabulous, special, BBC TV.
Noel's TV Years, BBC TV.
Today's the Day, BBC TV.

1997   *The News Huddlines*, two series, *Christmas Huddlines* and *The Huddlines Songbook*, BBC radio.
Gigi, BBC radio.
Tom Jones, TV film.
Out of Sight, children's TV, Carlton.
Get Fit With Brittas (with Chris Barry), BBC TV.
All Rise for Julian Clary, series, BBC TV.
Ab Fab 'A Life' (with Jennifer Saunders), BBC TV.
Funny Women, featuring June Whitfield, BBC TV.
The Almost Accidental Adventures of Bell and Todd, BBC radio.

Holiday Memories, BBC TV.
~~*Going Places*, BBC radio.~~

1998   *The News Huddlines*, two series and a *Christmas Huddlines*, BBC radio.
Friends, NBC TV.
Today's the Day, BBC TV.
Loose Ends (with Ned Sherrin), BBC radio.
The Newly Discovered Casebook of Sherlock Holmes (with Roy Hudd and Chris Emmett), series, BBC radio.
Lord's Taverners Tribute Lunch.
Women in Film and TV Lifetime Achievement Award.
CBE.

1999   *The News Huddlines*, two series, BBC radio.
The Newly Discovered Casebook of Sherlock Holmes, second series, BBC radio.
Like They've Never Been Gone (with Roy Hudd and Pat Coombs), first series, BBC radio.
Timekeepers of the Millennium, children's ITV.
The Secret by Catherine Cookson, drama, ITV.
Hale & Pace, LWT.
Days Like These, ITV
The Talkies Outstanding Achievement Award.
Inducted into the Royal Television Society's Hall of Fame.
The Last of the Blonde Bombshells (with Judi Dench and Ian Holm), film, BBC TV.

2000   *Mirrorball* (with Jennifer Saunders, Joanna Lumley, Julia Sawalha and Jane Horrocks), pilot sitcom, BBC TV.
The News Huddlines, two series, BBC radio.
Father Gilbert, USA radio.
Like They've Never Been Gone (with Roy Hudd and Pat Coombs), second series, BBC radio.

AUDIOTAPES

FOR CHIVERS:
The Blue Bedroom
The Adventures of the Little Wooden Horse
The Merman
Clever Duck and *Swooze*
The Witch of Blackberry Bottom
The Terrible Trins
The Stray
The Further Adventures of Gobbolino and the Little Wooden Horse
Sir Billy Bear and Other Friends

FOR HODDER:
Out of This World

FOR TELSTAR:
10 *Murder Mysteries*
10 *Chillers for Children*
10 *Stories of Love*

FOR PENGUIN:
Wind in the Willows
4 *Miss Read*
George's Marvellous Medicine

FOR CLASSIC FM:
100 Favourite Poems

FOR THE BBC:
June Whitfield at the Beeb
8 *Miss Marple*s

ANIMATED CARTOONS

HIT ENTERTAINMENTS PLC:
2 Brambly Hedge

COSGROVE HALL:
The Wyrd Sisters

GAME SHOWS AND PANEL SHOWS

FOR BBC TV:
4 *Call My Bluff*
Mish–Mash
The Generation Game
5 *Blankety Blank*
2 *That's Showbusiness*
2 *Telly Addicts*
All Over the Shop

FOR BBC RADIO:
Does the Team Think?
4 *Sounds Familiar*
Double or Quits
2 *A Rhyme in Time*
5 *Fair Deal*
The Petticoat Line
Twenty Questions
Pop Score
The Impressionists
6 *Punchline*
Pros and Cons
The 1978 Show
Just a Minute
The Zodiac Game
Million Dollar Bill
Which is Which

FOR HARLECH TV:
Funny You Should Ask

FOR THAMES TV:
3 *Whose Baby?*
3 *Looks Familiar*
2 *Whodunnit?*
3 *Give Us a Clue*
2 *What's My Line?*

FOR YORKSHIRE TV:
Jokers Wild

FOR ATV:
2 Celebrity Squares
The Golden Shot

FOR LWT:
2 Punchline

FOR TYNE TEES TV:
Crosswits

FOR GRANADA TV:
Cluedo

FOR CHANNEL 4 TV:

INDEX